DEFORESTATION:
Social Dynamics in Watersheds and Mountain Ecosystems

Deforestation has become a major environmental and development problem, as forests are cut in tropical and mountain areas and acid rain, pollution and disease wreak havoc in temperate zones. Some of the worst effects of deforestation have been changes in the world's climate system, erosion and flooding, desertification, wood shortages and the disappearance of some floral and faunal species. This book challenges the belief that deforestation is due entirely to rapid population growth and agricultural expansion and emphasises the effects of commercial exploitation and poor planning and management. It concludes with a programme for reforestation using agro-forestry, appropriate cottage industries, improved international programmes, local land reforms and community participation.

J. Ives is at the University of Colorado, USA and D.C. Pitt is with the International Union for the Conservation of Nature and Natural Resources, Switzerland.

DEFORESTATION:
Social Dynamics in Watersheds and Mountain Ecosystems

Edited by J. Ives and D.C. Pitt

ROUTLEDGE
London and New York

First published in 1988 by Routledge
Reprinted 1990 by Routledge
11 New Fetter Lane, London EC4P 4EE

Simultaneously published in the USA and Canada
by Routledge
a division of Routledge, Chapman and Hall, Inc.
29 West 35th Street, New York, NY 10001

Printed in Great Britain by
Antony Rowe Ltd, Chippenham, Wiltshire

British Library Cataloguing in Publication Data

Deforestation: social dynamics in watersheds
  and mountain ecosystems.
  1. Deforestation — Social aspects
  I. Ives, J.
  333.75   SD418

ISBN 0-415-00456-X

Library of Congress Cataloging-in-Publication Data

ISBN 0-415-00456-X

CONTENTS

v

LIST OF CONTRIBUTORS

J. Bandyopadhyay International Centre for Integrated Mountain Development (ICIMOD), Nepal

P. Blaikie University of East Anglia, Norwich, UK

M. Cernea World Bank, Washington, USA

L. Hamilton East-West Center, Honolulu, USA

J. Ives University of Colorado, USA

D.C. Pitt International Union for the Conservation of Nature and Natural Resources, Switzerland

A.J. Pearce Forest Research Institute, Christchurch, New Zealand

M.E.D Poore Formerly Professor of Forestry, University of Oxford

V. Shiva Research Foundation for Science, Dehradun, India

M. Thompson International Institute for Applied Systems Analysis, Laxenburg, Austria

PREFACE

The papers in this volume basically stem from the authors' and editors' participation in international projects particularly in the UN, UNESCO, World Bank, UNEP and the United Nations University. This latter institution has sponsored since 1977 a project on highland-lowland interaction which in recent years has focussed on deforestation, especially in the Himalaya region. In 1984 a workshop was held in Appenberg, Switzerland and in 1986 in Moherk, USA where there was detailed discussion of the deforestation problem. Readers are referred to Mountain Research and Development published by the United Nations University and International Mountain Society (1985-87) for more details. The editors are very grateful to the sponsoring organizations and to the IUCN and EEC for the opportunity to publish this volume and to the many scholars and officials who made contributions and comments. However it should be emphasised that the authors write here in their personal capacities.

J. Ives and D. Pitt

ACKNOWLEDGEMENTS

We are grateful to the Editors of <u>Mountain Research and Development</u> (Chapters 1, 6 and 7), <u>Commonwealth Forestry Review</u> (Conclusion) and the World Bank (Chapter 5) for permission to use materials.

INTRODUCTION

One has to justify a new book on deforestation, for the subject has been well worked over in recent years. But there are vital aspects of the problematique which have not been well covered. Most of the literature is about tropical deforestation and about the specific problem of tree felling. The wider social and ecological dimensions and their solutions have received much less attention, especially in upland watershed and mountains.

Many mountain areas (and not only in the developing world) are often on the periphery of the processes of social, economic and political development, even if vital for the provision of water and energy for the majority of the world's populations who live on the lowlands. The message of the book is surely that the focus on tropical deforestation studies has been misplaced or at least misleading. A significant proportion of deforestation is not in tropical ecosystems even if in tropical countries, but in mountain ecosystems which may have tropical elements. The World Resources Institute has recently pointed out (1) that over 160 million hectares of upland watersheds, nearly half the world's total, have been seriously degraded in over 30 countries in Africa, Asia and Latin America.

In some theories the loss of forest cover in the mountains (defined by altitude, slope, climate or sociological factors) is said to lead to massive erosion and flooding in which social factors are major causes and consequences. This theory has been applied particularly in the Himalaya, where the eroded materials from deforestation are said to threaten the lives of hundreds of millions of poor people on the Indo-Gangetic plain. In this book this thesis is questioned. Deforestation may not result in erosion (e.g. if there is appropriate agricultural terracing) and also the flooding in the plains may have other causes.

The mountain factor has also been underestimated in industrialized countries. For example, in Europe, for reasons not yet completely understood, massive forest death caused mainly by acid rain deposition has most affected trees in the 700m to 1200m altitude band.

Also, this book, unlike many deforestation treatises, is also about the solutions as much as the problems. These solutions again are multifaceted (not simply replanting trees), multidisciplinary and, perhaps most interesting of all, cross cultural and ideological boundaries. But in all cases there is a basic concern with putting people back in amongst the trees.

Although it is possible to show there is a problem, one can be less sure about its magnitude. We begin our book with a warning from Thompson, Warburton and Ives about how uncertain the situation and our knowledge of it is, in the Himalayas at least. Hamilton and Pearce continue by showing some of the complexities of deforestation and that reforestation may only be a partial solution. Blaikie argues that erosion has in fact fundamental socio-economic causes, whilst Pitt extends the socio-economic analysis by looking at two extremely deprived groups, women and young people. The book concludes with papers concerned with socially based solutions, involving both outside institutions as part of social forestry strategies (Cernea) or locally generated movements like Chipko (Shiva and Bandyopadhyay), where women led the way in 'hugging the trees' and preserving the forest for the people.

This book is only a beginning. Most of the contributors to this book have been participants in efforts by the International Mountain Society to open up both present discussion and future research on new approaches, often unconventional to deforestation. In the past it has been assumed, perhaps naively, certainly simplistically, that population pressure is the prime cause of deforestation whether in mountains or lowlands. The International Mountain Society (2) efforts have shown clearly that the situation is much more complex and will require much more research, careful interpretation and sophisticated models to talk confidently of critical causes or consequences. It is hoped this will stimulate future discussion and dialogue and readers are invited to send criticisms and contributions to

Dr. D.C. Pitt at the IUCN. 1196 Gland, Switzerland.

NOTES

1.   Tropical Forests - A Call for Action. 1985:
Washington, Pt. 1, p.26.
2.   Mountain Research and Development, v.7, no. 3,
August 1987 - The Himalaya Ganges Problem.   Special
Publication of the Commission on Mountain Geoecology,
International Geographical Union (eds J. and P. Ives).

UNCERTAINTY ON A HIMALAYAN SCALE

M. Thompson and M. Warburton

WELCOME TO UNCERTAINTY

> The spiral of tragedy has taken its own route. There is suffering in the hills now and there will be considerably more suffering in the future. The Himalayas might well change completely to a semi desert ecology. They might not. But things will get worse before they get better. (Cronin, 1979:222)

A complex series of interactions between man and nature in the Himalayan region has many experts from various disciplines speculating about the probable course of events in the area. The literature on the Himalayan 'eco-crisis' is replete with descriptions of rapidly expanding hill populations exploiting increasingly marginal land in an attempt to produce more food. As agriculture is extended so the forest cover is destroyed. Erosion and landslips decrease the productivity of soil, pasture and forest. There are all manner of self-reinforcing feedback loops in this system and traditional attempts by the farmer to better his lot or produce more food and fuel often lead to a worsening of the global situation in the hills and in the plains below (Eckholm, 1976; Lall, 1981). The lowlands are subjected to the silt and water runoff from the denuded land above, as well as all the attendant effects of migration by hill people. Because of growing populations in both the hills and plains, more and more people are displaced or otherwise affected by food and fuel shortages, changes in ground and surface water flows, and mass movements of land, water, and people in the area. Social unrest has also been increasingly intermixed with the effects of these processes. Regional and international attention has been focused on this situation, and many governments and organizations are already involved in trying to find a solution to a perceived crisis.

But describing the nature and the extent of the problem is fraught with complexity and uncertainty. There are many levels of interdependent cause-and-effect relationships to consider in the context of extremely fluid and complicated ecological and social systems. And uncertainty has become just as important a feature of the problem as any of its other attributes.

The problem, all agree, is that the Himalaya are caught in a downward spiral. Yet, when we look at the key variables in current models that attempt to define this spiral, we find that the uncertainties are so vast that we cannot even be sure that there is a spiral. For example, the expert estimates of two of these key variables - the per capita fuelwood consumption rate and the sustainable yield from forest production - vary by such enormous factors that it is but a slight exaggeration to say that, if the most pessimistic estimates are correct, the Himalaya will become as bald as a coot overnight and that, if the most optimistic estimates are correct, it will shortly sink beneath the greatest accumulation of biomass the world has ever seen. Despite our convictions as to the nature of the problem, the quantitative data can give us no guidance as to whether the spiral, if it indeed exists, is upward or downward. Far from the problem containing some uncertainty - a common enough situation in applied science - it is the uncertainty that contains the problem. The credible problem definitions, thanks to all this uncertainty, span such a wide range that it no longer makes any sense to use methods that attempt to tune to an already acceptable understanding of 'the problem'. Such a tunable understanding is possible only when the problem contains some uncertainty; it simply does not exist in the Himalaya.

Another way of talking about this switch from tunable to untunable problem that accompanies such a marked increase in the scale of uncertainty is to say that as we go from the one situation to the other so we go from science to trans-science (Weinberg, 1972). Trans-science is the science of messes, and the most important thing for the scientist who ventures into this region is that he be aware that he is entering it. This is because the tried-and-true methods that have long served him so well in situations that involve some messiness simply cannot be relied on to support him when he finds himself in a situation where there is nothing but mess. It is our contention that the Himalaya currently constitutes such a region and that the scientists who have ventured into it have failed to switch across to the methods appropriate to trans-science. Furthermore, since these scientists have entered the region at the behest of policy makers, there has been a knock-on effect and the policy formulations generated by this inappropriate science have been similarly flawed. Our argument, therefore, proceeds in two stages. Firstly, a critical stage in which we show that the Himalaya are currently well inside the realm of trans-science and that both research and policy formulation, having failed to concede this, have been inappropriately conceived. Secondly, a constructive stage in which we try to develop the methods and the policy implications appropriate to the trans-scientific realm.

Cis-science and trans-science

Policy issues can be approached in two ways. You can ask 'what are the facts?' and you can ask 'what would you like the facts to be?'. In a situation where there is already considerable certainty about the facts (and especially where there is a good prospect of increasing that certainty even further) the sensible approach is by way of the first question. As the noose of certainty is tightened so those who are advocating policies that, to be justified, would require the facts to be other than they are will be forced to abandon either their positions or their credibility. But in a situation where there is wide uncertainty about the facts (and especially where there is little prospect of decreasing that uncertainty) the sensible approach is by way of the second question. If those who are advocating the various rival policies can all justify their policies without losing their credibility, then they will simply stick to those positions. Here, in contrast to the first situation in which the problem contains some uncertainties, the noose is so loose that the relationship is the other way round and it is the uncertainty that contains the problems. This means that, try as you may, you cannot determine who is 'right'. But you can still do something - you can gain some understanding of why the various advocates take up their various positions.

When the noose of certainty is loose we are in the

realm of trans-science and, as it tightens, we move across into the realm of what we are accustomed to call science but which, if we are going to be following policy issues back and forth across this divide, we should get used to calling cis-science. That way we can give equal status to each - they are just two kinds of science - and we can concentrate on the different methods and modes of enquiry that are appropriate to each. Since cis-science is quite familiar to us, it is the methods and modes of enquiry that go with trans-science that will appear strange; and none stranger, perhaps, than the sociology of perception (by which is included the history, philosophy, and sociology of science and the sociology of everyday knowledge) and that has to do with the institutional forces that confer and withdraw credibility.

A science, it is often said, has reached maturity when it can afford to ignore its history but this comforting idea of an irreversible progression - for instance, from natural history to the various biological and earth sciences - is currently being undermined by the emergence of forest historians, risk historians, climate historians ... carbon historians in response to such pressing and largely trans-scientific problems as 'the greenhouse effect', and the whole question of the sustainable development of the biosphere. This distinction between (and even-handed legitimation of) cis-science and trans-science does not do away with the notion of scientific progress but it does reject the idea that it is always in the same direction. Cis-science, one could say, progresses by ignoring its history; trans-science cannot get along without it. Each has its part to play in the advancement of science. We are not opposed to cis-science; we are opposed to its misuse.

Is there a spiral?

Analysis in terms of physical facts - the appropriate method of cis-science - has first to identify all the components of the Himalayan system and all the connections between those components. The result is a qualitative model made up of numerous labelled boxes that represent the components of the system, connected together by a web of labelled arrows representing the dynamical pocesses that, in toto, sustain or transform the system. Before you can tell whether this system is being sustained or transformed (and, if the latter, the direction of that transformation) you need to know the relative rates of all these processes. At the very least, you will need to know the rates of those that can clearly be seen to be the key variables of the system. Uncertainty can enter into this analysis at several points. You may not have identified all the components of your complex system, you may not have identified all the dynamic processes that link those components, you may not have identified the key variables correctly and, lastly, you may not have achieved a sufficiently accurate measurement of the rates of these key variables. The Himalaya notch up impressively high scores on all of these possible sources of uncertainty.

For example, in trying to understand how fast the forested area is changing - one of the most important characteristics of the ecological structure of the region - you must first understand the pressures on the forest resource. One of the most significant demands is the need for fuelwood by farmers. In Nepal, farmers make up about 95 per cent of the population, and it has been calculated (by the Energy Research and Development Group at Tribhuvan University, Kathmandu, Nepal) that about 95 per cent of all wood taken from the forest is destined for use as fuelwood. Not only this, but the same group has estimated that about 87 per cent of total energy consumption for the whole country is in the form of fuelwood. Most attempts to quantify the impact of this factor have depended upon measuring the per capita rate of fuelwood consumption. This, according to the prevalent models, is one of the most crucial variables for understanding the whole system and many authors have used estimates of this rate to demonstrate the environmental impact of a growing population that must (they assume) depend on the land for meeting its subsistence needs.

A survey of estimates of this nationwide rate in Nepal over the last 26 years (Donovan, 1981) has revealed a range from $0.1 m^3$ (or 60 kg) to 6.67 m^3 (or 4,000 kg) per capita per annum - quantities separated by a factor of 67. Even when the two upper outliers are deleted (one of which may be a misprint) (1) we are still left with a range that differs by a factor of 26. Though the estimates do seem to cluster around the 1 cubic-metre level, Donovan's investigation of the range of expert opinion is very instructive for those trying to assemble previous research data on the Himalayan region. Uncertainty of this magnitude on a crucial system variable is quite rare in the systems with which we are familiar. Even the vast uncertainties associated with estimating oil and gas reserves (Schanz, 1978; Wildavsky and Tenenbaum, 1981) pale into insignificance when compared with this. And, in the case of fuelwood consumption, there is at least <u>something</u> that can be measured; in oil and gas reserves estimation there is nothing. (2)

Challenges to quantification

Such gross and persistent uncertainty, around something that is intrinsically measurable, demands some explanation. What obstacles, self-imposed and external, have got in the way of the fuelwood consumption estimators? The answers form a sad and familiar litany.

> All too often visiting consultants have neglected to explain the methods used to arrive at their expert opinions ... some estimates have been boldly quoted and requoted, often without citation, in ever more respectable documents, until a very casually contrived estimate has become the basis for policy formation and program planning. (Donovan, 1981: 5 and 14)

Donovan's own investigation into fuelwood use in the commercial sector sheds some more light on the uncertainty of figures related to resource consumption in the Himalayan region. Much information is gathered by asking local people how much they use.

> ... sometimes we felt the reply given was more socially or politically desirable than correct. At times there appeared to be an effort to present a facade of modernity; a few individuals preferred to guess weight, volume, or distance in international units rather than to report what they probably knew with greater confidence in traditional units ... Volume to weight ratios often vary from village to village, region to region and season to season. Time and distance are two additional variables presenting measurement problems, especially in a country where the average inhabitant does not own a timepiece and has little use for kilometers or miles. (Donovan, 1980:5)

On top of these difficulties in collecting data where

bookkeeping is practically non-existent, and where (as anyone who has travelled in the Himalaya knows to his cost) people always try to give the answer they think you would like to hear, there are some other powerful forces at work shaping the data.

> ... a universal dread of the tax collector appeared to hinder our attempts to secure accurate production and revenue data ... Although not as sensitive an issue as the more popular survey topics of family planning and farm management, the study focus on wood-fuel utilization did give rise to some degree of apprehension among those individuals questioned. Due to the rapid deterioration of Nepal's national forests during the last decade, the consumption of firewood and charcoal recently has come under scrutiny by government officials. In some districts where forest preserves have been established, local villagers now must obtain special permits to cut wood in areas which once were their common fuelshed; in Surkhet valley townspeople who have access to government fuel depots are denied such permits. Government forest regulations subject to enforcement by an inadequate, ill-equipped staff of field officers have had only limited success, however, in halting forest destruction. To our questions regarding forest utilization, I often felt informants gave a politically appropriate response rather than actual fact. Many times individuals were hesitant to name their suppliers or geographical source. In several instances we were told to return at dawn if we wanted to talk with the charcoal producers. Fearful of government surveillance these people carry their loads into the cities and towns under the cover of early morning darkness. (Donovan, 1980:8)

It is indeed difficult to gather factually accurate information under these circumstances. We say 'factually accurate information' because, of course, the information that is gathered does quite accurately reflect the various social forces that are at work in the Himalaya. In this sense, it is institutionally accurate and, as we shall argue later, perhaps institutional accuracy is more valuable (and more accessible) than factual accuracy. Though 'proper' research methods are supposed to control sources of bias such as these, they have clearly met their match in the Himalaya.

But, even assuming that the information that has been gathered can be controlled for bias, it still has to be assembled into a conceptual framework that is consistent with the context from which it was derived, and herein lies the next obstacle.

Challenges to conceptualization

When trying to fit a factor such as per capita fuelwood consumption into a quantitative causal model of impact on forest resources, the 'consumption' concept is often used as a proxy for 'demand' or 'need' in order to provide a gross measure of pressure on resources. This is probably a better proxy than many arbitrary guesses, but it has been noted that there are sometimes extreme variations in fuelwood use in relation to region (Donovan, 1981), availability (FAO, 1974), season (Kawikita, 1979), food-grain availability, and farm management styles (Bajracharya, 1983a, 1983b). People do not just <u>have</u> needs; they <u>manage</u> them. They use more wood when it is easier to get and less when it is more difficult to get. And, even when a number is put on a concept such as per capita fuelwood consumption, the researcher, focusing on numbers alone, 'may lose sight of their context, and thus, their relevance and reasonableness' (Donovan, 1981:14). The generalization of a locally derived figure is often unwarranted, and it often does not have any significance as a behaviour indicator under slightly different circumstances. None the less, many numbers, we find, are treated in just this manner.

> Firewood is used at a rate of 546.3 kg per capita per annum in Nepal. The estimated sustainable yield of firewood production from Nepalese forests is only 77.9 kg per capita per annum (1978). This represents a loss to the nation of 6.5 million tons of wood a year. With firewood scarce and expensive, the Nepalese are beginning to use dried animal manure for fuel, which results in lowered fertility on fields that previously were fertilized with manure. In addition, fewer people are boiling their drinking water, and eating hot meals because fuel is too precious. This leads to greater health problems because of poor nutrition and contaminated water. (Library of Congress, 1979:39)

Besides expanding on the logical consequences of fuel shortage, this sounds very authoritative and precise. But not only is there no feeling for the uncertainty of the consumption figure and its local contexts, there is also no mention of the inherent assumptions of forest productivity or even forest area which led to the 77.9 kg per capita per year figure for 'sustainable yield' of firewood. A cursory investigation of 'sustainable yield' calculations reveals that different forests grow at different rates, and that even the same sorts of forests grow at different rates in different areas. Yield calculations often involve the multiplication of several estimated quantities such as forest area, forest density, and average growth rates. Errors made in any one of these values are compounded in the product. Taking the value of 'forest growth' alone, it is not surprising that different methodologies and sample areas have produced estimates of 'forest growth' varying from less than 0.2 m^3/ha/yr (1976, Tribhuvan University study for areas near villages) through the 1978 World Bank Forestry Sector Review for Nepal which reports forest growth at 0.8 m^3/ha/yr, through 12.5 m^3/ha/yr (Levenson, 1979), through Wormwald's (1976) reports of 15-30 m^3/ha/yr for areas in west central Nepal.

On top of this, the very definition of what constitutes 'forest' (and other resource inventory classifications) adds still more confusion and technical uncertainty to the understanding of what is happening in the Himalayan region. Those who have taken the trouble to look in both places know that a forest on a bureaucrat's map is not always the same thing as a forest on the ground.

> In fact, even in the protected forest area, one finds considerable tracts of small shrub ... it is not uncommon to find vast areas of open ground which support only shrubs although they were formerly forested and are still counted as forests in official statistics because of unrecorded deforestation. (Parikh, 1977:1974)

> Published national forestry statistics are often misleading. They usually cover only those wooded areas officially designated as forest lands by governments and even the figures for those areas are sometimes grossly doctored. The United Nations researchers carrying out the 1963 World Forestry Inventory discovered that as

much as half the area reported as 'forest land' in many countries was also labelled 'unstocked' - generally a euphemism for partially or wholly denuded lands on which reforestation remains a hypothetical prospect. (Eckholm, 1978:37)

Because of this data problem, it is often difficult to assemble a picture of regional land-use patterns, or to even make intelligent estimates of potential forest production, because you need to know how much forest there is to do that.

Fuelwood consumption and supply, of course, is only one aspect of the Himalayan people-and-resources system and we should now move on to see whether the spectacular levels of uncertainty that surround it apply elsewhere in the system.

From measurement problems to causal uncertainty

Data derived from survey questionnaires can often be deceptive. The statistics used to quantify agricultural production and associated land-use patterns have been investigated by a team from the Research Centre for Nepal and Asian Studies at Tribhuvan University in Kathmandu:

In a study of the reliability of single visit surveys in Nepal, it was found that error on crop yields exceeded 180% for more than 20% of the farms ... (for all farms, 54% of the households reported erroneously their land holdings, with an average error of 240% ...). In a separate study, it was also found that 80% of the respondents did not fully understand the questions they were asked to answer ... These results which vary from village to village point to the fact that non-sampling errors are greater than sampling errors. (UNDP, 1980:27)

Further technical uncertainty is encountered in analysing the human components of erosion, flooding, and shifting hydrological patterns. Since only that part of a process that is caused by human agency can be altered by altering human behaviour, the whole question of how much of the damage inflicted by these processes is due to human activity in the hills and how much is due to events which would occur whether man were present or not has become increasingly important to policy makers.

In a paper presented at a seminar on the Himalayan region, several geologists agreed:

> The tectonic stresses which heaved up these mighty ranges in the recent past have not completely died down as yet, and provide additional impetus and vigour for the dynamic processes. These processes are manifested by intense seismic activity, floods and mass wastage observed in this region. (Department of Science and Technology, Government of India, 1978:9)

Obviously, flooding and erosion are part of the natural Himalayan environment. In the flooding case, the policy-relevant question has become: how are these massive floods related to the land-use activities of upstream people and has the problem become more serious in recent years because of upstream deforestation?

Upstream deforestation has been repeatedly, and categorically, labelled as a cause of catastrophic flooding:

> The major common factor is the increasing damage to the lowland agriculture of India, Pakistan and Nepal by floods loaded with debris from misused high altitude watersheds. These floods are due to increasing populations of subsistence farmers on steep mountain slopes in remote areas. (Pereira, 1981:3)

And, in much the same vein:

> In 1979, India suffered $2 billion in property damage and numerous lives in the Ganges Valley in part because of deforestation in northern India and Nepal. (Cultural Survival Quarterly, 1982:3)

But, in a monsoon-dominated climate, even forested watersheds can lose much of their protective effect when they become saturated. A study (Bruce Ross, 1982, personal communication) by a weather observer (Russell Ambrosiac of NOAA) has revealed that the weather pattern associated with the 1978-79 record floods of the Ganges released most of its moisture on <u>forested</u> land. If a heavy storm strikes when the 'sponge' is already full (a common enough occurrence during the monsoon) most of that precipitation will become runoff, there will be little buffering effect, and catastrophic floods will ensue. So it is oversimplistic to say that protection of forest in highland watersheds will put an end to flooding in the plains.

The bulk of the Himalayan literature paints a picture of increasing runoff from deforested slopes leading to ever increasing flood damage in the lowlands. It is actually very difficult to document whether catastrophic flooding is more serious now than before simply because flood damage statistics are usually published in monetary terms, and 'flood damage' is bound to increase along with increasing population and associated development in flood-plain areas. (And also with increasing disbursements, by government and international agencies, of flood damage compensation and relief. See Kunreuther (1969) for an account of how this has happened in the USA.)

> It is true that mountain torrents have increased as result of deforestation, but with widespread flooding, the connection has not been very well documented. The upstream problems alone justify reforestation projects, but if you try to justify them on the basis of downstream flooding, that could be vulnerable ground. (Erik P. Eckholm, 1982, personal communication)

The academic research community has prepared a whole battery of ongoing research projects to try and answer the question of how much human activities contribute to flooding and erosion (Unesco, 1977:28) but, in the meantime, the linkage between upstream deforestation and downstream flooding is a key policy consideration in the Himalayan region because 'upstream causes' are often located in one country and 'downstream effects' in another. The number of people who are affected is also an important consideration in this international framework because this number provides an initial guideline for the priority of disbursement of financial assistance to nations and organizations with interests in the region. In this economic and institutional context it is interesting to note the points emphasized by the Nepalese ambassador to the United States (Nepal is heavily dependent on foreign loans and grants), and by the international academic community concerned with scientific research in the Himalayan region (financed largely by UN organizations).

When asked if deforestation in the hills of Nepal led to

12

catastrophic flooding in India, the Nepalese Ambassador replied, 'It is obvious there is a very clear and direct link' (Bekh Thapa, 1982, personal communication). This perfectly legitimate position (given the current uncertainty) provides one more item in the list of justifications for the channelling to Nepal of increased financial assistance out of proportion to its own population. Likewise, all the academic experts who participated in the Unesco Man and the Biosphere Activity in Southern Asian Mountain Systems in Kathmandu adopted the statement:

> Although only about 40 million people live in the Hindu Kush Himalayan mountain lands, about 350 million live in adjacent large river basins and plains, and are seriously affected by conditions in the mountain areas. (Unesco, 1977:15)

Flooding figured prominently in their list of effects and, since so many people were affected, the participants (again, quite legitimately) concluded that this was one more reason why further research should be funded to study mountain problems. So the experts are just as busy assigning salience to the data in response to their institutional pressures as are the hill farmers, the ambassadors and anyone else with a stake in the region. In other words, they are biased.

The 'hard' scientist may find such a conclusion discouraging - insulting, even - but the sociologist of science sees it all in a more encouraging and complimentary light. First, it shows that the 'hard' scientist is only human and, second, it helps to reveal the patterns of institutional forces that sustain both the polarized positions of the various stakeholders and the wide uncertainty that allows them to legitimately take up those different positions. At the same time, it gives some clues as to why this uncertainty is so gross and so persistent. Uncertainty, we begin to realise, is not just the absence of certainty but, rather, a positive thing in its own right - something that can be socially generated and socially imposed in order to protect the legitimacy of established institutions and to prevent that legitimacy from being eroded by a creeping tide of certainty. Just as it would be naive to expect lawyers to tidy up the law, or the police to eradicate crime, so we should not place too much faith in the ability of 'hard' science to tell us what the facts in the Himalaya really are.

Crisis or no crisis?

A great deal has been written about the accelerated ecological deterioration in the Himalayan region. Most of it centres on the critical nature of the 'crisis'. One view which stands out is that of a former US Peace Corps Director in India who, in 1981, went back to the Khumbu region of Nepal which he had not revisited since his initial trip there in 1950. Instead of reporting critical deforestation and deterioration of the Sherpa lifestyle as is the usual custom in that area (Coppock, 1978; Lall, 1981) he said that, with the exception of a thicket of dwarf juniper at Pheriche, there was 'as much or more forest cover than there was in 1950 and I have the pictures to prove it.' As for the Sherpas, he felt they 'were better off and happier today than they were thirty years ago'. Though he said he could only speak authoritatively about Khumbu, he felt that the whole question of 'Is there really a problem that is more serious today than 30 years ago?' is an important one to consider (Houston, 1982).

Houston, in questioning the very existence of the crisis, has thrown his cap into the ring in much the same way that some bold spirits in the USA have seriously questioned the existence there of an energy crisis. All we are concerned with at this stage is to set the seal upon our argument that the uncertainty contains the problems by showing that even the existence of the crisis itself is open to doubt, but we will presently return to this particular challenge - the status of the Khumbu forests - and attempt some sort of resolution to it.

From fuzzy physical facts to the politics of polarized perceptions

Whilst this quick survey of uncertainty has not touched on many important aspects of the Himalayan system (it has not, for instance, gone into what happens to the key variables when the forest is viewed as a convertible rather than a renewable resource), it has served to draw attention to a few parts of that system where viewpoints, and hence problem definitions, can vary.

There are many individuals, organizations and governments that have become intimately involved in different aspects of the development challenges faced by the people of the Himalayan region, and each of them approaches the situation with a distinctive perspective - a perspective that is shaped by institutional structures and by past experience. Yet one of the most important perspectives in the whole system - that of the individual hill farmer himself - seldom gains entry to this arena. The reason is two-fold. First, the inappropriate cis-science approach, dealing in physical facts not socially-induced perceptions, cannot make room for him. Second, the hill farmer, lacking recognizable political or economic power, cannot force his way in. True, the hill farmer is often described, and a token place accorded to him, but, in a world where international balances of power are wavering, where internal political stability in a number of Himalayan countries is being eroded, and where the positions of economic and academic elites are always at stake, this viewpoint and its connection with the land that is actually threatened receive lowest priority.

The 'carrying capacity' of this land, despite the cis-science insistence to the contrary, is not simply 'given' by its bio-physical properties and by the state of the technology that is brought to bear on it. It must be locally perceived and interacted with. The local perception of the ecological situation is of extreme importance to any policy design, and as Edward Cronin has said 'to the villager's mind, the problem is not one of too many people but merely not enough food' (Cronin, 1979:216). This locally generated problem definition is not the result of a 'misperception' on the part of the hill farmer; it is deeply embedded in a particular cultural context and strongly buttressed by all sorts of local institutional supports. That is why it is credible to him. The policy maker who, for much the same sorts of cultural and institutional reasons, finds himself committed to the opposite problem definition - too many people - is being hopelessly optimistic if he expects the hill farmer to realign his perception once the 'real' situation has been revealed to him, and he is being hopelessly unrealistic if he expects to be able to push his policies through in the face of this perceptual mismatch. The policy maker, of course, will try to subsume the villager's problem definition within his own by pointing out that there is not enough food because there are too many people. But the villager does not make this connection. The fact is that, over the years, his seemingly inadequate problem definition has served him very well; it has, you could say, provided the strategic

15

underpinning for optimal migration. If there used to be enough food, and now there is not, then move on!

People have always moved about in the Himalaya, leaving places where the opportunities have declined and going to places where they are opening up. Population density is a very poor indicator of opportunity (and of its direction of change), nor is it something that is directly perceivable by the villager; hunger is an excellent, and readily perceived, indicator. (Its great drawback is that, by perpetuating the equation of land with wealth, it does not indicate those opportunities that are opened up by the severing of that equation.) Of course, it will be objected that this strategy is no longer viable because the population everywhere has increased to such an extent that there are no longer any opportunities left anywhere. This, as we will show, simply is not true. The strategy is not obsolete but it does need updating (particularly in its interaction with the other strategy that opens up the opportunities that it ignores).

Nor is this local perception, crucial though it always is, everywhere the same. Furer-Haimendorf (1975), in his study of Himalayan traders, has stressed a major cognitive and behavioural dichotomy between those - the 'cautious cultivators' - who equate wealth with land and those - the 'adventurous traders' - who do not make this equation. The result is a remarkable divergence of personal strategies: the pessimistic 'zero-sum game' of the conservative stay-at-home cultivator versus the optimistic 'positive-sum game' of the expansive and cosmopolitan trader. Since this distinction goes along with two of the crucial axes that characterize the whole region - the cultural axis between Buddhists and Hindus (the adventurous traders tend to be Buddhists and the cautious cultivators Hindus) and the physical axis between upstream and downstream (the Buddhists tend to occupy the high valleys and the Hindus the Middle Ranges and the Terai) - it has far-reaching implications for the design and implementation of policy.

Whilst Cronin's succinct characterization of 'the villager's mind' fits well enough with the institutional supports that sustain the 'cautious cultivator' strategy, it does not fit at all well with the very different institutional supports that sustain the 'adventurous trader' strategy. That is, not only is local perception a key consideration in the design of effective policy, but that local perception itself varies dramatically from one locality to another. The

16

tragedy of the classic ('what are the facts?') approach is that, by according the hill farmer just a token place in the arena, it commits itself to viewing the Himalaya as one enormous homogenized smear: 'the hill farmer', 'the villager's mind', 'the sustainable yield', 'the per capita fuelwood consumption rate' ... 'the carrying capacity'. But the Himalaya are not like that at all.

The state of empirical knowledge, patchy though it is, tells us that more trees are being cut down in some areas than in others, and that the same sort of variation holds for the soil that is indeed washing down the rivers, and for the population that is indeed increasing, but these relative rates and their significance have defied all attempts at global 'objective' analysis. That there is a problem is difficult to dispute but there are tremendous local variations in its manifestations and, more importantly, in its perception. In the Himalaya the ultimate clients of any programme of sustainable development are astonishingly diverse, and the interrelationships between all the brokers of economic and political power flows are remarkably complex. This is the arena in which data are being collected, models constructed, and projects launched. There is great technical uncertainty and the quality of the data reflects this but, even more importantly, different people are approaching the situation with different perceptions and with different ambitions.

The Himalaya may be poor in natural resources but they are extraordinarily rich in institutional variety - in contradictory perceptions, in multiple problem definitions, in plural rationalities, and in contending prescriptions - something which, alas, the classic approach, with its homogenizing assumptions and its inappropriate cis-science methods, is ill-equipped to handle. Perhaps the greatest single justification for the trans-science approach, and for its central preoccupation with institutions and credibility, is the simple recognition: where there is heterogeneity there is hope. This does not mean that there is no place for cis-science in the Himalaya; only that, at present, much of it is misplaced and misapplied. The essential heterogeneity of the region is precisely what the cis-science data capture - it makes sense of specific localized contexts. To then generalise that data across the region is simply to throw away all the understanding that it contains and to generate from it not policies but platitudes.

THE KHUMBU FORESTS REVISITED

It is worth pausing here for a moment to show how Houston's perception and the perceptions of those who argue for the existence of the crisis can be reconciled. Since a major strand in our argument is that cis-science is at present being misused, we should try to say more precisely what this misuse consists of. There are, it seems to us, two urges (both of which have their institutional origin at the macro-level of international bureaucracy and science) that should have been resisted. The first is the urge to generalize locally valid data across the region. The second is the urge to quantify what appear, from this lofty viewpoint, to be the key variables of the system.

Of course, the Khumbu forests are not at all typical - they are at a high altitude in a region that is not densely populated - and the forests that are causing most concern are those that extend (or used to extend) from the Middle Ranges down into the Terai. But, even so, we can use the example of the Khumbu forests to explain what we mean about the misuse of cis-science and to show the sort of progress that can be made by developing a sensitivity to contexts and by drawing upon the largely qualitative data of trained observers (and local inhabitants) who have detailed and often long-term experience of a particular locality.

On his second visit to Khumbu (in 1973), Furer-Haimendorf found that fires were lit only for cooking whereas, on his first visit (in 1957), they had been kept going all the waking hours. This must represent a fuelwood saving of at least a third and indicates that, sometime between 1957 and 1973, something happened to fuelwood supply. What? The forest productivity could not suddenly have changed, and the population did not suddenly increase. Nor is it very likely that this was the sudden cumulative result of gradual long-term misuse. The fact that the Sherpas had been living in Khumbu for 400 years or so without destroying the forest pretty well rules that out. One explanation that is sometimes advanced is that the increase in mountaineering and tourism had placed an excessive pressure on the forest resource but this, on closer inspection, does not bear up either.

Trekkers' permits are checked at Namche police station and in 1977 there were about 5,000 recorded. Since trekkers have been increasing rapidly year by year, the total must have been considerably less in 1973 when Furer-Haimendorf noticed the drastic reduction in fuelwood consumption. But, even if we take this high figure and assume that each trekker spends a fortnight in the area, we obtain an increase of only around 200 man-years consumption as against a saving of one third of the permanent population (which has long remained fairly constant at about 2,200). Since this works out at roughly 700 man-years of consumption (at the old rate) foregone - a sum that far exceeds the increased demand resulting from tourism - we must look elsewhere for an explanation. (3)

For 400 years the Sherpas were able to burn as much wood as they wanted and then suddenly, between 1957 and 1973, they had to cut back drastically. If it was not the tourists and it was not population increase, what was it? Well, in the 1950s the forests were nationalized. Management was taken out of local hands and transferred to central government - a reform which, we know, destroyed the indigenous management system (based on a rotating village office of forest guardians who managed the traditional village forest as a renewable resource) that had worked successfully for centuries and then did not work itself. Once this had happened the gentle controls were off and people began to take too much wood from the nearby forest and not enough from farther away. The thicket of dwarf juniper at Pheriche disappeared and so too, by Furer-Haimendorf's account, did some other areas of forest close to the villages and the trekking routes. But, on the other hand, Houston too is largely correct in that vast tracts of forest some distance from the villages and trekking routes are still intact. Indeed, large fallen trees lie rotting within them. If this is the case - if it is not a lack of forest but a lack of control of forest - then the solution is a temporary moratorium on taking wood from the nearby forest, and the best means of effectively doing this is probably a revival of the system of village forests and forest guardians backed up, if need be, by the sanctions that the local Everest National Park staff are already empowered by central government to exercise. At the same time, both institutions can probably collaborate in replanting the bits of forest that have disappeared and in gently enforcing the regulations that require trekkers to be self-sufficient in fuel (e.g. gas or kerosene) once they enter the park.

So here is a plausible, and testable, explanation of what has been happening to the Khumbu forests (4) - an explanation that closely relates such data as exist to their context, that makes use of detailed local observation and experience, that incorporates such historical facts and trends as are known, and that, by respecting the integrity of both Houston and those that he criticizes, is able to zero in onto the sort of fine-grained and critical shifts in collective resource management that alone can tell us what is wrong and what needs to be done to put it right.

Of course this is a very tentative explanation and prescription, based on just a few field studies that, moreover, were not even directed at the question of forest use, but, even so, it serves to highlight the meaninglessness of such generalizations as the per capita fuelwood consumption rate and the absurdity of the sort of premature quantification that tries to tell us that Nepal is losing 6.5 million tons of wood a year. (5)

GETTING TO GRIPS WITH UNCERTAINTY

The wide uncertainty surrounding Himalayan deforestation provides us with a wide choice of problems. We could, if we were so minded, simply choose the problem best suited to our approach and discard the rest; but that, of course, would mean claiming that that was the real problem and that all the others were unreal. If we want to preserve what is real about all these problems - the uncertainty as to which, if any, of them is the real problem - then we have to treat the problem we choose simply as a point of entry: a way of opening up and exploring the complex physical, social, and cultural system that is currently generating all this uncertainty. Since this whole idea of putting the problems inside the uncertainty runs so counter to the established patterns of applied science, we should make explicit the various steps that are involved in this sort of exploratory exercise.

The trans-science approach to uncertainty

The system that we wish to describe is, first and foremost, a system for generating uncertainty. This uncertainty, we would argue, is not inherent in the bio-physical properties of the system (though they, of course, are not irrelevant to it), nor is it generated just by accident, nor is it generated just for its own sake. It is generated by institutions for

20

institutions. The survival of an institution rests ultimately upon the credibility it can muster for its idea of how the world is; for its definition of the problem; for its claim that its version of the real is self-evident. And, for such credibility to be maintained, the institution must come tolerably close to delivering on the expectations that rationally flow from the system of knowledge that it promotes. (6) In this way, uncertainties to knowledge about physical processes are brought face-to-face with the creation of expectations by social processes. Social institutions are the means by which these two - knowledge and experience - are brought together, and only those institutions that manage to achieve some measure of consistency in this conflation can remain credible and viable.

If we have a system of plural institutions - a system that depends for its very existence on the contention of the diverse institutions that comprise it - then we should expect it to display a number of fundamental system properties: plural perceptions, plural problem definitions, plural expectations, and plural rationalities. And for such a system to go on existing it will, somehow or other, have to generate sufficient uncertainty to swamp all the contradictions that are inherent in the pluralized positions it contains.

To describe such a system you have to observe it, and herein lies the next difficulty. The observer is inevitably a part of the system he wishes to observe; there is no way that he can step right outside it and play the 'cosmic exile' (the traditional role of the cis-scientist). Our terms of reference and, indeed, the whole context within which the institutions we are embedded in were able to come together to conceive, approve, and fund this project predisposed us to grant credibility to one particular problem definition - that in terms of the trans-boundary properties of the silt and water runoffs in the Himalayan region. So we begin by treating this particular problem as if it is the real problem but, mindful of all the uncertainty we have already described, we try to resist the narrow parochialism that inevitably closes in around any single-problem definition by all the time asking ourselves how this particular definition might relate to some other possible definitions. By doing this we are able to list some practical reasons - some useful advantages - for choosing as our point of entry this trans-boundary problem. Then, as we try to generalize these advantages by placing this trans-boundary problem into its political and institutional setting, and by conceding that all sorts of other flows (technology 'transfers', for instance) also encounter boundary problems, we are able to translate these practical advantages into tactical and even strategic advantages.

In other words, we gradually detach ourselves from a particular set of trans-boundary problems - those involving water and silt flows between the countries of the region - and fasten finally upon trans-boundary problems of a much more general kind. Boundaries, we come to realize, are being generated (or actively maintained) all over the place and we end up by focusing on the perceptual and transactional boundaries that serve to separate and sustain all the various contending institutions. The physical boundaries between the nations of the region, of course, fall within this frame but, as our exploration has proceeded, so we have found them becoming less and less significant. And, as this particular trans-boundary problem has receded, so others have come to the fore. If we were to single out one particular type of trans-boundary problem as being the most significant, we would choose the problems of transfer between national and village-level institutions - between programme provision and programme delivery.

Point of entry: some credible problems

1.   Is the problem the environmental degradation of the Himalaya? If so, we must consider all the vegetated vertical zones - from the alpine pastures to the Terai. (These zones are not at all clear-cut; see Cronin (1979:22-25.)

2.   Is the problem the deforestation of the Himalaya? If so, we must consider the forest zones or, at least, those that are or may be subject to deforestation.

3.   Is the problem the downstream effects - the worsening impacts of flooding, the silting of dams, the clogging of turbines? If so, we have only to consider the increased runoff (from removal of the forest buffering), the increased erosion (from deforestation, over-grazing, over-terracing - over-extension of land use generally), and the increased transport of silt (from the combination of these two).

The serious trans-boundary problem is the last one. It is, of course, nested within the first two wider problems so far as the total physical/biological system is concerned, but it stands by itself as a <u>political</u> problem.

In one sense, of course, it really does not matter where we start. Whether we begin with the tail or the trunk, the systems approach, concerned all the time with the <u>connectedness</u> of the parts, should lead us to the same totality - the elephant. But there are, nevertheless, certain practical advantages in starting with this particular trans-boundary problem.

1.   Being political, it is directly concerned with 'the art of the possible' - with delineating what, if anything, can be done given the way people and nations are now and might be in the immediate future.

2.   It sets for its solution a clearcut and, by comparison with the other two problems, a modest goal - mitigating the downstream effects until they become roughly equivalent to what they were some years ago. With the other problems, by contrast, you run the risk of inadvertently committing yourself to the immodest and politically unreasonable goal of restoring the ecosystem to what it was before man arrived on the Himalayan scene.

3.   It places at the centre the whole system the agent responsible (in the physical sense of wielding the axe, that is, not in a social or political sense) for the problem - the individual hill farmer. In so doing it encourages us to understand his perceptions, his ecological theories, his strategies for coping with environmental dangers, his relations with his fellow men, and the way in which all these act so as to shape the options that are open to him and to guide him in his choice between them.

With this particular focus, the art of the possible becomes concerned with two things - the possibility of influencing his situation so that the options available to him are changed (either by adding new ones or removing old ones or both) and the possibility of influencing his choice between these options (by, somehow or other, changing their attractiveness relative to one another). Such influences can be brought to bear in two ways - by enforcement and by incentives. So far as the art of the possible is concerned, these sticks and carrots are the only instruments there are for reversing the downward spiral of degradation. If no combination of these instruments can achieve this, then there is no solution. If there is no solution, then there is no problem. It is important not to lose sight of this possibility; if there is no solution then resources, both financial and intellectual, should be redirected towards adapting to the inevitable.

In contrast to this art of the possible, where policy options have always to be measured against the solid (but locally variable) features of the hill farmer, there is what might be called the 'science of the possible' which simply ignores these obstacles. The challenge is, somehow or other, to explore both these - to experience the exhilaration and scope of what <u>could</u> be whilst, at the same time, gaining some sort of feel for the institutional barriers that may inhibit its attainment.

The crucial distinction between the 'science' and the 'art' is that the first sees the agent (in this case, the hill farmer) as a sort of zombie who just sits there having his life altered by the various ingenious policies that are targetted on him, whilst the second sees him as a responsive strategizing being who may be expected, not to just passively receive such policies, but to react to them as well. The science of the possible, therefore, has no place for perceptions, it sees cis-science as the only way to go, and it deals in technical fixes. The art of the possible, by contrast, accords a central place to perceptions - they are what makes <u>reactivity</u> possible - it leans towards trans-science, and it anticipates the institutional obstacles that may get in the way of the technical fixes. To understand just the fixes is to risk some nasty surprises once you start to implement them; to understand just the obstacles is to risk never getting to the point of implementing anything. The challenge, therefore, is not to choose one or the other but to usefully combine these two modes of understanding.

So let us start with the science of the possible and, ignoring the hill farmer and his heterogeneous perceptions, explore the range of solutions that are logically possible - solutions, that is, to the trans-boundary problem of increased runoff and silt transport from the hills causing increased flooding in the plains. But since we already know, from our exploration of the uncertainties surrounding this problem, that there may not <u>be</u> a causal connection between the human activities in the hills and the flooding in the plains, we should include alongside each of these 'solutions' a description of how they would look for this sceptical perspective.

Adherence to one or other of these perspectives is not haphazardly distributed, nor is it simply a function of personality. The view that there is a clear causal connection is the perspective to which those in the plains, close to the sources of power and its articulation, tend to subscribe. Behind it one can almost hear the irate administrator complaining about 'the debris from misused high-altitude watersheds' cascading down onto the plains as a direct result of the unruly behaviour of 'subsistence farmers on steep slopes in remote areas'. The view that there is no clear causal connection is the perspective of those whose precarious autonomy at the mountainous margin of all this power is sustained by the 'implicit compact' that guarantees the continued existence of the Himalayan buffer states. Since too much 'unruly behaviour' in the hills may cause those in the plains to abandon this implicit compact and move up to take control of the buffer, the autonomous margin has to do what it can to manage its relationship with the plains so as to lessen the likelihood of this happening.

Such management - the management of powerlessness - is often achieved by strategizing behaviour, by an actor, at certain moments and in certain circumstances, taking up a position that is not, in fact, his true position. For instance, that of the Nepalese ambassador who, by lending credibility to the existence of a clear causal connection, can further justify his claim to increased international aid, and hence autonomy, for the margin. The result of all this strategizing behaviour is an apparent blurring of the clear separation of perspectives between those in the plains and those in the hills - between centre and margin. The scientific expert, too, may find himself drawn into all this as, for instance, when he adopts the position of a sceptical observer in the hills and speaks out on behalf of remote villagers who otherwise would have no voice in the policy debate. That, to a considerable extent, is what we are doing here.

Of course, to speak in terms of just two fundamental perspectives - one from the plains and one from the hills - is to grossly over-simplify the patterns of socially induced perceptions in the region, and the fact that strategizing behaviour sometimes has the policy actors hopping back and forth between the various perceptual vantage points only complicates things still further. Though these underlying patterns and their overlays of strategizing behaviour can be sorted out, (7) we will not attempt to do much of that here. Instead, we will simply try to keep the idea of plural problem definitions alive by moving back and forth between just two of these socially induced perceptions - the 'irate administrator's' and the 'sceptical observer's'. What we are doing, in effect, is taking a crude geo-political slice through all these varied perceptions. We identify the axis between the plains and the hills, and its accompanying implicit compact, as one of the key variables in the whole system and we then collapse all the perceptions down onto that axis and explore the range of credible problems and credible solutions through the remarkably different perceptions that lie at each end of that axis. What follows, therefore, is not a complete analysis of problems and solutions but an exploratory range-finding exercise.

Some credible solutions

Solution 1: Restore the runoff (by increasing the tree cover) and restore the erosion rate (by reducing the landslides and gullying that are caused by human activity <u>and</u> by increasing the tree cover) so as to reduce the violence of the flooding to what it was ten, fifteen, thirty, or whatever years ago. This is an <u>upstream solution.</u>

The sceptical observer in the hills sees things rather differently. In his experience, 'the major effects are felt primarily at source. We don't count them because uplanders don't record the disappearance of their farms from landslip or burial or chronic deterioration' (Jeff Romm, 1983, personal communication). From this perspective, the distinction between upstream and downstream cannot be drawn just once - at the line that separates the hills from the plains. Rather, every point in the hills is upstream of somewhere and downstream of somewhere else, and the distinction is one that has to be drawn over and over again if we are to gain any valid understanding of what is happening there. This distinction between upstream and downstream is crucial because water flows downhill, and the critical issue becomes how to redistribute water consumption. The problem (in the hills, for the hills, throughout the hills) is that the present pattern of water distribution, when combined with the ethno-ecological knowledge and associated strategies of the hill farmers, tends to encourage 'extensive land use in land scarce conditions' (Jeff Romm, 1983, personal communication).

There is no magic solution. Rather it will be necessary to somehow or other encourage a gradual and pervasive shift in patterns of water distribution so as to steadily move away from widespread extensive land use towards a patchwork of

26

intensive use (where landslip hazards are low and other conditions are appropriate) and detensive use (where landslip hazards are high and other conditions render intensive use inappropriate). If there is a causal connection between human activity in the hills and flooding in the plains then, the sceptical observer would hold, this redistribution of water in the hills will do more to lessen that impact than anything else.

The irate administrator's perception leads him towards the integrated watershed management solution - a solution which presupposes that someone is in a position to do the managing. The sceptical observer's perception leads him towards a facilitated water redistribution solution - a solution which presupposes that no one is in a key position to do any managing. The sceptical observer is keenly interested in the ecological theories, land-use categories, and associated risk-handling strategies of the hill farmers because they provide the basis from which facilitation can start. The irate administrator shows little interest in such things and is often driven to distraction by the deviant and irrational behaviour of 'these people'. The irate administrator, you might say, sees the hill farmer as part of the problem; the sceptical observer sees him as part of the solution.

Solution 2. Reduce the impact of the increased runoff and silt transport to match what it was ten, fifteen, thirty years ago (by flood control engineering, relocation of settlements, and so on). This is a downstream solution.

The sceptical observer would point out that, though he is doubtful about there being an increase in the runoff and silt transport, this is probably still a sensible thing to do. It is, in fact, the traditional solution in the plains, and all those large-scale public works and resettlement schemes are just what is needed to keep the irate administrator happy and to divert his attention from the punitive expedition into the hills that he has been contemplating.

A little historical vignette may help to show the way in which the articulation of the political power that resides in the plains and the implementation of downstream solutions go hand-in-hand. Political power needs public works and public works need political power.

The Ganges Canal was the brain-child of Captain Proby

27

Cantley of the Bengal Engineers. He was convinced that it was possible to get water out of the Ganges and into the Doab, the land between the Jumna and the Ganges, an immense area which suffered from frequent and terrible famines. He made his first survey in 1836.

Then came the institutional obstacles - toes being trodden on in the efforts to co-ordinate departments that had not had to be co-ordinated before, and all the exquisite agonies of implementation:

> Every kind of difficulty had to be overcome: orders and counter-orders came from the authorities, civil and military, in bewildering confusion. One moment it was to be an irrigation canal, next for navigation only. Then it was not to be built at all; notwithstanding the fact that the East Jumna Canal which had originally been built by the Mughals in the eighteenth century had been extremely successful in combating famine in the country which it passed through.

Then there came the gloomy prognostications of the doomsters of the day:

> It was said that earthquakes would destroy the viaducts, that miasmas would hang over the irrigated lands, that malaria would become rife and that the navigation of the Ganges would be affected. (This last objection was the only one that proved to be right.)

In overcoming all these obstacles the great empire was able to demonstrate its power and to impress upon those who were affected by the project the full extent of their incorporation into that empire.

> Twelve years after its commencement the Ganges was finally admitted into the canal at Hardwar in April 1854 ... By the eighties it had been extended as far as Allahabad and the irrigation of the Doab was complete. Its completion marked the end of serious famine in the area. (This and preceding quotes, Newby, 1966:61).

Solution 3. Some politically and physically optimal combination of Solutions 1 and 2. This is an <u>upstream and</u>

28

downstream solution.

The sceptical observer in the hills will probably identify as optimal a combination somewhat different from that identified by the irate administrator in the plains. But, even so, when the notion of the appropriateness of different solutions as we go from downstream to upstream - from centre to margin - is fed into this combination, a surprising amount of agreement can be reached.

The sceptical observer, for his part, can approve of the large-scale downstream solutions whilst the irate administrator, well aware that the implementation of integrated management schemes is much more easily achieved in areas where his control is effective than in areas where it is not, may well be relieved to have the hills taken off his hands. Provided he can bring himself to accept (and justify) that other, less managed solutions, are appropriate in the areas to which his writ will not run, then the irate administrator may well be prepared to let the facilitated solution take precedence over his managed solution. Disagreements, of course, will remain but at least this matching up of institutional obstacles and technical fixes allows us to fractionate the issue and to avoid demanding an answer to the question, 'Who is right?'. With this debilitating demand safely out of the way, the administrator can now become a little less irate and the observer a little less sceptical. But that is not the end of it. We still have to consider the unthinkable solutions.

Solution 4. Let it collapse. If the Himalaya are desertified their population will decrease dramatically and human impacts will similarly decrease. But, quite apart from the human misery this would entail, perhaps the runoff and silt transportation - the non-human impacts - would be even worse than before.

It is not easy for the layman to gain any clear conception of what the desertified Himalaya would be like. We could, of course, look at those parts of the Himalaya (like Ladakh, the Karakorum, and Dolpo) that are deserts now, but these regions are deserts because they lie beyond the reach of the monsoon. It is the idea of the wet desert that is so difficult to grasp. A first reaction is that it must be a contradiction in terms - an emotional but scientifically indefensible outcry against environmental degradation - but, no, the north of Scotland, once covered by a rich forest of

Scots pine, is now a wet desert and in many parts of Southeast Asia denuded hills, their fragile soils leached by the heavy rains, now support little but coarse lalang grass. So wet deserts do exist and it is possible, perhaps inevitable, that the Himalaya will (in whole or in part) become one.

Neither the irate administrator nor the sceptical observer confronts this possibility head-on. Given their prior commitments to their respective restorative policies their eyes are inevitably averted from a prospect in which these policies will be rendered totally useless. As they urge their various prescriptions they use the wet desert as a sort of bogeyman: 'If you persist in disregarding what we are telling you, the wet desert will get you'. This is not to say that they should change what they are doing; only that, like the Hudson Institute's study of nuclear war and its accompanying megadeaths and overkills, there is also a need for someone to think the unthinkable in the Himalaya.

Of course, it could be argued that such a study would be a waste of time and money because even the most cursory survey of what is likely to happen if the Himalaya are desertified is sufficient to convince us that to deliberately allow such a thing to happen could never be a sensible policy. But to take up that position is to assume that the choice is ours. It may be, but what if it is not?

Solution 5. If the collapse is unavoidable anyway then the problem is one of adapting to the inevitable. What would and could such adaptations entail? Exploration of this question will open up some unfamiliar and surprising policy options - the development and settlement of the new island that is forming in the Bay of Bengal, for instance, and the possibilities of controlling the silt flow through the Ganges delta to create and stabilize further new land. The deployment of capital-intensive projects undergoes a similarly dramatic switch - from gulley-plugs in the Siwaliks (the Himalayan foothills) to seawalls in the Sunderbans (the alluvial islands of the delta (Fazal, 1983).

Though neither the sceptical observer in the hills nor the irate administrator in the plains would wish to concede the inevitability of collapse, both may nevertheless seek to benefit from some of the policy options that are opened up by its contemplation. Nepal, for instance, has already tried to establish its claim to this new island (on the grounds that it is Nepalese soil) and, if it is successful, it might be well-advised to seek Dutch aid in place of the Swiss and Austrian aid that it sees as appropriate now.

Again, a little historical vignette may give us some feel for the awesome processes that are at work in the region:

> A Victorian engineer, Sir Charles Lyell (an eminent geologist, in fact), estimated that 350,000,000 tons of silt were discharged each year at Ghazipur on the Middle Ganges. 'Nearly the weight of sixty replicas of the Great Pyramid'. A useless comparison. 'It is scarcely possible', he goes on, 'to present any picture to the mind which will convey an adequate conception to the mind of the mighty scale of this operation, so tranquilly and almost insensibly carried out by the Ganges'. Whether some smallholder in Bihar, watching his half-acre slipping noisily into the water and his family being swept downstream on top of a haystack would regard the operation as being either tranquil or insensible is open to question. No one knows for certain the depth of the alluvial silt in the Delta. (Newby, 1966:16).

These sixty pyramids per year have over the millenia created the Delta and, if they are to some extent the product of human activity in the Himalaya, then that land, far from being a 'given' - a part of nature's endowment - is to a considerable extent 'the flesh and blood and sweat of men' (quoted by Simon, 1981:85). While it has been well said that God made the Dutch but the Dutch made Holland, the trans-boundary properties of this Himalayan system give an extra twist to the relationship. God may have made the Bangladeshis but the Nepalese (with some help from the forces of gravity) made Bangladesh!

Solution 6. Even if the collapse is not unavoidable we should still consider various combinations of these adaptive policies with the restorative policies of Solutions 1, 2 and 3 above.

Somewhere, between the undoubted good sense of putting a few bamboo stakes into a river bank in Bhutan to prevent a valuable rice paddy from being swept away and the undoubted stupidity of carting alluvium from Bangladesh back up into the hills to rebuild a little terraced field on a ridiculously steep and landslip-prone slope, there is a line that can and should be drawn.

31

The sociology of perception (which is what we have been relying on to guide us as we have tried to feel our way through all these credible solutions), whilst it does argue that problems and solutions are shaped by institutional forces, does not argue that they can be shaped into anything at all. It does not require us to take up a position so relativistic as to deny the existence of the line. No, all of the socially induced perceptions can agree that the line can be drawn; their disagreements are over just where it should be drawn. And the definition of the problem, the credibility of the solution, and the formulation of sensible policies are all directly related to the position of that line. (If they were not - if, as sometimes happens with some policy issues, the noose of certainty was so tight that such variability and polarization was not possible - then the whole issue could be dealt with in terms of cis-science and there would be no need for the application of this trans-science approach.)

So this whole exploration of alternative Himalayan realities does fit inside some physically imposed frame. Whatever we might argue about the social malleability of physical facts we would not wish to argue that physical facts can be whatever we want them to be. Water, for instance, we concede does flow downhill. Or, to avoid any criticism for being over-positivistic, let us say that, if we assume that it does, we get quite good results, and quite good results, not perfect enlightenment, is all we are seeking.

Putting these problems and solutions into a physical frame

Since all these credible problems fit inside a physical frame, it does not matter which particular credible problem we use as our point of entry for the exploration of that frame. So we stay with our initial 'as if' approach in terms of the trans-national boundary transfers of silt and water.

We have, in the first instance, to take the entire drainage basins of the Indus, the Ganges, and the Brahmaputra. But, since runoff and catastrophic flooding are caused by the monsoon rains, we do not really have to consider those parts of the basins that lie beyond the limits of the monsoon (but could the monsoon change? Is it changing?). Nor do we need to bother too much about those areas that are above the cultivation limit (approximately 2,300 m, but it varies with latitude and with culture). Nor, so far as cause is concerned, do we need to bother about the plains. We are left with a long, narrow winding strip all the way from Kashmir in the west to the Naga hills in the east. Which countries are involved? Pakistan (perhaps only marginally), India, Nepal, Bhutan (India presently responsible for foreign policy), India again ... Burma (has the same problem but does not drain into the Brahmaputra - the frontier lies along the watershed). Also, in several places (for example, Sun Kosi and Arun valley in Nepal, north of Sikkim, and north of Assam and Arunachal Pradesh in India) China is involved. In some of these areas the frontier currently is not clearly defined or is in dispute.

But what this long, narrow strip does not reveal is the convolution of the landscape that it contains. Though the cause lies within this strip, it is far from evenly distributed along it. The oft-quoted statistic that the volume of silt disgorged into the Ganges by the Karnali is equivalent to the annual removal of a layer of land one and three-quarter millimetres thick from the entire drainage basin of the Karnali River should not be interpreted as a valid description of what is actually happening. (8)

The convolutions of the Himalayan landscape, and its underlying geology, render some localities particularly prone to mass wastage and others virtually immune. (9) And some localities are actually subject to mass deposition; that is where the Kathmandu Valley came from. Far from the cause being evenly spread, ninety per cent of the 'damage' may result from ten per cent of the land. Recognition of this profound heterogeneity within the long, narrow strip helps us to introduce a strategic perspective. What is needed is a rejection of homogenizing generalizations and their replacement by a sensitivity for local contexts. On the one hand, we will just be throwing scarce resources away if we approach the problem in terms of generalized data and, on the other hand, we will simply be wasting our efforts if we persist in packaging land by administrative units, map grids, and fence lines. Instead, we must recognize that any set of data is meaningful only in relation to its context and we should allow the data themselves to tell us what are the appropriate (that is, meaningful) land packages.

So much for the cause; now what about the effects? Where are the serious (and, perhaps, worsening) floods? The floods occur in India (in the Ganges, Brahmaputra, and Indus plains), in Bangladesh (fairly widespread throughout the delta) and, to a lesser extent, in Pakistan (in the Indus and

Figure 1.1: Schematic representation of cause and effect.

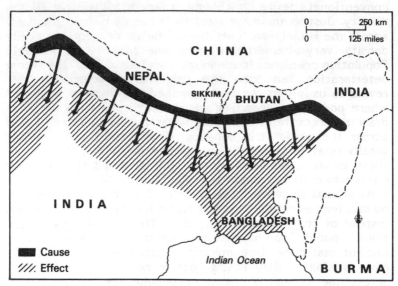

Punjab river plains) and in Nepal (in the Terai). As with the cause, we obtain a fairly clearly-defined geographical area for the effect.

Figure 1.1 makes salient a number of key features:

1. Cause and effect are clearly separated geographically. (For schematic clarity, they are shown as more separate than they probably are.)
2. This separation, in several instances, coincides with national frontiers and thereby gives rise to the transnational properties of the system. Moreover, the direction of causation defines 'giver' and 'receiver' nations (for example, Nepal and Bhutan are givers, Bangladesh is a receiver, India is both a giver and a receiver but receives more than it gives).
3. The areas of both cause and effect are densely populated (the area of cause perhaps 40 million, the area of effect perhaps 350 million). So the problem is first and foremost a people problem; it is a social, economic, and political problem set against a dramatic physical backdrop - the greatest mountain range in the world.

But to state the problem baldly like this is to feed the conventional desire to blame everything on population density. Just as the mass wastage is not evenly skimmed off across the Himalayan foothills, so the effects of population density vary dramatically from one locality to another. Population pressure often enough does lead to environmental deterioration, but what this long, narrow strip does not reveal to us is that the best managed lands are often found where population densities are also high. We simply cannot draw a direct relationship between population and effect across the whole strip because the effect of population is totally relative to institutional and technical capacities, and these social capacities vary from village to village and from culture to culture across the region. So long as technical and institutional capacities advance ahead of population there is no problem; eventually we can all be living in space colonies instead of on Himalayan hillsides. The trouble only comes when population seriously outstrips technical and institutional capacities and this situation, like proneness to mass wastage, is something that is not uniformly present across the region. To identify population density as the problem, without developing any feel for the localized variations in institutional arrangements that everywhere modify its effect on the land, is to compound on the social level the misdirection of effort engendered by homogenizing assumptions about mass wastage at the physical level.

Now, with this physical frame and its heterogeneous properties established, we can reverse the procedure of our earlier exploration (in which we simplified the perspectives so as to open up the variety of problems and solutions) and move on to explore more fully the ways in which this dramatic physical backdrop can be perceived.

Some credible perspectives

One perception might be that the problem is the collective responsibility of the countries that are physically affected, in which case the patterns of cause and effect - of giver and receiver nations - could provide a first tentative framework for the necessary international negotiations between them. But such a perception is unrealistically static in that it ignores the grand process that has created, and is still transforming, the present state of affairs.

The forest historian (Tucker, 1981) will point out that,

at one time, most of the Indian sub-continent was covered in forest and that, over the centuries, this forest has been gradually rolled back (under the combined influence of population increase, technological development, and political development) across the plains and up into the foothills. What we are witnessing now is simply the final stage of this awesome historical process. From this dynamic perspective, halting and, to some extent, reversing this trend is an even more formidable task than that revealed by the more static perspective. In particular, preserving and restoring the forests along the Himalaya, without at the same time doing something similar in the plains, looks like a very artificial and processually naive thing to try to do. Historical processes, of course, seldom do have 'final stages'. What looks like a final stage often turns out to be simply a turning point. In North America and in Europe the forests, after being rolled back for centuries, are now actually rolling forward. The point we wish to make is that a feel for this historical momentum is crucial for anyone who is trying to hasten this turning point (if it exists) in the Himalayan region.

Another virtue of placing the problem within its historical context is that it provides us with some guidance on the critical uncertainty as to whether the forested land in the system now is being treated as a renewable resource or as a convertible resource (in much the same way as the waters of the Ganges were converted by public works into a means for the extension of political influence). Clearly, the whole rolling-back process depends upon the forests being treated as a convertible resource. Only in the case of the little pockets that remain is there any likelihood of renewable resource treatment. If what is happening in the Himalaya now is essentially the continuation of this rolling-back process, then this would suggest that much of the forested land is being treated as a convertible resource but, at the same time, the physical contortion and the political marginality of the region should result in many more (and larger) pockets of renewable resource being left behind than has been the case in the plains.

The strategic implications of this historical insight are profound. The rolling-back process imposes a complex pattern of heterogeneity - renewability here, convertibility there - on the Himalayan forests. In the pockets, all the institutions will be geared toward renewal and will only need sufficient encouragement and support for their forests to remain intact. Elsewhere, all the institutions will be geared toward conversion and will first of all have to be 'turned round' for conservation to become feasible.

From a wider international perspective, the idea that the problem is the concern only of the directly affected countries is similarly naive. The Himalaya, for better or for worse, exert a powerful fascination over people and organizations many thousands of kilometres from the Indian sub-continent. At the level of the global community, the Himalaya enjoy (or suffer) a status that is little short of a de facto International Park. The English garden is largely composed of Himalayan plants originally collected by Sir Joseph Hooker; Nanga Parbat is a German Mountain, K2 an American mountain, Annapurna a French mountain, Everest a British (and New Zealand) mountain (not, we hasten to add, in any colonial sense but in the sense that these nations' relationships with, and understanding of, the region are to a considerable extent shaped through their historic involvements with these mountains). There are Californian monks in Tibetan monastries in Kathmandu, Spanish nuns in Lahouli nunneries in Kulu, and world travellers of every nationality, colour, and creed spaced out all the way along the trails from Pokhara to Miktinath and from Lama Sangu to Everest Base Camp. The Himalaya are to this modern Grand Tour what Italy was to its eighteenth-century counterpart.

One exercise that might be worth taking seriously, as a way of exploring the wider international pressures that bear upon the region, would be to treat the Himalaya as an International Park and to enquire, first, into what sorts of park management techniques would be appropriate in different institutionalized settings within the developed world and, second, into how those techniques (and the recipient) might fare when they are transplanted from the centre out into what is really the margin of the periphery of the global economic system. It is ironic that, whilst those individuals who embark upon this Grand Tour do so in the hope of putting a little distance between themselves and the elaborate institutional arrangements (especially the bureaucratic ones) of their highly developed home countries, those who are responsible for the delivery of international and national government aid programmes are drawn almost exclusively from those irksome institutional reaches. In consequence, the exploration of these various transplants may well reveal more about the institutional disjunctions within the highly developed North than about the cultural gulf that separates it from the less developed South. If it does, then that is all to the good; aid can then flow one way and self-understanding the other.

In the nineteenth century the Alps became 'the playground of Europe', and it is this idea that has shaped them into the sporting, convalescing, and recreational paradise (nightmare) that they are today. In America, the idea of 'the wilderness' so dominates the National Park scene as to make the Alps look like Disneyland-with-Snow. So stern is this ideal that, not only cog railways, ski-lifts and sumptuous mountain huts, but even the presence of natives in the landscape is frowned upon. In the lavishly illustrated Time-Life book The Himalayas (Nicholson and the editors of Time-Life Books, 1975), there is not a single Himalayan inhabitant of the species Homo sapiens to be seen. (10) In Britain the absence of wilderness and the presence of Wordsworth has led to a park ideal in which the appearance of man's interaction with nature is frozen at just the point where 'all is peace, rusticity, and happy poverty, in its neatest and most becoming attire' (Gray's Journal in the Lakes quoted by Wordsworth, 1810:70).

In the projects, the proposals, and the prescriptions currently aimed at the Himalaya all these park ideals can be discerned and, since their combined impact is likely to be considerable, an understanding of the various contending aesthetic orientations that underlie international concern for the Himalaya may well prove to be a useful evaluative aid.

A tentative synthesis

Possible problems and possible solutions do not meet up with one another in some value-free void; they come together only when there exists a possible perspective for them to come together in. Then, and only then, can appropriate and socially viable management styles emerge. Such possible perspectives are socially-shaped, value-impregnated, and aesthetically-articulated. Surprising though it may seem, it is aesthetics and not economics, or engineering, or applied science, or systems analysis, that has to be accorded the central role in formulating an approach to the problems of the Himalaya. It is writers, painters, and poets who profoundly change the world; economists, engineers, scientists, systems analysts, and, be it said, international agencies, just tinker with it (Boulding, 1983). Rather than succumbing to the temptation to see ourselves as the saviours of the Himalaya, we should heed Lord Keynes' salutary advice and aim to be 'like dentists' (Keynes, 1931).

Aesthetics, of course, is to the artists what ornithology is to the birds but, even so, it can help us to tinker in a more effective way. Parks, like other social and cultural institutions, have followed a developmental path. We have had private parks, municipal parks, national parks, binational parks (for example, between Canada and the USA) and now, for the first time, we have in the Himalaya a de facto international park. Since the same aesthetic forces that have shaped the parks we already have are, even now, shaping the parks we are about to get, there is much to be said for trying to understand these forces - the different perspectives within which possible problems and possible solutions can come together, and the different park management styles that can emerge from these conflations.

The aesthetic of the playground shapes the Euro-park; the aesthetic of the wilderness shapes the New World park; the aesthetic of man-and-nature-in-rustic-harmony shapes the British park. All three aesthetics (and, perhaps, others as well - the Japanese park?) are currently competing to shape the Himalayan park. We should enquire whether these competing aesthetics are inherently contradictory. If they are, then it is a waste of time trying to create a single management style out of them, and the solution is to fractionate the Himalaya (along the lines of the pattern in terms of renewable and convertible resources) and to encourage the application of the appropriate aesthetic and management style to each fraction - the wilderness style in the parts that are (or could feasibly become) sparsely populated (Hongu, for instance), the playground style in the areas (like Khumbu) that have already evolved in that direction, and the man-and-nature-in-rustic-harmony style in those more densely populated areas where man's impact is greatest.

If, on the other hand, the rival aesthetics are not entirely contradictory then, to the extent that they are not, it may be possible to negotiate (or, more properly, facilitate) between them with a view to moving toward a new synthetic aesthetic appropriate to the Himalaya. Or, rather, since the Himalaya are far from homogeneous, toward a number of distinct aesthetics - one (or more) appropriate to the Indian Himalaya, one appropriate to the Nepal Himalaya, one appropriate to the Bhutan Himalaya. Such negotiations, of course, are already being attempted - in the social forest/commercial forest distinction highlighted by the Chipko Movement in India (Tucker, 1981; Agarwal, 1982; Gadgil and Sharma, 1982), in the experimental efforts to establish National Parks in Nepal (where development zones have already been parcelled out to different national aid missions so as to avoid conflicts between their different, and perhaps irreconcilable, approaches), and in the careful preparations for the development of tourism in Bhutan (Jest and Stein, 1982).

The tentative conclusions that can be drawn from these negotiations suggest that there is little prospect for achieving any viable synthesis of these aesthetics. In its early attempts at establishing National Parks, Nepal would seem to have fallen foul of these contradictory park ideals by choosing (under external aid pressure, no doubt) one that was inappropriate. In many cases, it can be argued, the British ideal of man-and-nature-in-rustic-harmony would have been more appropriate than the American (and New Zealand) wilderness ideal that was initially chosen. Furer-Haimendorf states:

> National parks can be recommended only if the rights of the local inhabitants can be safeguarded. A totally misguided proposal to evacuate the Sherpa inhabitants from a Khumbu National Park has fortunately been abandoned. But the tragedy of the Rara National Park must be a warning to planners prepared to sacrifice human needs to the establishment of wildlife sanctuaries.

> On the banks of Rara Lake there used to be two medium sized Thakuri and Chetri settlements, which greatly contributed to the attractiveness of the locality. Neither had encroached on the surrounding forests, and the cultivation of crops of barley and potatoes utilized only a small area. The lake was full of fish which the local people caught only by spearing. Such was the position in the early 1970s. When a Wild Life Sanctuary was established, the inhabitants of the two villages, who had lived there for many generations, were forcibly evacuated, and moved from an environment situated at 10,000 feet above sea level to

the lowlands of Terai without being provided with adequate aid for their resettlement. It is reliably reported that the communities disintegrated and many perished within a short span of time. (Furer-Haimendorf, 1983, personal communication).

International aid and inadvertent cultural imperialism

The first thing to notice about these various park management styles is that they all involve management, not facilitation. As such they are antithetical to a political margin that has to sustain its precarious autonomy by playing off against one another (in the nicest possible way) the various external pressures that bear upon it. As long as it is successful in doing this it will keep itself largely free from hierarchical patterns of control. Of course, there is some control in the margin, and it is hierarchically organized, but it is remarkably undeveloped. A comparative study (Schloss, 1983) of Russian, American, Chinese, British, and Indian road construction projects in Nepal shows that, though each country adopted a distinctly different management style, they all encountered serious and unexpected difficulties in matching their styles to a situation where the machinery for administrative and financial management and control scarcely existed.

Their surprise is rather like that of the British colonial powers who, having chosen the principle of indirect rule as the best means of extending and consolidating their empire, found themselves up against some peoples in West Africa and the Sudan, the celebrated acephalous societies, who simply did not have any chiefs - any permanent positions of leadership - through which that indirect rule might be channelled. There are two ways of coping with such a surprise: keep the external style and change the indigenous organization, or keep the indigenous organization and change the external style. The first way leads to cultural imperialism; the second way leads to appropriate institutional development.

If we assume that imperial aggrandisement is not the aim of those who provide development aid, then what we are faced with is a facilitation problem on a global scale. At the macro-level an international park looks like a good idea but, as it moves from this provider level down to the delivery level, it starts running into difficulties. The challenge is to resist the temptation to push it through regardless (a temptation that, alas, it is particularly difficult for the bureaucrat to resist) so as to allow a learning process to move up in the reverse direction and modify the initial design to suit the local conditions.

A successful buffer draws a sharp distinction between itself and what lies outside it. Although governments in the Himalaya can do very little to directly control their hill farmers, they can (and do) exercise considerable direct control over their foreign tourists (and other visitors). They issue them with visas, they count them in and out, they grant or withhold trekking permits for various areas, they add and remove mountains from the list of available peaks, they insist on trekkers taking kerosene or gas fuel with them in the Everest region, and they demand that adequate insurance be taken out on the lives of high-altitude porters, engaged for mountaineering expeditions (they also exercise much the same sort of control over research and aid projects). There are, of course, certain constraints on their freedom to channel this alien influx - to irrigate their land with tourists. Just as water will only flow downhill, so tourists (with a few notable exceptions - the Chitwan Game Reserve in the Terai, for instance, and river rafting) will only flow uphill, toward the mountains that are the object of their pilgrimage. Tourists are also very localized, culturally and spatially. They all want their four-minute breakfast eggs and they all want to go to the honey-pots of Leh, Kashmir, Kathmandu, Annapurna, and Everest, and in consequence, the very considerable sums of money that they spend are not at all evenly spread throughout the villages. And much of it, of course, never reaches the villages but stays in Kathmandu and even in California.

But, even so, by closing to tourist traffic this airstrip here and opening up that airstrip there, by stipulating that if you fly into the Everest region you must walk back (or vice versa), by granting or withholding trekking permits for different areas ... by initiating or discontinuing tourist buses along different roads, those who manage the powerlessness of the buffer are able to gain considerable scope to ease the tourist flow this way and that. In so doing they modify the social contexts, and hence the strategic behaviour, of remote villagers whose lives they are scarcely able to touch by any direct means (and it is, of course, an excess of <u>direct</u> control that is inimical to the inner workings of the buffer).

So the sharp distinction between the inside and the

outside of the buffer is the key to the successful modification of the park management styles as they make the transition from the provider to the delivery level. By fractionating the issue, so that direct control is exercised over the alien tourist and only indirect control over the indigenous hill farmer, the buffer is able to have the best of both worlds. The tourists, as they are carefully channelled to the places where they are needed, can enjoy all the blessings of an International Park whilst the hill farmers, pretty well immune from any such controls, can get on with their lives in what is for them a working and lived-in landscape. Just as, to the Sherpa, mountaineering is simply another kind of trading so, to the hill farmer, the International Park can be simply another way of making some of his natural resources more valuable to him.

HOW HAVE WE GOT TO GRIPS WITH UNCERTAINTY?

Quantification and science are often bracketed together, and it is indeed true that they are often in one another's company, but quantification is not a necessary condition for science. This is just as well because, if it was, we could not develop any scientific approach to uncertainty, apart from that which aims to convert it into certainty or into risk - an approach that, at present, is making little headway in the Himalaya. But fortunately science proceeds, first and foremost, by reducing the arbitrariness of description and this is what we have tried to do in getting to grips with uncertainty.

The Himalaya, we can safely say, abound in heterogeneity. There is the ecological heterogeneity that results in perhaps ninety per cent of 'the problem' being caused by perhaps ten per cent of the land; there is the social and cultural heterogeneity that, by endowing or withholding technical and institutional capacity, dramatically modifies the environmental effect of population; there is the resource treatment heterogeneity that transforms the raw material of the forest into a patchwork of renewable and convertible resources; there is the aesthetic heterogeneity generated by the social and political forces that shape the various contradictory park ideals; there is the geo-political heterogeneity that results in such markedly different control modes as we go from the inside to the outside of the buffer. In recognizing this heterogeneity, in uncovering the patterns in which it is arranged, and in identifying the processes that lie behind those patterns, we can discard all the conceptual baggage that assumes homogeneity. We are left with remarkably little; a description in terms of linked patterns at three levels (physical, social, and cognitive) and of the institutional forces that sustain and transform those patterns, and a strategy for intervention based on a limited number of management styles and their appropriateness in relation to the heterogeneity that is revealed by that description. Though we may sometimes despair at the inability of our institutions to cope with the complexities of our world, there remains the simple fact that, like it or not, those institutions are all that we have. Rather than despair we should make the most of them.

A closer look at 'the problem'

The wide uncertainties that currently exist at the biophysical level - uncertainty as to whether the consumption of fuelwood exceeds or is comfortably within the rate of production, uncertainty as to whether deforestation is a widespread or localized phenomenon, uncertainty as to whether it is population pressures or inappropriate institutional arrangements that lie behind instances of mismanagement of renewable resources ... uncertainty as to whether deforestation in the hills (if it indeed exists) has any serious impact on the flooding in the plains - mean that a wide range of mutually contradictory problems are credible. The Nepalese ambassador to the United States, for instance, can claim that there is widespread deforestation in the hills and that there is also a strong connection between it and the flooding in the plains, whilst Charles Houston, for his part, is convinced that the forests of Khumbu are in as good shape now as they were thirty years ago. These positions, given their policy implications, are inevitably thrown into contention. One position justifies one policy, the other position another policy, and the stage is set for the acrimonious exchange of accusations of self-interest. If, by remedying what is happening in a nation of 14 million souls, the welfare of 350 million more can be assured then, of course, resources should be committed to the small root of the huge problem. But, if the forests are not really disappearing then who, we should ask, stands to gain by convincing us that they are? The whole international eco-lobby, of course - the professional foresters, conservationists, agronomists, and so on who need serious (but curable) environmental problems every bit as badly as anti-poverty campaigners need poor (but deserving) clients.

The perhaps unpalatable point we wish to make (and it is the point on which the whole trans-science approach rests) is that, if we wish to retain any shred of scientific integrity, we must extend legitimacy to each and every problem definition that can be formulated in such a way that all its assumptions lie within the current bounds of uncertainty. To demand to know which of these problems is the right one is simply to encourage the arbitrary tyranny of one uncertain position over all the others. On the other hand, if the price of keeping an open mind on the subject is the acceptance of a world view so cynical that it can see behind these rival positions nothing other than the ill-disguised and predatory advancement of craven self-interest, that too is an unattractive option. So is it a straight choice between Arbitrary Tyranny and Cynical Resignation?

No. We can, as they say in international negotiation, fractionate the issue; we can separate current certainty from current uncertainty and handle each by its appropriate mode. We can visualise the boundary between certainty and uncertainty moving this way and that in response to two opposing forces - the drive toward certainty that advances under the banner 'what are the facts?' and the drive toward uncertainty that is the inevitable by-product of people variously choosing, from among available (but contradictory) facts, those that comport best with their various socially induced predilections.

Only those who subscribe to the sociological fallacy, and believe that the universe can be anything they want it to be, could seriously consider a situation in which this boundary was pushed so far out that nothing was certain; only those imbued with the positivistic optimism of Victorian science could trust in the foreseeable arrival of the day when all uncertainty will finally be squeezed out of our environment. Not wishing to position ourselves at either of these polar extremes, we began by conceding that in any policy debate uncertainty will always be contained within a noose of certainty and that two complementary modes are available for the progress of that debate: we can strive to tighten the noose and we can strive to understand the forces that resist that tightening. The first is the <u>adversary mode</u>, familiar to us in such grand institutions as the courts of law and the scientific method (but not in science itself which is a complex mix of adversary and exploratory modes), in which we ask 'what are the facts?'; the second is the <u>exploratory mode</u>, less familiar to us perhaps but subtly built into most constitutions and into many political systems, in which we ask (in effect) 'what would you like the facts to be?' The first, when successfully applied, allows us to get rid of what we cannot live with; the second, when successfully applied, allows us to live what we cannot get rid of.

When we apply this sort of fractionating approach to the policy debate over Himalayan deforestation we see that the noose of certainty is, at present, rather loose and that, since there are many important variables (like local fuelwood consumption rates) that (unlike oil and gas reserves) are intrinsically measurable, there is clearly much progress to be made by the pursuit of the adversary modes (especially if data are not torn from their contexts). At the same time, the scientist who operates within this mode soon becomes aware of all sorts of institutionally mediated pressures (from the granting and withholding of resources by the agencies that fund his research, through the screening processes built into the editorial policies of the journals in which he aspires to publish, to the systematically biased responses of the villagers he interviews in order to assemble his data). The institutions, you might say, have got there ahead of the scientist and have interposed themselves between him and the facts he is so anxious to uncover. Thus, there is a very real sense in which the institutions <u>are</u> the facts.

So what is the problem?

The first part of the problem (and perhaps the most difficult part to grasp) is that there is not <u>a</u> problem. There is a plurality of contradictory and contending problems - each one focused by the shared credibility it enjoys in the eyes of those who subscribe to it, and each held separate from the rest by the mutual incredibility that is the inevitable global corollary of locally focused credibilities. The reason, of course, is that if the institutions are pluralized so too will the facts that those institutions mediate be pluralized.

The second part of the problem is to accept this state of affairs; to stop demanding a problem when there is not a problem, and to take up a conceptual position from which diversity, contention, and contradiction, far from being undesirable qualities that must be eradicated before any progress can be made, can be seen for what they really are - our ultimate resource.

The outline of a strategy

It is not an either/or choice between cis-science and trans-science - between the adversary and exploratory modes. Both are essential. The choice lies in their appropriateness in any given situation. At present, in the policy debate surrounding Himalayan deforestation, there is clearly much scope for both modes but, at the same time, the rich institutional plurality (and, in particular, the institutional 'spread' between the provider and delivery levels) that is the inevitable accompaniment of the 'many agents' problem suggests that the biggest payoff will come from the exploratory mode.

So what does the exploratory mode look like? First and foremost, it is tolerant of contradiction, not in a spirit of anything-goes eclecticism, but with a view to uncovering patterns of contradiction and contention (such as those that are generated through local credibility and global incredibility). It uncovers those patterns, not for their own sake, but for the policy capabilities that may be embedded in the dynamical systems that sustain them (within the 'cautious cultivator' and 'adventurous trader' strategies, for instance, that provide the dynamic basis for the widespread Hindu-Buddhist geographical and cultural pattern). Then the exploratory mode has to turn away from the sort of legitimacy-conferring and legitimacy-withdrawing processes that are appropriate to the adversary mode. Learning, mediating, facilitating, interacting - these are the sorts of processes that characterize the exploratory mode.

Into the garbage can

The classic Operations Research approach proceeds in three stages: problem formulation, problem analysis, and problem solution. Although such an approach is often highly effective when applied to well-structured problems, the scale of uncertainty in the Himalaya renders it a non-starter. The plurality of problem definitions ('too many people' ... 'not enough food') means that we cannot even get Stage 1 - the formulation of problem - sorted out. Fortunately, there is another approach: the delightfully named 'garbage can model' of decision (March and Olsen, 1976).

In the garbage can we have all imaginable shapes and sizes of problems and all imaginable shapes and sizes of solutions. Not only is the classic approach's neat threefold package ripped apart, the linearity - the progression from problem to solution - goes out of the window too. If solutions and problems are all in there looking for one another then the whole thing becomes not just plural but circular as well. Time's arrow points in both directions: from problem to solution and from solution to problem. Since each is looking for the other, to ask which comes first is to ask a meaningless question. Though March and Olsen, the inventors of the garbage can, have spoken of this as <u>organized anarchy</u>, there is as it stands no organization in it, just anarchy. So, if we take the garbage can as our starting point, the crucial question becomes: 'how is this anarchy organized?' This is the question we have answered in this paper.

The wide uncertainty that everywhere pervades the Himalaya allows a wide range of problems and solutions to lie comfortably within it. But the set of all <u>possible</u> problems and solutions (pure anarchy) is not the same as the set of all <u>credible</u> problems and solutions (organized anarchy). Possible problems and possible solutions do not come together in some value-free void; they can meet up only when there exists some perspective for them to meet up in. So it is perspectives that organize the anarchy, that tease out the credible - the socially viable - conjunctions of problem and solution. For instance, the perspectives of the irate administrator and the sceptical observer clearly have this social viability, and we have gone to some exploratory lengths to tease out the particular social and cultural circumstances under which each becomes credible and incredible. The divergent strategies of the cautious cultivator and the adventurous trader, similarly, furnish perspectives that impose an impressive degree of order on the anarchic contents of the garbage can. So it is institutions - the value-determined choices of fact - and not simply the facts themselves that we must deal with when we seek to promote the sustainable development of a region that, like it or not, is awash with uncertainty.

NOTES

1. Donovan (1981:4) makes the following observation: On page 144 of Rieger 1981, under the section entitled 'Forest Administration in Practice', the authors report that according to the 'Divisional Forest Offices ... firewood demand is 50 bundles per family per year'. Possibly then the authors' subsequent estimate on page 152 of 'per capita annual fuel consumption ... (of) 50-100 bundles of 40 kilograms each' is a misprint.

2. The fact that it simply is not possible to figure out whether or not this is a misprint is, perhaps, the most telling indication of all that the uncertainty contains the problem.

The scientific guesswork in oil and gas reserves estimation is '... akin to going to an unfamiliar supermarket on a foggy night and trying to estimate the total amount of asphalt used in paving the parking lot with no other data than a cubic inch sample of the blacktop used'. (Schanz, 1978:333).

3. Of course, there is also the spin-off - the cooks, porters and so on who accompany some of these trekkers. But the Tamang, Rai (or whatever) porters usually get replaced by Sherpas (and/or yaks) once a trek reaches Khumbu, in which case the spin-off effect is comparatively slight.

4. An additional factor in the breakdown of the control system may be the partial erosion of the two great stabilizing ideals of Sherpa life: the proper utilization of acquired wealth and the cultivation of courtesy, gentleness, and a spirit of compromise and peacefulness. Both Sherpa business involvement in Kathmandu and central government's involvement in the local affairs of Khumbu contribute to this erosion.

5. Much more data of this type is now available. There is the experience of the National Park wardens (Jeffries, 1982) and of the leaders of the two hydroelectric projects in Khumbu (Hinrichsen et al., 1983; Coburn, 1983). Recently there have been detailed studies of how fuelwood is used in Namche village (Adam Stern) and of how that

wood is obtained (Barbara Brower). Furer-Haimendorf has just completed another field trip to Khumbu, aimed at documenting the changes that have occurred since his previous visits, and Sherry Ortner has recently revisited the area to study the effects of mountaineering and tourism on the Sherpas' Buddhist belief and practice. Then there is the less formal, but every bit as useful, on-the-ground experience of various programme staff and of the Sherpas themselves, many of whom are multi-lingual, well-educated, and extraordinarily well-travelled. In every local context in the Himalaya there is knowledge and experience of this type waiting to be tapped. All that is missing is the recognition by international agencies, organized science, and national governments that this is the level at which data becomes information. That is, it begins to tell you something.

6.   'Tolerably close' means that the system of knowledge that an individual is supplied with in return for granting credibility to a particular institution comes closer to delivering on the expectations it creates for him than would any of the systems of knowledge that would be available to him if he were to switch his allegiance to other institutions. For a fuller treatment of this, see Thompson (1982a, especially p.56).

7.   For an illustration of how this can be done in the context of the energy debate in the West, see Thompson (1982b) and Wildavsky and Tenenbaum (1981).

8.   To draw such a comparison is to mislead and to repeatedly requote it without any qualification is to deliberately mislead. The image of a 1.75mm thick layer of Karnali basin is as unreal a picture of what is actually happening as is Sir Charles Lyell's image of sixty great pyramids floating down the Ganges each year. The difference is that, in Sir Charles' case, the bizarre imagery has been drawn so as not to mislead the reader.

9.   The 'denudation rate', the unit used by soil scientists to describe the effects of erosion over a wide area, is itself a homogenizing measure which tends to average out the impact of individual events such as landslides, but the rate calculated for one drainage basin in Nepal was more than an entire order of magnitude greater than the rate generally calculated for that part of the Himalaya (Caine and Mool, 1982). In other words, the particular geologic structure of this area was contributing to a far higher level of erosion than that generally assumed for the larger area.

10. This is not quite correct. There are some tiny specks to be seen walking up the Western Cwm of Everest in a photograph wrongly captioned 'Annapurna'.

REFERENCES

Agarwal, A. (1982), Introducing new techniques - try asking the women first. Ecodevelopment News, International Research Centre on Environmental Development, New Delhi

Bajracharya, Deepak (1983a), Fuel, food or forest? Dilemmas in a Nepali village. World Development, 11(12), 1057-74

Bajracharya, Deepak (1983b), Deforestation in the food/fuel context: Historical and political perspectives from Nepal. Mountain Research and Development, 3(3), 227-40

Boulding, K.E. (1983), National Defence Through Stable Peace (Lectures delivered at IIASA). IIASA, A-2361, Laxenburg, Austria

Caine, N. and Mool, P.K. (1982), Landslides in the Kolpu Khola Drainage, Middle Mountains, Nepal. Mountain Research and Development, 2(2), 157-73

Coburn, B.A. (1983), Managing a Himalayan World Heritage Site. Nature and Resources, 19(3)

Coppock, R. (1978), The influence of Himalayan tourism on Sherpa culture and habitat. Zeitschrift fur Kulturaustausch, 3(7)

Cronin, E.W. (1979), The Arun. A Natural History of the World's Deepest Valley. Houghton Mifflin, Boston

Cultural Survival Quarterly, (1982), Deforestation: The Human Costs, vol. 6, no. 2. Published by Cultural Survival, Inc., Cambridge, Mass., USA

Department of Science and Technology, Government of India (1978), Proceedings. National Seminar on Resources, Development and Environment in the Himalayan Region, New Delhi, April 10-13, 1978

Donovan, D.G. (1980), Research Trials in Nepal, Newsletter (DGD 9), Institute of Current World Affairs, Hanover, New Hampshire

Donovan, D.G. (1981), Fuelwood: How Much Do We Need? Newsletter (DGD 14), Institute of Current World Affairs, Hanover, New Hampshire

Eckholm, E.P. (1976), Losing Ground: Environmental Stress

and World Food Prospects. W.W. Norton & Co., New York

FAO (1974), Forest Development, Nepal: Marketing. Based on Work of A.J. Browning FO. DP 1, NEP/69/513, Tech. Rep. No. 1, Rome

Fazal, M. (1983), Farakka: An Alternative Policy, Transnational Perspectives, 9(2)

Furer-Haimendorf, C. von (1975), Himalayan Traders: Life in Highland Nepal, John Murray, London

Gadgil and Sharma (1982), Ecology Is for the People. Centre for Science and Environment, Report no. 73, New Delhi

Hinrichsen, D., Lucas, P.H., Coburn, B. and Upreti, B.N. (1983), Saving Sagarmatha, Ambio, 12(3-4)

Houston, C.S. (1982), Return to Everest ... a sentimental journey. Summit, March/April 14-17, 28

Jeffries, B.E. (1982), Sagarmatha National Park: The impact of tourism in the Himalayas. Ambio, 11(5)

Jest, Corneille and Stein, J.A. (1982), Preliminary notes and observations on development of the Bumtang area of Bhutan. Mountain Research and Development, 2(2):223-6

Kawikita, Jiro (ed.) (1979), A Study of the Development of Remote Areas in Conformity with Environmental Conservation. Association for Technical Cooperation to the Himalayan Areas (ATCHA), Tokyo

Keynes, John Maynard (1931), Essays in Persuasion, Macmillan, London

Kunreuther, H.C. (1969), Economics of Natural Disasters, New York, Free Press

Lall, J.S. (ed.) (1981), The Himalaya: Aspects of Change, India International Centre, New Delhi, Oxford University Press, Delhi, Bombay, Calcutta, Madras

Levenson, B. (1979), Fuelwood Utilisation: A Study of the Demand and Available Fuelwood Resources at Six Selected Villages. Phewa Tal Technical Report no. 9, Kathmandu

Library of Congress (1979), Draft Environmental Report on Nepal prepared by the Science and Technology Division of the Library of Congress with the U.S. Man and the Biosphere Secretariat in Washington, DC

March, J.C. and Olsen, J.P. (1976), Ambiguity and Choice in Organisations, Bergen Universitetsforlaget

Newby, E. (1966), Slowly Down the Ganges, Picador, London (paperback edition, 1983)

Nicholson and the Editors of Time-Life Books (1975), The

World's Wild Places Series: The Himalayas

Parikh, Jyoti K. (1977), Environmental problems of India and their possible trends in future. Environmental Conservation, 4(3)

Pereira, Sir Charles (1981), Feasibility Study for High Altitude Agricultural Research, FAO, Rome

Reiger, Hans (1981), Man versus mountain, in Lall, J.S. (ed.), The Himalaya, Aspects of Change, Oxford University Press, pp.351-76

Schanz, John J. (1978), Oil and gas resources: Welcome to uncertainty, Resources, no. 58

Schloss, Aran (1983), The Politics of Development: Transportation Policy in Nepal, University Press of America

Simon, Julian L. (1981), The Ultimate Resource, Oxford, Martin Robinson

Thompson, Michael (1982a), 'A Three Dimensional Model' and 'The Problem of the Centre' in Douglas, M. (ed.), Essays in the Sociology of Perception, London, Routledge and Kegan Paul

Thompson, Michael (1982b), Among the Energy Tribes: The Anthropology of the Current Policy Debate. IIASA Working Paper, WP-82-59, IIASA, A-2361, Laxenburg, Austria

Tucker, R. (1981), British Colonialism and Forest Utilization in the Indian Himalaya. Paper for International Union of Forest Research Organisations International Congress, Kyoto, September 7-11, 1981

UNDP (1980), Project Document, National Farm Management Study, no. NEP/80/035/01/A

Unesco (1977), Regional Meeting on Integrated Ecological Research and Training Needs in Southern Asia Mountain Systems, particularly the Hindu Kush-Himalayas, MAB Report Series, no. 34

Weinberg, A. (1972), Science and trans-science, Minerva, 10:209-22

Wildavsky, A. and Tenenbaum, E. (1981), The Politics of Mistrust: Estimating American Oil and Gas Resources, Beverly Hills and London, Sage

Wordsworth, William (1810), Guide to the Lakes, Reprint and edited by Ernest de Selincourt, 1970, Oxford University Press

Wormwald, T.J. (1976), Village Forestry in the Hills of West Central Nepal, Lumle Agricultural Centre, Pokhara, July, P.A.I.

2

DEVELOPMENT IN THE FACE OF UNCERTAINTY (1)

Jack D. Ives

INTRODUCTION

The small kingdom of Nepal occupies a critical position in the Himalaya-Ganges region. With an east-west extent of 900 km it encompasses the central sector of the Himalayan ranges accounting for about one-third of their total west-northwest to east-southeast length between the river gorges of the Indus and the Yarlung-Tsangpo/Brahmaputra. From a climatological point of view the Nepalese central third serves as an extensive transition between the wetter Eastern Himalaya of Arunachal Pradesh, Assam, Bhutan, West Bengal, and Sikkim, and the drier Western Himalaya of Uttar Pradesh, Himachal Pradesh, Jammu and Kashmir. This transition is displayed most effectively by the vegetation map compiled by Schweinfurth (1957).

Nepalese territory also extends from the upper Ganges and Brahamputra plains (Terai) across the topographical grain of the entire Himalaya and onto the Tibetan Plateau. Given the great east-west extent and the enormous range of altitude (100 to more than 8,000 m), Nepal encompasses an almost infinite variety of landscapes, vegetation types, and micro-climates. Similarly, a large number of ethnic groups with their various adaptations to the array of landscapes and particular cultural evolution, results in a complex mosaic of man-land relationships.

Since 1950 this complex of interrelated cultural and physical landscapes, that collectively is Nepal, has been subjected to increasing influences of the 'outside' world. A particular concern of this paper is the way in which one set of these influences, the foreign aid and development assistance set, has responded to the perceived deepening crisis that Nepal is facing. It is not proposed to examine this topic exhaustively since space does not permit. However, what is proposed is an attempt to identify and discuss some of the major generalizations that have come to be widely accepted as truisms and which appear to have had significant impact on the policies that have been generated to combat the perceived crisis. Even this smaller topic can only be developed as an exercise in tentative geographical assessment.

WHAT IS THE NATURE OF THE PERCEIVED CRISIS?

A synoptic response to the question: what is the nature of the perceived crisis? can be compiled from numerous reports in the news media, internal reports of aid and development agencies, and countless published papers available in the scientific and conservationist literature. The most compelling written characterization is that published by Erik Eckholm (1975, 1976), and the most startling visual representation is contained in the movie The Fragile Mountain produced by Sandra Nichols (1982). Any such synthesis would include all, or most, of the following points:

1.   Consequent upon the introduction of modern heath care, medicine and malaria suppression after 1950 there occurred an unprecedented wave of population growth that does not yet appear to have peaked, reaching 2.6 per cent per annum for the 1971-81 census decade (Goldstein et al., 1983).

2.   This population explosion, with a current doubling period of 27 years, is augmented by uncontrolled and uncounted illegal migration into the Terai across the open frontier with India. Furthermore, upwards of 90 per cent of the 1981 total of 15 million is rural and subsistence. This has led to increasing demands for fuelwood, construction timber, fodder (the domestic livestock has experienced a parallel or even greater population explosion to that of the human population), and agricultural land on which to grow more food.

3.   The next step in what has been described as a vicious circle, is that the increasing pressures on the forest cover have led to massive deforestation, amounting to a loss of half the forest reserves of Nepal within a 30-year period

and a prediction that by AD 2000 no accessible forest cover will remain.

4.   The deforestation and the cutting of agricultural terraces on steeper and more marginal slopes has led to a catastrophic increase in soil erosion and loss of land through acceleration of debris flows and disruption of the normal hydrologic cycle.

5.   This, in turn, has led to increased run-off during the summer monsoon with attendant increase in disastrous flooding and massive siltation on the plains, and lower water levels and the drying up of springs during the dry season.

6.   The increased sediment load of the rivers emanating from the Himalayan system is extending the Ganges and Brahmaputra delta and causing islands to form in the Bay of Bengal.

7.   The constant loss of agricultural land in the mountains leads to another round of deforestation. Yet as the labour of walking greater distances from the village to cut fuel increases with the receding forest perimeter a critical threshold is reached whereby the available human energy becomes progressively overtaxed and an increasing quantity of animal dung is used for fuel.

8.   Thus a second vicious circle, within the first one, is set up: terrace soils, deprived of natural fertilizer - the animal dung now being used for fuel - induces lower crop yields, and the weakened soil structure augments the incidence of debris flows (landslides). Thus more trees are cut on increasingly steeper slopes to make room for more agricultural terraces to feed the growing subsistence population.

Thus it follows from this 8-point scenario that there is a progressive shift from potential instability to massive actual stability and, in face of these irreversible destructive processes, out-migration increases, which adds to the already heavy pressure on the resource base of the Terai. Extensive mountain desertification ensues, with increased and calamitous downstream effects and, as the worst-case scenario foresees, Nepal will flow down the Ganges by the year AD 2000. In preparation for such an event His Majesty's Government should transfer its request for advice from Swiss to Dutch engineers and begin a political struggle to reclaim (and claim) land below sea level in the Bay of Bengal.

The last sentence of the preceeding paragraph has been inserted to demonstrate both the seriousness and the science-fiction attributes of this powerful hypothesis of 'Himalayan Environmental Degradation'. This has already been expressed in earlier publications (Ives, 1985a and b). The broad hypothesis, however, is an intellectually satisfying concept and, as a working hypothesis, it seems so reasonable that it is hardly surprising that it is widely accepted as fact.

The development of my argument has now reached a rather critical point of departure. I believe that the foregoing hypothesis of 'Himalayan Environmental Degradation' may be based, at least in part, upon a large element of latter-day myth - a quarter century of emotion and repetition of first impressions. I feel comfortable about raising this serious criticism because it is directed against my own published first impressions as much as anyone else's. But we must now begin to ask ourselves some hard questions. Is the eight-point statement <u>true</u> and if so <u>how true?</u> More specifically, has deforestation from 1950 to 1980 across the length and breadth of Nepal proceeded in the manner envisaged and will the process lead to complete practical deforestation by AD 2000? Is it correct to assume that deforestation in the mountains leads to increasing soil erosion and landsliding, and this in turn to the perceived devastation on the plains downstream? Perhaps more importantly, is this assumed man-induced erosion and sediment transfer more significant in total volume than the product of the 'natural' processes operating in an extremely <u>geologically</u> unstable mountain range? It is even necessary to challenge the assumption that the post-1950 population explosion has been the cause of the bulk of the deforestation. And we must also question whether or not this set of assumptions can be applied to other sectors of the Himalaya, and the mountain systems of South and Central Asia in general (Tucker, 1986).

All of this begs the question of development aid: have the real problems been correctly identified and are they being tackled effectively? Each of these difficult questions must be raised within the context of Nepal as an exceedingly complex mosaic of man-land relationships. What are the facts? Mauch (1983) has argued that when the scientist does not know what to do he collects more data. This has been countered (Ives and Messerli, 1984): the scientist often perceives the developer and the decision-maker as someone who prefers no data because then the decision-making process is easier. Thompson and Warburton

(1985a and b) have argued that the problem is one of 'uncertainty on a Himalayan scale' and that few facts are available. Pitt (1986) has demonstrated that the 'bibles' of the international agencies are replete with manufactured facts. I hope that the preparation of this paper can be regarded as an excusable prelude to an international conference, being organized by the United Nations University and the International Mountain Society (6-11 April 1986) on 'The Himalaya-Ganges Problem', and intended to challenge some of these assumptions.

SELECTED ELEMENTS OF THE CRISIS

Population trends: 1950-85

In 1950, when Nepal first opened its borders to the outside world, the population was about 8 million. By 1971, it had reached 11.5 million and was growing at a rate of 2.0 per cent per annum. Between 1971 and 1981, despite what was believed to be a highly successful government family planning programme, the rate in population growth increased to 2.6 per cent per annum, giving a 1981 total of 15 million. Goldstein et al. (1983) predict that, if this trend continues, Nepal's population will exceed 25 million by 2001. Also significant is the rapidly accelerating growth in the urban sector, as well as the increase in lowland-based population.

Goldstein et al. (1983) predict a growth in the urban sector from 2.8 per cent of the total in 1952-54 to 20 per cent in 2001, and in the lowland sector from 35 per cent in 1952-54 to 56 per cent in 2001: in other words Goldstein et al. indicate that Nepal is changing from a mountain-rural society to a lowland-urban one.

Despite the growth in urban centres, especially Kathmandu and Biratnagar (urban population in 1981 was still only 6.4 per cent of the total), over 90 per cent of Nepal's rapidly growing population is rural and subsistence. And despite possible criticism of the reliability of the census data, the orders of magnitude are likely correct. However, estimates of the total and annual increments of illegal immigrants into the Terai from India vary widely. Informal commentary in Kathmandu in July/August 1984 provided unsupported estimates as high as 'over three million'. This figure is so high that it may be discounted as alarmist. Nevertheless, it is within the bounds of possibility that this form of population increase may equal the acceleration in the nation-wide increase from 2.0 per cent per annum in 1971 to 2.6 per cent per annum in 1981. The many implications of the open frontier policy are critical to any review of the status of Nepal, as evidenced by the strong political reactions in 1984 to the findings of the Royal Commission set up to review this situation.

Increase in extent of agricultural land and population growth (2)

Given: that the population of Nepal has probably doubled between 1950 and 1985 and, at present rates, will double again in 27 years; that the area under forest has been at least halved in the same period; that the area cultivated has been greatly expanded (an increase of 34 per cent, 1975-80); it is instructive to examine the trends in levels of productivity and total food produced.

In 1950 it has been estimated that rice productivity (per unit area) in Nepal was amongst the highest for South Asia and yet by 1980 it was amongst the lowest. Despite the increase in area cultivated and the large capital inputs into commercial agriculture, total production has barely increased, or has remained essentially level. This is presumably a reflection of declining yields in the Middle Mountains and the low yields from marginal steeplands that are being terraced at the expense of the forest cover. There has been an increase in the number of hill/mountain districts in deficit, in terms of subsistence food production and up to 250 million N.Rs per annum spent in food subsidies. In addition, much of the commercial agriculture on the Terai is controlled by Indian capital and destined for transfer to, and processing in, India. Much of the poor showing of agricultural production on the Terai is due to inadequate fertilizer inputs and to inefficient development of irrigation potential and unsatisfactory management of developed facilities. 'Despite the abundance of water, less than 15 per cent of the cultivated area has irrigation facilities, and those that do exist have varying standards' (ADB, 1982, Vol. 2, p.30). For example, during the Fifth 5-Year Plan, 95,000 ha were to be added to the total irrigation command area, yet only 21,000 ha are estimated to have received water. The real causes of these failures are perceived by ADB as organizational and institutional. Water delivery schedules frequently do not coincide with periods of peak water demand in terms of the agricultural cycle.

From the foregoing, it would appear that Nepal is facing a growing crisis in terms of population growth, declining food production, and accelerating deforestation, despite increasing capital input based upon a progressive increase in foreign aid. Moreover, the argument so far has been grossly oversimplified; it has not taken into account animal husbandry, fodder production and fodder requirements, fuel needs, land ownership, taxes and rent, all of which compound the difficulties described above and lead us toward an increasingly pessimistic scenario.

Fodder trees and tree fodder in Nepal

This topic is the object of a special publication by Dr K.K. Panday (1982), so will not be elaborated here. Suffice to say, that it is estimated that: (1) Nepalese animal husbandry is a vital part of its standard mixed-farming subsistence economy (contributes about 25 per cent of the agricultural G.D.P. and provides almost all the draught power); (2) 90 per cent of the fodder used is required merely to keep alive the very poor quality stock; (3) that there is a close interdependency between animal numbers, quality, fertilizer production, fuel requirements and uses, and deforestation; and (4) Panday predicts that proper management and development of tree fodder sources can increase production by 15 to 20 per cent. There was a total lack of recognition of the importance of tree fodder production by development agencies (foreign aid and H.M.G.) until the last few years, and organizational and institutional difficulties remain major obstacles to improvement.

Land tenure, rents and taxes

Fifty-five per cent of Nepal's farmers own less than 12 per cent of the land. The average farm size for this group is 0.21 ha. Six per cent own 44 per cent of the land with an average holding of 6.8 ha - mostly absentee landlords who organize share-cropping under which the share-croppers have neither resources nor motivation to increase productivity.

The 1964 Lands Act placed a ceiling on amount of land ownership and provided for the redistribution of the excess. Less than 1 per cent of the excess was actually redistributed. Rents were set at a maximum of 50 per cent of farm produce. In fact, in many cases they are probably much higher, and it has been argued that many poor subsistence farmers quietly pay rents in excess of legal requirements out of personal pride and entrenched family generational tradition.

The small farmer tends to borrow money privately at the village level at interest rates as high as 150 per cent, thereby placing himself and his descendants into debt-bondage and eventual landlessness. This practise continues despite Government efforts to counter it through making available loans at 6-15 per cent from co-operatives and banks.

It can be argued that much of the deforestation is driven by the need to grow crops to pay rents and interests on loans. This statement represents a partial challenge to the assumption that deforestation is the direct response to rapid population growth.

Fuelwood requirements and deforestation

Bajracharya (1983a and b) has made a detailed examination of the fuelwood/food dichotomy in relation to deforestation based upon extensive survey of a single panchayat in eastern Nepal. Only a few salient points are introduced here:

1. Fuel requirements in Nepal are met over-whelmingly from trees.

2. Inability of small holders to produce enough food has led to a great increase of illegal wood-cutting for sale, especially near urban centres, such as Kathmandu.

3. Development agencies seem to be paying undue attention to the introduction of alternate energy sources on the assumption that wood-cutting is the primary cause of deforestation when Bajracharya (1983a) has argued that, at least in parts of Eastern Nepal, deforestation is primarily due to the need to build more agricultural terraces to produce more food. This leads to a vital concept introduced by Thompson and Warburton (1985a:129). It is critical to consider the issue of how the forests are perceived. Development agencies and Government perceive them as a renewable resource; some subsistence farmers appear to

perceive them as a convertible resource. Unless these diametrically opposed perceptions can be harmonized, no amount of legislation nor any number of development projects will lead to successful reforestation.

4.   The vicious circle illustrated initially by Eckholm (1975) - fuelwood gathering - increased walking distance - increased use of animal dung - reduced fertilizer input, is grossly oversimplified (Bajracharya, 1983b). In the Kathmandu Valley, for instance, fuelwood is the main growing-season staple fuel, while dung is used for fuel in the winter when less is needed for fertilizer and would be wasted otherwise (pers. comm., K.K. Panday, 1984). The use of dung for fuel is related to ethnicity and not to pressure on forests (Thompson and Warburton, 1985a).

Development of hydro-electricity

It has been estimated that Nepal's hydro-electricity potential is equal to the combined developed and potential capacity of the USA. Regardless of the accuracy of this statement, Nepal has enormous hydro-potential (est. 83 TWH: Sharma, 1976). Only 2 per cent of the national energy requirements are being met by electricity, indicating that much less than 1 per cent of the potential has been harnessed.

H.M.G. regards development of the hydro-electric potential as a means of reducing the heavy costs of oil imports, accelerating industrial development, reducing pressure on forests, increasing the irrigated area, providing a major export item (sales to India), and improving the quality of life of its people. Consequently, the Seventh 5-Year Plan calls for massive development of hydro-electricity with a high dam on the Karnali River as a primary objective. This will require a 850 m long dam and a 10-year construction period with an estimated 36 TWH generating capacity. It is necessary, therefore, to examine the implications of this policy decision, not only in terms of its basic economics, but also in terms of social and environmental impacts.

The following remarks are based, in part on Bjønness's (1982-84) investigations of the Kulekhani Project, by comparison with Karnali, a second order project with a generating capacity of 60,000 kwh. Delivery of electricity began in March, 1982.

The Kulekhani River is a tributary of the Bagmati. The extent of the watershed above the dam is 212 km^2 with a 1971 population of about 30,000 growing to about 36,000 by 1979. Kathmandu is the primary market. The upper Kulekhani River has been diverted by tunnel into the Rapti River, giving a hydraulic head of about 600m. The study of Bjønness concentrated on the environmental and socio-economic impacts of the power project. A few of her main findings are itemized:

1. 1,200 people in 235 houses had to be removed from the land that would be submerged by the reservoir. Compensation was offered in cash or by provision of land in the Terai. More than 80 per cent accepted the cash option; payment was not completed until two years after dispossession, during which time land values had risen sharply and much of the cash had been spent on subsistence; this led to pauperization and landlessness.

2. No consideration was given in terms of downstream effects yet, below the dam site, villages and households were presented with a dry river channel resulting in the loss of irrigation water, and the rendering useless of many water mills.

3. Above the dam the reservoir severed many households from access to markets and water mills, or enforced a long detour.

4. No account was taken of the importance of communal facilities.

5. Progressive deforestation of the upper watershed and landsliding into the reservoir will reduce the design life of the project through accelerated siltation.

The implications of this study for the Karnali Project are significant, especially since the latter has been declared technically and economically feasible and a multi-million dollar exploratory study is currently being set up for tenders.

This raises the broader question of large dams in Developing Countries. A review of the Indian experience would indicate the need for caution. In particular, the problem of regular sale of large volumes of electricity outside of Nepal and the frequent disassociation between a major power supply and the minute needs of scattered mountain people need attention. Finally, it is remarkable that hydro-electricity, and other mega-engineering works, are rarely viewed holistically.

Sri Y.K. Murthy, Chairman of the Central Water

Commission, India, made the following statement during a seminar on environmental problems of water-resources development in the Himalayan region:

> with our circumstances and needs we cannot cry halt to the development of water resources merely for the fear of impinging on the environmental balance. A large segment of our population, which resides in the Indo-Gangetic plains, is dependent on the Himalayan resources for its survival. For any programme aimed at bettering the lot of these people, the exploitation of the resources of the Himalayas is a primary requirement. We, therefore, cannot afford the luxury of totally stopping development with a view to preserving the environment. (Murthy, Y.K. 1978, pp.67-8).

Reforestation

Present forest cover is estimated in the Asian Development Bank report at 4.1-4.5 million ha or 30 per cent of total area of Nepal (25 per cent reduction over last 10 years). The actual situation is assumed to be far worse, and the projection is that accessible forests in the hills will disappear within 14 years and in the Terai within 25 years. However, the Canadian Land Resources Management Project indicates twice the area of production forest compared with the estimate by the H.M.G. Department of Forestry. Thompson and Warburton (1985a) challenge the entire data base.

Canadian Land Resources Management Project in the Far Western District indicates that the ratio of demand to forest supply is 2.3:1 and in some districts as high as 4:1. But there are also serious problems facing attempts to reforest. For example, the Fifth 5-Year Plan showed a reforestation target of 20,000 ha, grossly inadequate in itself, yet only 9.864 ha were planted. During the last 15 years, 2 million ha are presumed to have been deforested and only 20,000 ha reforested. Even in replanted areas it is claimed that the 'target mentality' indicates success once seedlings are planted; little attention is paid to irrigation, leading to a very high rate of loss.

It is also important to consider the projects of introduced exotic species - usually fast-growing pines and eucalyptus. Dr J. Bandyopadhyay has led an attack and exposé of the World Bank's attraction to fast-growing exotics (Shiva et al., 1981).

While this report deals with a district in southern India, it indicates that subsidized introduction of fast-growing exotics benefits the relatively wealthy farmer, pauperizes the small farmer who depends on wages from labouring on larger holdings, and reduces the area under food crops. Eucalyptus, for instance, is too expensive to be used as fuelwood and is purchased by plastics and pulp and paper industries. This progression is now being studied in sections of the Indian Himalaya where local people have accused the World Bank of destroying their livelihood, a focus that has been taken up by the Chipko Movement. Finally, Mahat et al. (1984, 1986) have argued with telling effect and impressive documentation that, at least for the Sindhu Palchok and Kabhre Palenchok districts east of Kathmandu the most massive deforestation occurred during the 18th and 19th centuries. This was the result of pressure from the government to levy large quantities of iron production and the policy of promoting the conversion of forest to agricultural land in order to maximize agricultural surpluses and land taxes superimposed upon subsistence farming requirements. Deforestation since 1950 has been insignificant in comparison.

Rainfall intensity, rates of soil erosion, location of eroded areas

There is a widely accepted assumption that soil erosion intensity and incidence of landsliding is directly related to rainfall intensities and rainfall amounts. Rainfall intensities of between 100-200 mm per 24 hours probably occur frequently almost anywhere in Nepal (Nepali, 1981, unpub.). Laban (1978) has calculated erosion rates varying from 420 t/ha/yr down to 30 t/ha/yr. He has also estimated that erosion rates from degraded forests and cultivated fields vary between 31.5 t/ha/yr and 140 t/ha/yr (cf. also Laban, 1977). Nepali recounts that for the three main tributaries of the Kosi, in eastern Nepal (Tanur, Arun, and Sun Kosi) the silt load is 172 million t/yr (171,702,400), citing Laban (1978) as his source for field measurements on erosion and sedimentation in Nepal. This figure of 172 million t/yr is used by Sterling (1976) to account for the formation of 40,000 km^2 of land in the Bay of Bengal (Sterling, 1976).

Laban stipulates that soil erosion rates of 10-20 t/ha/yr are acceptable. Starkel (1972) has indicated that major catastrophes in the Himalaya occur 4 or 5 times a century with precipitation amounts exceeding 400 mm in 24 hours. He also indicates that 100-200 mm/24 hr may cause local failures on an almost annual basis (Starkel, 1972).

Nelson (1979) conducted a national watershed inventory:

> The inventory, even in its early stage, confirms the observation that watershed problems are far from uniformly distributed in Nepal. The Humla-Jumla example shows an area of few watershed problems. A blanket indictment of Nepal for high erosion rates is obviously unwarranted. It is probable that of the 14 ELUAs (Ecological Land Unit Associations) 3 or 4 will be the site of most of the watershed problems. This complex picture means that watershed management in Nepal must be a mix of educational, remedial, and protection activities which must vary by geographic location. Our observations indicate that a considerable amount of erosion in Nepal is natural, i.e. caused by the natural slope-forming processes active in the area.

Laban (1979) provides the following significant statements:

1. Fifty per cent of landsliding in Nepal is due to natural causes;
2. Least affected areas are the Middle Mountains because they are densely populated and terraced, and the terraces, for the most part, are well maintained;
3. Due to the scale of the survey, aircraft reconnaissance plus satellite imagery, smaller landslides may have been missed.

At least in partial disagreement with some of the foregoing statements Caine and Mool (1982) have effectively demonstrated in the Kakani area of the Middle Mountains close to Kathmandu that there is no direct correlation between 24 hour rainfall amounts and landsliding. Heavy rainfalls early in the summer monsoon season generally do not produce landslides; significant landsliding is delayed until ground water recharge brings the watertable to within less than 1 m of the surface. The phenomenon of piping is also important in some lithologies and generally defies prediction.

Professor Peter Rogers (pers. comm., 1984) indicated that the Kosi dam close to the Nepalese border with Bihar effectively checks far distant downstream silt transfer, so that the Kosi sediment load, calculated at 172 million t/yr within Nepal, can hardly influence the formation of islands in the Bay of Bengal. Nelson's (1979) comments substantiate the generalization of Rom (quoted in Thompson and Warburton, 1985b) to the effect that 90 per cent of the soil erosion losses may occur in 10 per cent of the area.

Going beyond the limits of Nepal, Professor Peter Rogers (pers. comm., 1984) contested the common stipulation that the Brahmaputra floods and siltation rates, as with the Ganges, are progressively increasing because of deforestation in the Himalaya. Rogers maintains that the level of the annual floods along the Brahmaputra have actually decreased since 1975 at an average rate of about 15 cm/yr. While they had increased over the 20-year period preceding 1975 the 1952 earthquake had raised a section of the Brahmaputra's bed by about 4m. Thus the increase may have been the natural result of the river adjusting to this disturbance and bore no relationship whatsoever to mountain deforestation.

DISCUSSION

The selected 'elements of the crisis' facing Nepal that were introduced in the preceding section, while only outlined in cursory fashion, raise some significant questions. Primarily they indicate that the 8-point scenario of Himalayan Environmental Degradation requires rigorous re-examination. It is instructive to carry this line of discussion somewhat further. To assist in this process some of the conclusions of a selection of more recent Nepalese research projects will be introduced.

The United Nations University (Highland-Lowland Interactive Systems Project), in collaboration with the Nepal National Committee for the Unesco Man and the Biosphere (MAB) Programme began a series of small studies in 1979 aimed primarily at producing proto-type mountain hazards maps at various scales (Ives and Messerli, 1981). This led to the production of maps at a scale of 1:10,000 for the Kakani area near Kathmandu (Kienholz et al., 1983, 1984), a study of the subsistence farmers' perceptions of local hazards and the traditional strategies designed to combat them (Johnson et al., 1982), and some studies of specific hill slope processes (Caine and Mool, 1981, 1982). Subsequent work in the Khumbu Himal was designed to modify but essentially repeat the Kakani strategy in a high-mountain setting (Zimmermann et al., 1986; Vuichard, 1986; Byers, 1986). A number of general conclusions can be derived from this interdisciplinary effort:

1.   Rates of land loss, landslide initiation, and landslide expansion can be derived for the specific study areas, but they are appreciably less than the generalizations inferred by the 8-point scenario.

2.   The subsistence farmers of the Kakani area have accumulated over generations an effective understanding of, and response to, landsliding. Initial impressions of rates of land loss were reduced once the importance of the stabilizing and reclamation efforts of the local people were realized following several years of fieldwork and observation.

3.   Possible depopulation of apparently unstable areas ordered by government authority to prepare for reforestation as a project-sponsored stabilization measure, could be disastrous and lead to catastrophic increases in erosion once terrace construction and maintenance was withdrawn.

4.   Ethnographic studies demonstrated great differences in the effectiveness of hazard-coping strategies between different ethnic groups within the same small area.

5.   In the Khumbu, the hitherto widely proclaimed sentiment of serious deforestation and high rates of soil erosion is an over-estimate (Byers, 1986). The most dangerous mountain hazard is the catastrophic outbreak of ice-dammed and moraine-dammed lakes, and subsequent landsliding due to the undercutting of talus slopes and alluvial fans along the river's course (Ives, 1986; Zimmermann et al., 1986; Vuichard and Zimmermann, 1986).

6.   There is widespread distrust of government agencies.

CONCLUSION

The central theme of the 8-point scenario of Himalayan Environmental Degradation, that massive deforestation, caused by post-1950 explosive population growth, has not only produced extensive environmental and socio-economic losses in the hills, but also has caused serious impacts on the Ganges and Brahmaputra plains and delta, must be challenged at all levels. As the second generation of Himalayan research moves into more precise, detailed, and much more exacting studies of small areas, a number of site-specific conclusions can be drawn:

1. Extensive deforestation in some regions occurred long before 1950 (Mahat, unpubl., 1985; Mahat et al., 1986). This is also true of areas far beyond the boundaries of Nepal, for example in the Western Himalaya (Tucker, 1986) and in the Hengduan Mountains of northwestern Yunnan (Messerli and Ives, 1984; Ives, 1985c).

2. Recent acquisition of reliable data on soil erosion throughout the summer monsoon period in the Khumbu (Byers, 1986, 1987) indicates that previous assumptions of soil loss have greatly exaggerated actual circumstances.

3. The subsistence farmer has often been castigated as the reckless and ignorant despoiler of his own land resources (H.M.G. Nepal and ADB, 1982:34) which is an especially unfortunate fallacy (Ives, 1985d).

4. The Himalaya-Ganges system is a natural and highly active system. The plains are the product of uplift of, and erosion in, the mountains and the recently added increment due to human misuse may be insignificant (Starkel, 1972; Ives, 1970, 1981; Carson, 1985). The implications of this final point are of critical significance.

Nevertheless, the most important conclusion is the simple and obvious one anticipated in the descriptive introduction to this paper: Nepal, in particular, and the Himalaya, in general, represent one of the most complex mosaics of man-land interrelationships on earth. To base development policy on facile generalizations can lead only to disaster. This is compounded when the 'data' utilized are unreliable, in some cases manufactured, and in all cases serve only to conceal the extent of the prevailing uncertainty (Thompson and Warburton, 1985a and b; Hatley and Thompson, 1985; Pitt, 1986). There is no doubt that Nepal is facing a serious crisis that demands an equally serious response. The arguments introduced in this paper to illustrate that the rates of loss may have been exaggerated must not be taken to imply that the crisis is not so serious. The very nature of the uncertainty is a large element of the 'Himalaya-Ganges Problem'. The way to solve the problem must be sought through institutional channels based upon a better appraisal of the extent of the uncertainty.

ACKNOWLEDGEMENTS

The ideas expressed in this paper have been influenced by discussions with many colleagues but principally with Professor Bruno Messerli, and Drs David Pitt and Michael Thompson, collaborators in the organization of the April 1986 UNU/IMS Conference on The Himalaya-Ganges Problem.

NOTES

1. First published as 'The status of Nepal: Development in the face of uncertainty' In S.C. Joshi (ed.) Nepal Himalaya: Geo-ecological Perspectives, 1986: Himalayan Research Group, Naini Tal, U.P. India, pp. 265-81.
2. Much of the information in this, and subsequent, sections has been obtained from the Asian Development Bank/H.M.G. Nepal report: Nepal Agricultural Sector Strategy Study, December 1982, 2 volumes.

REFERENCES

Bajracharya, D. (1983a), Deforestation in the food/fuel context: historical and political perspectives from Nepal. Mountain Research and Development, 3(3), 227-40

------, (1983b), Fuel, food or forest? Dilemmas in a Nepali village. World Development, 11(12), 1057-74

Bjønness, Inger-Marie, Kulekhani Hydro-Electric Project, Nepal: Research Working Papers. No. 1, 1982: Theory and Method, 67 pp.; No. 2, 1983: Energy and Development, 62 pp.; No. 3, 1983: Socio-Economic Analysis, 94 pp.; No. 4, 1984: Strategies for Survival, 83 pp. Department of Geography, University of Oslo, Blindern, Oslo 3, Norway

Byers, Alton (1986), A geomorphic study of man-induced soil erosion in the Sagarmatha (Mount Everest) National Park, Khumbu, Nepal: report on the activities of the UNU-MAB (Nepal) Mountain Hazards Mapping Project,

Phase II. Mountain Research and Development, 6(1) pp.83-87

Byers, A. (1987), A geomorphic study of Man-induced soil erosion in the Sagarmatha (Mt. Everest) National Park, Khumbu, Nepal. Unpub. PhD dissertation, Dept. of Geography, Univ. of Colorado, Boulder

Caine, N. and Mool, P.K. (1981), Channel geometry and flow estimates for two small mountain streams in the Middle Hills, Nepal. Mountain Research and Development, 1(3-4), 231-43

------, (1982), Landslides in the Kolpu Khola Drainage, Middle Mountains, Nepal. Mountain Research and Development, 2(2), 157-73

Carson, B. (1985), Erosion and Sedimentation Processes in the Nepalese Himalaya. International Centre for Integrated Mountain Development (ICIMOD), Occasional Paper No. 1, Kathmandu, Nepal

------, (1976), Losing Ground. Worldwatch Institute. W.W. Norton & Co., Inc., New York

Eckholm, E. (1985), The deterioration of mountain environments. Science, 189, 764-70

Goldstein, M.C., Ross, J.L. and Schuler, S. (1983), From a mountain-rural to a plains-urban society: implications of the 1981 Nepal Census. Mountain Research and Development, 3(1), 61-4

Hatley, T. and Thompson, M. (1985), Rare animals, poor people, and big agencies: a perspective on biological conservation and rural development in the Himalaya. Mountain Research and Development, 5(4), 365-77

His Majesty's Government of Nepal and Asian Development Bank (1982), Nepal Agricultural Sector Strategy Study, 2 Volumes. Kathmandu, December 1982

Ives, J.D. (1970), Himalayan highway. Canadian Geographical Journal, LXXX(1), 26-31

------ (1981), Applied high altitude geoecology. Can the scientist assist in the preservation of the mountains? In Lall, J.D. (ed.), The Himalaya: Aspects of Change. India International Centre, Oxford University Press, New Delhi, pp.377-402

Ives, J.D and Messerli, B. (1981), Mountain Hazards Mapping in Nepal: introduction to an applied mountain research project. Mountain Research and Development, 1(3-4), 223-30

------, (1984), Stability and instability of mountain ecosystems: lessons learned and recommendations for the future, Mountain Research and Development, 4(1), 63-71

------, (1985a), The mountain malaise: quest for an integrated development. In Singh, T.V. and Kaur, J. (eds.), Integrated Mountain Development, Himalayan Books, New Delhi, pp.33-42

------, (1985b), Himalayan environmental regeneration: an overview. What are the problems and how can they be tackled? In Singh, J.S. (ed.), Environmental Regeneration in Himalaya: Concepts and Strategies. The Central Himalayan Environment Association, Naini Tal, India, p.1-11

------, (1985c), Yulongxue Shan, Northwest Yunnan, Peoples Republic of China: a geoecological expedition. Mountain Research and Development, 5(4), 382-5

------, (1985d), Mountain environments, Progress in Physical Geography, 9(3), 425-33

------ (1986), Glacial lake outburst floods and risk engineering in the Himalaya, International Centre for Integrated Mountain Development (ICIMOD), Occasional Paper No. 5, Kathmandu

Johnson, K., Olson, E.A. and Manandhar, S. (1982), Environmental knowledge and response to natural hazards in mountainous Nepal. Mountain Research and Development, 2(2), 175-88

Kienholz, H., Hafner, H., Schneider, G. and Tamrakar, R. (1983), Mountain hazards mapping in Nepal's Middle Mountains with maps of land use and geomorphic damages (Kathmandu-Kakani area). Mountain Research and Development, 3(3), 195-220

Kienholz, H., Hafner, H. and Schneider, G. (1984), Stability, instability, and conditional instability: mountain ecosystem concepts based on a field study of the Kakani area in the Middle Hills of Nepal. Mountain Research and Development, 4(1), 55-62

Laban, P. (1977), A preliminary appraisal of mass movement in Nepal. Proceedings of a seminar on Mountain Ecosystems, Kathmandu

------, (1978), Field measurements on erosion and sedimentation in Nepal. Department of Soil Conservation and Watershed Management, PAO/UNDP. IWM/SP/05

------, (1979), Landslide occurrence in Nepal. Phewa Tal Project Report No. SP/13. Integrated Watershed Management Project, Kathmandu

Mahat, T.B.S. (1985), Human Impact on Forests in the Middle Hills of Nepal. Unpublished doctoral dissertation submitted. Australian National University, January 1985, 2 Volumes, Canberra

Mahat, T.B.S., Griffin, D.M. and Shepherd, K.R. (1984), An historical perspective of the forests of Sindhu Palchok and Kabhre districts of Nepal. Proceedings of a Symposium on Forest History. International Union of Forest Research Organizations, Zurich, 3-7 September 1984

------, (1986), Human impact on some forests of the Middle Hills of Nepal I: Forestry in the context of the traditional resources of the state. Mountain Research and Development, 6(3):223-32

Mauch, S.P. (1983), Key processes for stability and instability of mountain ecosystems: is the bottleneck really a data problem? Mountain Research and Development, 3(2): 113-19

Messerli, B. and Ives, J. (1984), Gongga Shan (7556m) and Yulongxue Shan (5596 m). Geoecological observations in the Hegduan Mountains of Southwestern China. Erdwissenschaftliche Forschung, Bd. XVIII:55-77. Franz Steiner Verlag Wiesbaden GmbH, Stuttgart

Murthy, Y.K. (1978), Environmental problems of water-resources development in the Himalayan region. In: National Seminar on Resources, Development, and Environment of the Himalayan Region, Proceedings, April 10-13, 1978, New Delhi. National Committee on Environmental Planning and Co-ordination, Department of Science and Technology, Government of India, pp.67-8

Nelson, D. (1979), A national watershed inventory. Journal Nepal Res. Centre, 2/3, 81-96

Nepali, S.B. (1981), Unpublished manuscript

Nichols, S. (1982), The Fragile Mountain (privately published by author)

Panday, K.K. (1982), Fodder Trees and Tree Fodder in Nepal. Swiss Development Corp. and Swiss Federal Inst. Forestry Research, Birmensdorf, Switzerland, 107pp.

------, (1984), Personal communication

Pitt, D. (1986), Crisis, pseudocrisis, or supercrisis: poverty, women and young people in the Himalaya: a survey of recent developments. Mountain Research and Development, 6(2)

Rogers, P. (1984), Personal communication

Schweinfurth, U. (1957), Die horizontale and vertikale Verbreitung der Vegetation im Himalaya. Mit mehrfarbiger Vegetationskarte 1:2,000,000 auf 2 Blättern mit Profilen. Bonner Geogr. Abh., H.20, 1957

Sharma, C.K. (1976), Landslides and Soil Erosion in Nepal, Mrs Sangeeta Sharma (publisher), 23/281 Bishalnagar, Kathmandu, Nepal

Shiva, V., Sharatchandra, H.C. and Bandyopadhyay, J. (1981), Social, economic and ecological impact of social forestry in Kolar. Indian Institute of Management, Bangalore, India (mimeo)

Starkel, L. (1972), The role of catastrophic rainfall in the shaping of the relief of the Lower Himalaya (Darjeeling Hills). Geographia Polonica, 21

Sterling, C. (1976), Nepal. Atlantic Monthly (Oct.), 238(4): 14-25, New York

Thompson, M. and Warburton, M. (1985a), Uncertainty on a Himalayan scale, Mountain Research and Development, 5(2), 115-35

------, (1985b), Knowing where to hit it: a conceptual framework for the sustainable development of the Himalaya, Mountain Research and Development, 5(3), 203-20

Tucker, R. (1986), The evolution of transhumant grazing in the Punjab Himalaya, Mountain Research and Development, 6(1) 17-28

Vuichard, D. (1986), Geological and petrographical investigations for the Mountain Hazards Mapping Project, Khumbu Himal, Nepal, Mountain Research and Development 6(1) 41-51

Vuichard, D. and Zimmermann, M. (1986), The Langmoch flash-flood, Khumbu Himal, Nepal. Mountain Research and Development 6(1): 90-4

Zimmermann, M., Bichsel, M. and Kienholz, H. (1986), Mountain Hazards Mapping in the Khumbu Himal, Nepal, with prototype map, scale 1:50,000. Mountain Research and Development, 6(1) 29-40

3

SOIL AND WATER IMPACTS OF DEFORESTATION*

L.S. Hamilton and A.J. Pearce

At the outset, we wish to set forth an important semantic ground rule concerning the harvesting of forest products. This activity has frequently been called 'deforestation' in the press and indeed in some technical writing. It is our contention that use of the term 'deforestation' must be discontinued, if scientists, forest land managers, government planners and environmentalists are to have meaningful dialogue on the various human activities that affect forests, and the biophysical consequences of those actions.

The generic term 'deforestation' is used so ambiguously that it is virtually meaningless as a description of land-use change. It has been used at times to refer to any or all of the following activities with respect to existing forest: fuelwood cutting; commercial logging, shifting cultivation; forest clearing for conversion to continuous annual cropping, to grazing, to food, beverage or industrial tree crops, to forest plantations; and finally where burning has produced a degraded forest. (Bowonder (1982) in an article 'Deforestation in India' includes these and a host of other activities such as: gathering medicinal plants, killing of wildlife, and flooding by reservoirs.) Though each of these activities will have different hydrological and erosional effects, they are too often undifferentiated, and one reads or hears generalizations that deforestation results in erosion, in floods, in droughts, in accelerated reservoir

* A version of this paper was originally presented to the 16th Pacific Science Congress, Seoul, Korea, August 1987

sedimentation, in drying up of wells and springs, in desertification, and in nutrient impoverishment of the area.

The effects of fuelwood cutting where the products are manually carried out of the forest are greatly different from those of commercial logging where large and heavy equipment may be used and where skidding trails and logging roads may cover as much as 16 to 30 per cent of the area. Similarly, in conversion of forest to annual crops, after the initial soil and water impacts of land clearing (see for instance Lal 1981), it makes a great difference whether the subsequent agricultural cropping follows conservation practices (e.g. properly constructed and maintained terraces) or is heedless of soil and water conservation.

We must more precisely describe the land-use change or activity under consideration, before we can estimate its water and soil effects. Only in this way can we differentiate those activities that have undesirable effects from others that currently are on an unwarranted blacklist. For example, it is usually not the cutting of trees per se that causes large increases in on-site erosion - it is the way the tree products are removed from the area. When this is clearly recognized, it properly shifts concern about erosion from how much of the tree canopy is removed to how the skid trails, landings and logging roads are located, constructed and maintained (or whether elephants, bullocks, helicopters, balloons, or caterpillar tractors are used in wood extraction). Cutting of trees alone does not directly cause erosion (Hamilton 1983) except in cases of sites prone to shallow landslips. (1) In these instances, root decay in non-coppicing species following cutting can, by reduction in soil shear strength, reduce the safety margin and thus permit more shallow landslips under saturated soil conditions (O'Loughlin and Ziemer 1982).

In most forests of the Pacific/Asia region (particularly the moist temperate or tropical forests), harvesting activity should not be described as 'deforestation'. With the exception of dry zone forests, most forests will either have advanced understory growth prior to cutting, or following cutting will have fairly prompt establishment of new reproduction. Although the age and size structure are altered by harvesting, the area remains forested. That is, it remains forested <u>unless</u> other land-use activities are going on. If burning occurs, if livestock are permitted to graze, if agricultural crops are planted - then a process of conversion is taking place, and there will be a loss of forest area or at least a serious forest density decline. The biophysical consequences of these conversion activities are quite different from those of fuelwood or timber harvesting. For example, the common claim that fuelwood cutting in the Middle Hills of Nepal is 'deforesting' the hills, decreasing forest area, and initiating a series of erosional and hydrologic effects that lead to destruction and death in the lower Ganges, is inaccurate on several counts. In the first place, recent surveys have shown that the major loss of forest in the Middle Hills occurred long ago (Mahat et al. 1986), and that loss of forest between 1964 and 1977 has been insignificant (Robinson et al. 1983). Fuelwood cutting accompanied by converting land gradually to grazing or agriculture may together be responsible for loss of forest, but a complex process other than meeting fuel needs is going on (see Bajracharya 1983). Burning and overgrazing rather than fuelwood cutting and fodder lopping are more likely causes of accelerated on-site erosion. Desirable reductions in erosion entail actions aimed at the former activities rather than the latter. The linkages between these land-use changes and inferred effects many hundreds or thousands of kilometers downstream are tenuous and poorly documented (Hamilton 1986).

These are but a few examples of how using the term deforestation masks the various land-use changes that may be taking place. In an attempt to clarify some of the semantic fogginess surrounding deforestation, Hamilton (1983) developed the following activity headings for chapters in a book on the hydrologic and soils aspects of tropical forested watersheds:

Uses or Alterations	1.	Harvesting minor forest products
	2.	Shifting agriculture
	3.	Harvesting fuelwood and lopping fodder
	4.	Harvesting commercial wood
	5.	Grazing on forestland
	6.	Burning forestland
Conversions of Forest	7.	Conversion to forest tree plantations
	8.	Conversion to grassland or savanna for grazing
	9.	Conversion to food or extractive tree crops

	10.	Conversion to annual cropping
	11.	Conversion to agroforestry
Restoration	12.	Reforestation or afforestation
of Forest		

Even with this degree of specificity, the biophysical consequences of these actions are generally complex, unknown or ambiguous. The emotive term 'deforestation' compounds the problem and should be eliminated from both technical and popular thinking unless used with qualifying adjectives or phrases to indicate the real nature of the forest land-use change.

In this presentation we will discuss primarily items 1, 3 and 4 in the above list: harvesting minor forest products, harvesting fuelwood, and mechanized wood harvesting. Each of these is discussed with respect to what we know, or can professionally judge from our general understanding of hydrological and erosional processes, about its effect on water and soil resources. The focus will be on Pacific/Asian tropical moist forests, a forest biome of major concern due to its rapid rate of alteration and of conversion to other uses.

HARVESTING NON-WOOD (MINOR) FOREST PRODUCTS

In Asia and the Pacific, people dwelling in or near the tropical forest derive from it many food, tool, and shelter products. In some instances, an entire tribal people may essentially be forest dwellers who obtain almost all of their sustenance from the forest; for example, the Semang forest people in the Orang Asli group of Peninsular Malaysia (Rambo 1983).

Some examples of minor forest product use include: food (e.g. wild yams, bamboo shoots, fruit and nuts); medicinal and ceremonially important plants; poisonous plants (for use in fishing); leaves for wrapping food; leaves and twigs for thatching; various plant parts for tanning or dyeing; rattan for making baskets and furniture; tapping trees for resins, oils and turpentine; gathering wild honey or using forest tree flowers for apiary purposes; wild fauna for food and ornamentation and for skins to be used as clothing, shelter and utensils; and removal of forest litter for various uses.

The lengthy list, even in any one locality, is often truly

amazing (e.g. Lert et al. 1985 for Thailand), and is basically the array of products harvested by traditional forest dwellers or nearby agriculturalists including shifting cultivators. World-wide, these products in providing food and other materials for the well-being and daily lives of millions of people, are comparable in importance to the use of wood for structural purposes and for fuelwood. Foresters must not ignore these products, many of which have become substantial items of commerce, even though still harvested by rather primitive means. For instance, the rattan products from Indonesia alone represent an export trade worth one-half million US dollars annually. The worldwide rattan end-product trade is estimated to be about a 1.5 billion US dollar per year business (Spears and Ayensu 1984). The modern pharmaceutical industry uses extractives from tropical humid forests probably amounting to 100 million US dollars in retail trade (Spears and Ayensu 1984). Tewari (1982) reported that 36 per cent of the revenue of the Forest Department in India in 1980-81 came from non-wood forest products.

Non-wood forest product harvesting is usually a 'benign' use of the tropical forests of the region. The continuation or even expansion of non-wood forest products harvesting is unlikely to have any major detrimental impact on water regime, soil erosion, or sediment; nor is it likely to be a source of nutrient impoverishment when carried out on a sustainable basis. One instance of utilization which has created problems in tropical forest plantations of mahogany, teak and gmelina is the gathering of forest litter. In Cebu in the Philippines, leaf litter of these species is harvested to make mosquito repellent coils (Yao and Nanagas 1983) and they warn of problems. Litter collection for livestock bedding and even cooking fuel is gathered in many parts of the Himalayas, and is a practice which should be reduced if erosion is to be reduced. Litter is not only important in nutrient cycling but has an extremely important role in protecting the soil from raindrop impact and therefore minimizing splash erosion, and the beginning of a serious erosion sequence. The litter is often far more important than the high forest canopy in this function, and in fact a high forest canopy of large-leaved species can increase raindrop impact (Lembaga Ekologi 1980, Mosley 1982).

Leaves and the young shoots that bear them are used as animal fodder in many parts of the Asia/Pacific region. In most cases fodder lopping is practiced on individual trees on the farm, on tree agroforestry systems or on specially planted fodder hedges (or fodder/fuel hedges). Such fodder sources in agricultural or grazing areas are an important link in the animal feed/manure/crop fertilizer system. Leaf fodder is often harvested from forests, especially as dry season animal feed when grasses and forbs have dried and withered. If carefully carried out, this can be a sustainable use, reducing wood production by the trees, but producing successive crops of leaf fodder. Where this is carried off site as in stall feeding of animals, it can represent a nutrient drain that may reduce future production. Moreover, where it prevents leaf litter cover from protecting the soil against splash erosion, it may induce serious surface erosion on sloping land. Much depends on the intensity of the leaf harvesting (both the severity per tree and the extent of lopped trees on an area). If overdone, it gradually kills the trees that are then often used for fuelwood. If reproduction is not presented (due to grazing perhaps?) then forest is being steadily converted to grazing land. It is no longer non-wood forest harvesting, but conversion, and the impacts are of a new order of magnitude.

HARVESTING FUELWOOD

Fuelwood harvesting, unless accompanied by burning and/or grazing, or unless followed by a true conversion that attempts sedentary agriculture, can be sustainable forest use. Even after clearcutting in one sub area, the harvesting area generally remains essentially forested (i.e. advanced reproduction or subsequent regeneration of the stand keeps the area vegetated). In the Asia/Pacific region fuelwood harvesting is usually a non-mechanized activity since the bulk of fuelwood is harvested manually or with the use of animals. If machinery is used, there is a marked change in the water and soil impacts and this kind of activity and these associated impacts are dealt with under 'Mechanized Wood Harvesting'.

In the drier parts of the Asian tropics, a common pattern of fuelwood cutting follows a scenario of overcutting of growth capacity (often with fodder lopping for livestock), burning, and grazing (or sometimes cultivation). This scenario is a deliberate conversion to another land use. It commonly leads to deterioration of productivity, soil erosion, stream sedimentation, reduced groundwater levels and increased local flooding. This should not be labelled 'fuelwood cutting' but should be identified as land abuse. This land abuse over large areas has unquestionably aggravated local flooding, but to state that major floods in the lower Indian subcontinent were caused by fuelwood harvesting in the Himalayas (Openshaw 1974) is simply not defensible (Hamilton 1986).

In the forests of Southeast Asia and the Pacific (in contrast to South Asia), fodder lopping is not an important activity, and fuelwood cutting impacts are fairly modest. The major hydrological impact of sustainable fuelwood cutting occurs because of a reduction in the evapotranspiring canopy. The major soil impact is due to whatever roads or tracks are employed to remove the products.

Water effects

Forest canopy reductions through tree cutting reduce the evapotranspiration losses from the water budget of forest watersheds, resulting in increased water yield in streams from the harvested area. Bosch and Hewlett (1982) reported on this effect from a review of 94 catchment experiments (most, but not all, in the temperate zone). They also found that the increase in total yield was proportional to the reduction in canopy, that it was greatest in high rainfall areas, but that the effect was shorter lived in high rainfall areas due to more rapid regrowth. They suggest that for each 10 per cent reduction in forest cover there is roughly a 40 mm increase in total water yield for conifer and eucalypt types, and approximately 25 mm increase for deciduous forest. The increase diminishes rapidly as the forest grows back and as the trees grow larger. Where soils have only limited water storage capacity (e.g. 20 cm or less), research in tropical rain forests in Australia indicates that increases in yield are only slight following tree cutting (Gilmour et al., 1982). This is probably true for most shallow soils.

Almost all studies have shown that tree cutting similar to fuelwood harvesting (no mechanical logging) resulted in increases in peak flows, and often, but not always, an increase in stormflow volumes (Hamilton 1983). The relative magnitude of these effects diminishes as either storm magnitude, intensity or duration increase. There may be some slight impact in aggravating <u>local</u> stream flooding in the lower intensity or shorter duration storms that occur frequently. But in the rarer large storm events there is little impact. Most studies have shown that the greatest percentage increase in yield occurs in the low-flow periods. Some streams that ceased to flow in the dry season remained perennial following cutting (Gilmour 1977a). These effects are temporary and diminish as the forest regrows, until cut again.

Following cutting, due to the reduction in evapotranspiration, the free water table beneath forests moves closer to the surface (Wicht 1949, Boughton 1970, Gilmour 1977a).

Fuelwood cutting in 'cloud' forests represents a special case. Reduction in canopy and vertical structure temporarily decrease the capture of 'occult' precipitation (Zadroga 1981). This phenomenon could lead to a decrease in total water yield with adverse implications for the low-flow periods and possibly lower groundwater levels.

Soil effects

Fuelwood harvesting temporarily breaks the nutrient cycling process, and some part of the nutrient budget can be lost through leaching and water movement out of the stand (e.g. Likens et al. 1970). Moreover, removal of the wood represents a nutrient loss, especially if foliage is removed with the wood. The period of forest regrowth restores the nutrient budget unless the period between harvests is too short. Fuelwood harvesting is similar in this respect to traditional stable shifting agriculture. Fast-growing fuelwood plantations which are totally harvested on a short rotation can cause problems of declining productivity on many tropical soils (Jorgenson and Wells 1986).

Reduction of the upper tree canopy increases the throughfall of rain but does not necessarily increase raindrop impact and 'splash' erosion. Forest floor litter and understorey vegetation are much more effective in reducing splash erosion than is a tall tree canopy layer, which may, in fact, increase drop size and total energy (Lembaga Ekologi 1980, Mosley 1982). If fuel gathering removes understorey and forest-floor debris and litter, then an increase in splash erosion will move soil material downslope. Stream sediment levels may show little increase except where the cutting activity is adjacent to the stream channel or where any access trail or road conducts water and erosion material downhill and into watercourses. Again, in non-mechanized operations this increase will probably be modest. Uncut streamside buffer strips of at least 10 m on both sides of a stream will eliminate most of the adverse impact on soil of this kind of fuelwood harvesting (Bosch and Hewlett 1980, Hamilton and Pearce 1986).

Areas prone to shallow debris slides because of steep slopes and soils with low or no cohesion are provided with a degree of stability by tree roots. O'Loughlin and Watson (1981) showed a substantial reduction in soil shear strength following cutting in New Zealand beech forests due to decay of the tree roots. In similar situations, intensive fuelwood cutting could accelerate landslide activity. Prompt regrowth minimizes the risk. Any ground disturbance, such as skidding or roading, not only greatly increases the risk of shallow debris slides but also of deep-seated slides. This mass soil movement hazard will be discussed further in the section where commercial forest harvesting is considered. Areas prone to mass soil movement are 'areas of risk' where even cutting fuelwood and removing it manually has some likelihood of initiating erosion.

MECHANIZED WOOD HARVESTING

The impact of commercial wood harvesting on the watershed variables considered here depends on several factors, including:

1. the amount of canopy removed;
2. the promptness with which regeneration occurs;
3. the methods of slash disposal and site preparation;
4. the amount of biomass removed (including how much slash remains on the area);
5. the product removal methods;
6. the timing with respect to wet and dry season;
7. the extent, nature, and usage of roads, skid trails and landings;
8. the presence or absence of adequate riparian buffer strips;
9. the soil, geological conditions, and topography;
10. the nature of climatic events following disturbance.

Since the major effects on water and soil resources

have less to do with the silvicultural system (items 1-4) than they do with logging (items 5-8), most attention will be focussed on 'how' the products are removed rather than on the type of cutting. Furthermore, it is helpful to distinguish, within the logging activity, between commonly used practices that give scant regard to impacts on soil and water, and those 'improved' harvesting methods that include a major component of environmental protection with regard to watershed values. Unfortunately, much of the commercial logging in the Pacific and Asia has been of the former type. Furthermore, most of the adverse watershed effects are a result of hydrologically insensitive logging irrespective of the amount of canopy removal. It is encouraging to note, however, that recently promulgated harvesting specifications of the Forestry Department for Peninsular Malaysia address the erosional consequences of poor logging by guidelines for conservation logging (Mok 1986). Queensland (Australia) has adopted watershed-sensitive harvesting guidelines for both rainforests and plantations in the tropics (Cassells and Bonell 1986 and Appendix 1 in Pearce and Hamilton 1986). Moreover, the Sabah Foundation is adopting a series of comprehensive guidelines for planning and harvesting in Sabah (Tang 1985).

Water effects

In general the effects of commercial harvesting on water resources are similar to those that were summarized in the previous section on fuelwood. This is true because the greatest effects occur due to changes in evapotranspiration from tree cutting. In addition, however, the exposure of bare soil and its compaction by machinery has effects on water recharge and on speed of delivery to the streams. In the interests of more completeness, some of the material will be repeated below.

Groundwater: Reduced stand density from felling results in reduced evapotranspiration until it is gradually restored by regrowth from 6-12 years after cutting (Hamilton 1983). This reduction in ET normally results in higher stored soil moisture and thus more water available to recharge groundwater, springs and wells. Throughfall is usually increased because of the reduction in interception, thus allowing a greater percentage of the rainfall to reach the forest floor (particularly important during light-intensity, short-duration precipitation events, and of lesser consequence during high-intensity and prolonged storms). Any additional precipitation reaching the forest floor will either infiltrate the soil, contribute to surface runoff, or evaporate. Increased raindrop impact will be minimal if it is possible to retain understorey vegetation, forest root mat, and litter, and in such cases, reduced infiltration rates should not occur. Thus, water movement processes in forests should result in a net increase in groundwater following canopy reduction, with the effect persisting until full canopy is restored. If, however, much of the area is exposed and compacted by heavy logging machinery, the infiltration rates may be decreased, more water may be quickly channelled off-site, and there may not be an increase in groundwater levels.

A special situation exists where 'cloud forests' capture occult precipitation and add it to the water budget of the system. Removal of the canopy may result in decreased groundwater recharge as previously pointed out.

Aside from cloud forests, increasing heights of water tables have usually followed cutting of forests in areas where permanent free water tables are found (Wicht 1949). Gilmour (1977a) showed, in a tropical rain forest situation, an approximate 10% increase in groundwater storage after logging. Boughton's (1970) review of experience in Australia and elsewhere showed almost total consensus on increases in groundwater following clearing. Roads are a compounding element, however, as they may cut across shallow, unconfined groundwater aquifers or springs, and channel the water off-site or store it on-site. Careful road layout in improved watershed protection logging generally can avoid this problem.

Water yield in streams: Almost every well-designed experiment has shown increased water yield in streams as a response to forest cutting, and, in general, the increase was proportional to the amount of canopy removed. The increase declines as full forest returns to the site. The most recent review of catchment experiments has been undertaken by Bosch and Hewlett (1982). In assessing the results from 94 catchments, they have added the results of 55 experiments to those assessed by Hibbert (1967) and came up with the same conclusion; namely, no experiments in deliberately reducing vegetative cover (i.e. by logging) caused reductions in yield. Unfortunately, there are few long-term paired-catchment study results in the humid tropics, and none that we are aware of in the Pacific and Asia, which have measured impacts of logging on water, though a few have recently been initiated - notably in Malaysia (Baharudin and Low 1982) and the Philippines (Saplaco and Perino 1982). One carefully monitored nearby study in humid tropical northeastern Australia proved to be one of the few exceptions to the general rule. Gilmour et al. (1982) found only a marginally significant increase in annual water yield (although there was a small increase in peak discharge). They attributed this anomaly to the relatively minor role of vegetation changes in a situation of intense monsoon storm pattern, soil with only 20 cm of water storage capacity and overland flow even under undisturbed forest. Where there are very shallow soils, forest removal makes little difference in water yield.

Increases in total yield decline as forest regrows and may disappear within 6-10 years. Then, during the period of rapid increase in biomass in young polewood stands, the forest may actually 'use' more water than did the old growth forest from which it was derived (Langford, Moran and O'Shaughnessy 1980). This has led the Melbourne Water Board to adopt a protection and long rotation forest policy because they obtain more water from old growth forests than from the young forests that follow tree harvesting.

Streamflow distribution and timing: Almost all research on timing of streamflow in deep soils has shown that, proportionally, the greatest increase occurs in the low-flow period, or dry season. Few data, however, are available from locations with very prolonged dry seasons. This result has important forest management implications if low flows are a major water resource problem. Cutting could be beneficial, provided it was repeated when water yields had declined due to regrowth. Hough (1986) has given management suggestions involving tree removal in the semi-arid miombo woodlands of Southern Africa in order to increase dry season flow.

Stormflow volumes, peak flows, and stormflow durations are also usually increased by harvesting, and these effects may increase local upstream flash flooding in, and downstream of, the logged areas. Logging roads, skid trails, and log landings can increase these stormflow parameters further if they are not well planned, not well constructed, and not well maintained.

These stormflow effects must not be extrapolated to support statements that appear in the press (and the misconception commonly held) that logging in upper watersheds is the principal cause of serious and widespread flooding in the lower reaches of major river basins. If the whole major river basin were to be logged at once, this situation could be true on occasion, but such a situation is unrealistic. Hewlett (1982) has reviewed the relationship and he concluded that forest operations (not conversion to agriculture) in upstream catchments have not been shown to increase flood flows seriously in major streams. He also suggested that this conclusion is applicable to the tropics as well as the temperate zone, from which has come most of the experimental evidence. Hewlett indicated that the cumulative downstream effects of fairly widespread forest harvesting in a basin can be calculated by streamflow routing techniques and that they will prove to be minor in comparison with the influences of rainfall and basin storage (and, in our opinion, the direction the storm moves over the basin, the amount of sediment that has accumulated in the channel, the density and location of roads and structures, and the tinkering we have done with the river itself). If a storm event of magnitude 400 mm in 24 hours occurs on soils that can accommodate only 200 mm even if there were no antecedent storage, there will be flooding even if undisturbed forest covered the entire drainage basin.

Soil effects

On-site erosion: Soil surface erosion is not usually an important process in the undisturbed forest, but it can occur, as has been shown in tropical rain forests in Australia (Gilmour et al. 1982) and in Malaysia (Peh 1980). However, wood extraction by ground transportation (as opposed to helicopter or balloon) inevitably increases erosion rates substantially.

In general, skyline logging systems are least damaging of the conventional systems. In general, in spite of some exceptions seen in Malaysia, aerial-high lead logging methods are more benign than tractor logging in steep terrain. While damage to residual trees, especially close to spar trees or the crane may be high, keeping the logs off the ground reduces the amount of soil disturbance and compaction. It also usually reduces the number of roads, and roads are particular trouble spots in regeneration. Chauvin (1976) suggested that for ground logging it requires approximately 4 km of roads and 8 km of trails for 1,000 ha of logging in low volume harvesting in poor forests, but can reach 8 km of roads and 22 km of trails for 1,000 ha of logging in rich forests. Rough terrain limits road density but increases skidding trails, unless aerial cable logging is used. The 'san tai wong' or 'king-of-the-forest' winch lorry used in Peninsular Malaysia hill forests requires a dense network of logging roads. The percentage of a heavily logged (but not clearcut) forest involved in tracks and roads may range from 16 to 30% (Burgess 1973 for Malaysia; Kartawinata 1978 for Indonesia; and Gilmour 1977b for Australia). An enlightening study of the variation in bare area under different methods comes from the humid Northwestern United States and has relevance for the tropics (Rice et al. 1972). For jammer logging group selection - 25 to 30% bare; for high lead clearcut - 6%; for skyline clearcut - 2%; and for helicopter clearcut - 1%.

Plot studies have shown the seriousness of logging-induced erosion in Southeast Asia's rain forests - for instance, Lim Suan (1980) in the Philippines, and Ruslan and Manan (1980) in Indonesia. Excerpts from the skid road study in Indonesia are shown in Table 3.1.

It is worth noting that elephant logging is rather benign compared to other methods of timber extraction on slopes, provided that the road density is not increased. Thailand has used elephants from its elephant training camp, and these have recently been introduced into Sumatra (Jurvelius 1987, pers. comm.).

The practice of cutting on unstable steep slopes that are prone to mass wasting can increase the risk of shallow landslips because of a reduction in root shear strength (O'Loughlin and Watson 1981). Wood extraction exacerbates the situation, even if carefully done, by oversteepening slopes in road cuttings. Aerial logging has been used in some areas in developed countries in such situations, but will probably be impractical for most situations in the Pacific/Asia region. The best answer is to avoid forest harvesting on these areas. Methods of identifying these mass-erosion prone areas have been given by Megahan and

Table 3.1: The influence of the regrowth that occurs in erosion rates on skidding roads in an Indonesian logging situation*

Plots/Treatments	Erosion (tons/ha/month)	Run-off (m^3/ha/month)
Newly constructed and used skid road	12.90	189.14
Newly constructed but unused skid road	10.80	148.56
Two years abandoned skid road	6.15	42.70
Three years abandoned skid road	3.20	19.22
Forest undisturbed - no skid road	0.00	2.09

* Slope 8-10%; Precipitation 2,429 mm/yr; latosol; plot size: 4m x 2m; observation period, 5 months.

Source: Adapted from Ruslan and Manan (1980).

King (1985), and are summarized:
   1.   Slope, steepness - most landslipping occurs on slopes of 40 to 70%.
   2.   Slope shape - most critical areas are those spoon-shaped concavities where there is convergence of drainage near the heads of a drainageway.
   3.   Soil layers - a more permeable layer atop a layer of restricted permeability or bedrock, where there is sharp discontinuity in texture, structure, and drainage.
   4.   Erosivity - the greater the erosivity (combination of rainfall intensities, frequency, and total amount) the greater the potential for failure (an erosivity threshold can be established).

Sediment in streams: While it is virtually impossible to prevent some increase in erosion from forest harvesting (except on level land), increased stream sediment is not necessarily a consequence of logging. This has been shown by careful logging in the Melbourne water supply catchments (Catchment Hydrology Research Coordinating Committee 1980). As currently carried out in the tropics,

89

however (and usually in the temperate zone also), logging is usually followed by increased sediment in streams. This has potentially deleterious impacts on aquatic life, reservoir siltation rates, altered stream channels that may increase flooding and reduce navigability, and reduced water quality for domestic and industrial use.

For Indonesia, Karawinata (1981) reported that no convincing studies have been carried out to show the effects of logging on stream sediment loads, but he stated that sediment loads of rivers within deforested areas were extremely large and a cause of national concern. Hamzah (1978), however, has made some empirical observations on the effects of mechanical logging in east Kalimantan and reported increasing silt content in the river, the closer the measurements were made to the logging area. O'Loughlin (1985) has reviewed the sediment production situation with respect to roads for tropical and temperate forest logging, and summarized several studies, particularly in Peninsular Malaysia. At a north Queensland site involving heavy logging of virgin tropical rain forest, peak concentrations at sampling stations below the logging area, during high intensity rains, increased 6- to 12-fold (Gilmour 1971). The sediment derived from streams flowing through undisturbed forest was largely organic, in contrast with the dominantly mineral sediment in streams coming from the logged area. Gilmour reported that the principal sources of sediment were from poorly located, undrained roads and skid trails, from log landings, and from earth- and log-filled stream crossings. He also indicated that, as a result of this study, conditions were placed in the timber sale agreements to minimize the effect of these sediment-producing areas and that they were effective in reducing sediment level. These conditions were enunciated as guidelines in the FAO publication, Guidelines for watershed management (Gilmour 1977b).

Sediment problems can be reduced substantially during and after harvesting by a number of conservation logging practices. For instance, it is obvious that roads and skid trails should be kept out of water-courses, or should at most cross them at right angles using bridges or culverts. In addition to the FAO Guidelines (Gilmour 1977b and Megahan 1977) more recent ones have been proposed by Megahan and Schweithelm (1983) and officially promulgated for selective logging in Queensland, Australia (Cassells and Bonell 1986) and in Malaysia (Mok 1986). In all of these and in other studies, the importance of streamside buffer strips is emphasized. These strips can reduce streambank erosion and can trap sheetwash and rill sediments (but not gully material) from upslope (Hamilton and Pearce 1986). Moreover, this streamside vegetation moderates light and temperature levels with benefits to many kinds of aquatic life. Terrestrial and arboreal wildlife also benefit because cover is provided with access to water supply. Rules of thumb suggest strips 20 to 40 m each side of perennial streams (Bosch and Hewlett 1980), although in some instances narrower strips of 10 m have proven effective (Hamilton and Pearce 1986).

Nutrient loss: What was said about nutrient loss from harvesting fuelwood applies to commercial wood harvesting. The nutrient cycling is temporarily disrupted, and most studies have shown nutrient export increases in the streamflow from increased leaching following harvest (Bormann et al. 1974). In addition, the potential for larger increases in soil erosion means that commercial logging has more potential for serious impacts on site productivity, because eroding soil takes nutrients with it. Minimizing erosion will reduce nutrient loss from the disturbed area. The export of nutrients in harvested material is a further drain, and the more complete the biomass utilization, the more serious this drain becomes. Until recently, the long interval between successive harvests has allowed recovery. Logging of secondary forests or plantations on short rotations now brings this problem into the area of concern (Hase and Foelster 1983, Jorgensen and Wells 1986).

Obtaining prompt and adequate regeneration, maintaining as much advanced reproduction as possible, and keeping bare areas to a minimum not only reduce erosion caused by productivity decline, but get the nutrient cycles returned to pre-harvest levels in the shortest time.

CONCLUSIONS

It is misleading and counter-productive to treat as though they were alike the impacts of the very disparate array of activities that have been labelled 'deforestation'. The consequences of fuelwood cutting and product removal by non-mechanized methods are vastly different than those of mechanical clearing of forest and converting the area to maize or rice. Yet this emotion-provoking word 'deforestation' has been used to describe these and other very different kinds of alteration or elimination of forests. Only by more precisely naming the action can we estimate some of the probable effects and thus achieve better planning and management policies for forestlands in the development process.

Generalizations about the effects of harvesting in forests are difficult to make because of the many variables in precipitation patterns, topography, methods of product extraction, and a number of other factors. It is re-emphasized that the greatest effects, especially in erosion, are due to the way in which the material is removed rather than in the amount cut. Because of its comparatively benign effects, the harvesting of non-wood products was elaborated upon as an enterprise with unplumbed potential. It is emphasized that only the soil and water impacts of these activities have been considered, and not the myriad of broader questions of great importance, including impacts on existing forest dwellers or nearby users, on biological diversity, on sustainable forest industry, and others.

The on-site effects on soil and water are important, particularly as they relate to the ease of obtaining regeneration and the need to maintain nutrients in order to maintain productivity. However, it is the off-site impacts that tend to capture societal concerns and galvanize people into actions which might prohibit or regulate harvesting in forests. Some of these perceived adverse impacts have been based on assumptions with no foundation (e.g. cutting forests causes catastrophic floods on large rivers). Others are valid observations and the negative impacts can be severe (e.g. logging increases sediment in streams coming from the area). Forest managers and planners need to be able to separate myth from reality, and then take action on those legitimate public concerns where they can reduce negative effects. They should insist that planned and managed forest harvesting not be labelled 'deforestation', because in the moist tropics, if fire, grazing and agriculture are not initiated, regeneration of forest on harvested areas is prompt. Harvesting may, of course, be followed by conversion to agriculture or grazing where there are serious land hunger pressures. Solutions to this major global problem lie in the realms of population planning, land reform, and equity in economic development. Banning forest product harvesting on the basis of the harmful soil and water consequences of 'deforestation' is aiming at the wrong target.

NOTE

1.   Those who might argue that removal of the upper forest canopy exposes the ground surface to greater raindrop impact, soil detachment and splash erosion, should note the research reported by Lembaga Ekologi (1980) showing greater raindrop impact on bare soil under a tall forest canopy than on bare soil in the open. Mosley (1982) showed greater kinetic energy of raindrops per unit area under tall forest than in the open because of larger drop size. Wiersum (1984) has summarized several studies that show that ground cover such as forest litter rather than tree canopy has a greater effect in reducing erosion.

REFERENCES

Anonymous (1980), Rules on harvesting, cutting of rattan out; rattan incentives out, The Philippine Lumberman 26(7):30

Baharudin, J. and Low, K.S. (1982), Forest influences research in Malaysia, in Hamilton, L.S. and Bonell, M. (eds), Country Papers on Status of Watershed Forest Influence Research in Southeast Asia and the Pacific, Working Paper, Environment and Policy Institute. Honolulu: East-West Center, 174-85

Bajracharya, D. (1983), Deforestation in the food/fuel contest: historical and political perspectives from Nepal. Mountain Research and Development 3(3):227-40

Bormann, F.H., Likens, G.E., Siccawa, T.G., Pierce, R.S. and Eaton, J.S. (1974), The export of nutrients and recovery of stable conditions following deforestation at Hubbard Brook. Ecological Monographs 44:255-77

Bosch, J.M. and Hewlett, J.D. (1980), Sediment control in South African forests and mountain catchments. South African Forestry 115:50-55

Bosch, J.M. and Hewlett, J.D. (1982), A review of catchment experiments to determine the effect of vegetation changes on water yield and evapotranspiration. Hydrology 55:3-23

Boughton, W.C. (1970), Effects of land management on quantity and quality of available water: a review. Australian Water Resources Council Research Project 68/2, Rep. 120. Manly Vale: University of New South Wales

Bowonder, B. (1982), Deforestation in India. International Journal of Environmental Studies 18(3,4):223-36

Burgess, P.F. (1973) The impact of commercial logging on the hill forests of the Malay Peninsula. Proc. Symposium on Biological Resources and National Development, Kuala Lumpur, 131-6

Cassells, D.S. and Bonell, M. (1986), Logging operations in forest watersheds: an Australian perspective, in Pearce, A.J. and Hamilton, L.S. (eds), Land Use, Watersheds and Planning in the Asia Pacific Region, Bangkok: FAO Regional Office, 44-58

Catchment Hydrology Research Coordinating Committee (1980), Water supply catchment hydrology research, summary of technical conclusions to 1979. Melbourne and Metropolitan Board of Works Rept. No. MMBW-W-0012, Melbourne

Chauvin, H. (1976), Opening up the tropical moist forest and harvesting the timber. Unasylva 28(2,3):80-5

Gilmour, D.A. (1971), The effects of logging on streamflow and sedimentation in a north Queensland rainforest catchment. Commonwealth Forestry Review (Australia) 50:38-48

Gilmour, D.A. (1977a), Effect of logging and clearing on water yield and water quality in a high rainfall zone of north-east Queensland, in The Hydrology of Northern Australia, Institution of Engineers, Australia, National Conference Publ. No. 77/5:156-60

Gilmour, D.A. (1977b), Logging and the environment, with particular reference to soil and stream protection in tropical rainforest situations, in FAO Conservation Guide No. 1, Guidelines for Watershed Management, Rome: FAO, 223-35

Gilmour, D.A., Cassells, D.S. and Bonell, M. (1982), Hydrological research in the tropical rainforests of north Queensland: some implications for land use management. Proc. First National Symposium on Forest Hydrology, Institution of Engineers, Australia, National Conference Publication 82/6:145-52

Hamilton, L.S. (with King, P.N.) (1983), Tropical Forested Watersheds: Hydrologic and Soils Response to Major

Uses or Conversions, Boulder: Westview Press

Hamilton, L.S. (1986), What are the impacts of deforestation in the Himalaya on the Ganges-Brahmaputra lowlands and delta? Relations between assumptions and facts. Presented at Conference on the Research and Policy Recommendations, Mohonk Mountain House, New Paltz, N.Y., April 6-11, 1986. To be published

Hamilton, L.S. and Pearce, A.J. (1986), Biophysical aspects of integrated watershed management, in Easter, K.W., Dixon, J.A., and Hufschmidt, M.H. (eds), Watershed Management: An Interdisciplinary Approach, Boulder: Westview Press, 33-52

Hamzah, A. (1978), Some observations on the effects of mechanical logging on regeneration; soil, and hydrological conditions in East Kalimantan. Proc. Symposium on Long-Term Effects of Logging in Southeast Asia, BIOTROP Spec. Publ. 3, Bogor, 73-8

Hase, H. and Foelster, H. (1983), Impact of plantation forestry with teak (Tectona grandis) on the nutrient status of young alluvial soils in West Venezuela. Forest Ecology and Management 6(1):33-57

Hewlett, J.D. (1982), Forests and floods in the light of recent investigation. Proc. Canadian Hydrological Symposium, 14-15 June 1982, Fredericton, 543-60

Hibbert, A.R. (1967), Forests treatment effects on water yield, in Sopper, W.E. and Lull, H.W. (eds), International Symposium on Forest Hydrology, Oxford, Pergamon Press, 527-43

Hough, J. (1986), Management alternatives for increasing dry season base flow in the miombo woodlands of Southern Africa. Ambio 15(6):341-46

Jorgensen, J.R. and Wells, C.G. (1986), Tree nutrition and fast-growing plantations in developing countries. International Tree Crops Journal 3(1986):225-44

Kartawinata, K. (1978), Biological changes after logging in lowland Dipterocarp forest, in Suparto, R.S. et al. (eds), Symposium on the Long Term Effects of Logging in Southeast Asia, BIOTROP Spec. Publ. 3, Bogor, 27-34

Kartawinata, K. (1981), The environmental consequences of tree removal from the forest in Indonesia, in Sutlive, V.H., Altshuler, N. and Zamora, M.D. (eds), Where Have All the Flowers Gone? Deforestation in the Third World, Publ. 13. Williamsburg: College of William and Mary, 191-214

Langford, K.J., Moran, R.J. and O'Shaughnessy (1980), The

North Maroondah experiment pretreatment phase comparison of catchment water balances. Journal of Hydrology 46:123-45

Lembaga Ekologi (1980), Report on study of vegetation and erosion in the Jatiluhur catchment, 1980. Bandung: Institute of Ecology, Padjadjaran University

Lert, C., Prin, S.A. and Wuthipol, H. (1985), Non-Wood Forest Products in Thailand, FAO GCP/RAS/106/JPN Field Document 5

Likens, G.E., Bormann, F.H., Johnson, N.M., Fisher, D.W. and Pierce, R.S. (1970), Effects of forest cutting and herbicide treatment on nutrient budgets in the Hubbard Brook watershed ecosystem. Ecological Monographs 40:23-47

Lim Suan, M.P. (1980), Technical feasibility and economic viability of selective logging in the Insular Lumber Company. Forest Research Inst. Annual Report, College, Laguna, Philippines, 142-3

Mahat, T.B.S., Griffin, D.M. and Shepherd, K.R. (1986), Human impact on some forests in the Middle Hills of Nepal. 1. Forestry in the context of the traditional resources of the state. Mountain Research and Development 6(3):223-32

Megahan, W.F. (1977), Reducing erosional impacts of roads, in Guidelines for Watershed Management, Conservation Guide 1, Rome: FAO, 237-61

Megahan, W.F. and King, P.N. (1985), Identification of critical areas on forest lands for control of nonpoint sources of pollution. Environmental Management 9(1):7-18

Megahan, W.F. and Schweithelm, J. (1983), Guidelines for reducing negative impacts of logging, in Hamilton, L.S. with King, P.N., Tropical Forested Watersheds: Hydrologic and Soils Response to Major Uses or Conversions, Boulder: Westview Press, 143-54

Mok, S.T. (1986), Sustained use and management of forests: a Malaysian perspective, in Pearce, A.J. and Hamilton, L.S. (eds), Land Use, Watersheds and Planning in the Asia-Pacific Region, Bangkok: Food and Agriculture Organization in East-West Center, 34-43

Mosley, M.P. (1982), The effect of a New Zealand beech forest canopy on the kinetic energy of water drops and on surface erosion. Earth Surface Processes and Landforms 7(2):103-7

O'Loughlin, C.L. (1974), The effect of timber removal on the stability of forest soils. Hydrology 13:121-34

O'Loughlin, C. (1985), The Influence of Forest Roads on Erosion and Stream Sedimentation - Comparisons Between Temperate and Tropical Forests. Working Paper, Environment and Policy Institute, Honolulu: East-West Center

O'Loughlin, C.L. and Watson, A.J. (1981), Note on root-wood strength deterioration in Nothofagus fusca and N. truncata after clearfelling. New Zealand Journal of Forestry Science 11(2):183-5

O'Loughlin, C.L. and Ziemer, R.R. (1982), The importance of root strength and deterioration rates upon edaphic stability in steepland forests, in Waring, R.H. (ed), Carbon Uptake and Allocation: A Key to Management of Subalpine Ecosystems, Corvallis, 84-91

Openshaw, K. (1974), Woodfuels in the developing world. New Scientist January 31:271-2

Pearce, A.J. and Hamilton, L.S. (eds) (1986), Land Use, Watersheds and Planning in the Asia Pacific Region, Bangkok: FAO Regional Office

Peh, C.H. (1980), Runoff and sediment transport by overland flow under tropical rainforest conditions. The Malaysian Forester 43:56-67

Rambo, A.T. (1982), Orang Asli adaptive strategies. Implications for Malaysian natural resource development planning, in MacAndrews, C. and Chia, L.S. (eds) Too Rapid Development: Perceptions and Perspectives from Southeast Asia, Athens: Ohio University Press, 251-99

Rice, R.M., Rothacher, J.S. and Megahan, W.F. (1972), Erosional consequences of timber harvesting: an appraisal. Proc. National Symposium Watersheds in Transition, Fort Collins, 321-9

Robinson, Merritt and deVries Limited (1983), The forests of Nepal. A study of historical trends and projections to 2000. Report No. 4/2/2007 83/1/1, Kathmandu

Ruslan, M. and Manan, S. (1980), The effect of skidding road on soil erosion and runoff in the forest concession of Pulan Lant, South Lakinanton, Indonesia. Seminar on Hydrology in Watershed Management, Surakarta, unpublished

Saplaco, S.R. and Perino, J.M. (1982), Status of watershed research in the Philippines, in Hamilton, L.S. and Bonell, M. (eds), Country Papers on Status of Watershed Forest Influence Research in Southeast Asia and the

Pacific, Working Paper, Environment and Policy Institute, Honolulu: East-West Center, 219-62

Spears, J. and Ayensu, E.S. (1984), Sectoral paper on forestry. Background paper for 'The Global Possible' conference, Washington, World Resources Institute

Tang, H.T. (1985), Watershed Considerations in Tropical Forest Planning and Harvesting, Working Paper, Environment and Policy Institute, Honolulu: East-West Center

Tewari, D.N. (1982), Minor Forest Products in India. Paper at US AID Conference 'Forestry and Development in Asia,' Bangalore, unpublished

Wicht, C.C. (1949), Forestry and water supplies in South Africa. Department of Agriculture South Africa, Bull. 58

Wiersum, K.F. (1984), Surface erosion under various tropical agroforestry systems, in O'Loughlin, C. and Pearce, A. (eds), Proceedings, Symposium on Effects of Forest Land Use on Erosion and Slope Stability. Honolulu: East-West Center, 231-9

Yao, C.E. and Nanagas, F.N. (1983), Litter fall commercialization: a threat to Cebu reforestation. Canopy International 9(8):6-7

Zadroga, F. (1981), The hydrological importance of a montane cloud forest area of Costa Rica, in Lal, R. and Russell, F.W. (eds), Tropical Agricultural Hydrology, New York: John Wiley and Sons, 59-73

4

FORESTRY AND WATERSHED MANAGEMENT

L.S. Hamilton

INTRODUCTION

Existing forests in upper watersheds produce a number of substantial benefits which should not lightly be discarded, as increasing amounts of forest come under planned or unplanned forest conversion to agriculture and grazing. Foresters and others, however, must not be guilty of exaggerating those benefits or claiming spurious benefits because they want to weigh the balance in favour of retention of forests. For instance, forest benefits do not extend to creating rain nor to preventing major disastrous floods in the lower reaches of large river systems. They do, assuredly, in undisturbed form, provide the greatest vegetative protection against erosion and mass movement, yield the least sediment, and usually reduce local stream peak flows from storms of shorter duration and lower intensity which occur with a high frequence (i.e. not those that occur perhaps once in 30 years or less nor for the annual torrential monsoon rains when there is total soil saturations for long periods of time). In certain physiographic situations where frequent cloud cover occurs at upper elevations, forests can 'capture' moisture by condensation and add it to the watershed system as increased 'effective' precipitation. These situations are the well-known 'cloud' or 'wet dwarf' forests of the tropics. In addition, natural undisturbed forests are habitat for a rich array of indigenous fauna and flora (other than trees) that constitutes not only a national but a global patrimony. The genetic bank represented by natural tropical forests may be one of their principal values.

These forests may be harvested for nonwood forests products such as rattans, fruits and nuts (if done in moderation) without sacrificing any of the benefits of importance in watershed management. Tribal forest dwellers using such produce at the hunter-gather level are not usually of concern in terms of soil and water conservation. These forests may also provide opportunities for scientific research, nature study and tourism without decreasing their hydrologic and soil conserving functions, while clothing the landscape in aesthetically pleasing fashion.

However, as the intensity of forest modification increases to include such activities as stable shifting agriculture, light forest grazing and wood product harvesting, some of the protective watershed functions are at risk unless high standards of performance are induced or enforced. The paper discusses some of the guidelines and methods of maintaining a high degree of hydrological and erosional safety under such uses. Of particular importance for minimizing erosion and sediment yield from a watershed are: the maintenance of undisturbed streamside buffer strips; maintenance of continuous tree roots on landslip-prone sites; care in location, design and maintenance of roads for harvesting; protection from fire; maintenance of the litter layer and understory vegetation (including continuous grass cover if the forest comes under a light grazing use - a situation extremely difficult to achieve where pressures of humans and livestock are high). It is suggested that with high performance standards, direct wood product harvest and stable shifting agriculture do not significantly increase the incidence nor severity of major catastrophic lower basin floods, and may result in greater yield of water from the watershed through reduction in evapotranspiration losses.

Conversely, there are many watershed benefits to be garnered from putting forests on denuded lands (forestation) or in introducing trees or groups of trees into agricultural or grazing systems (agroforestry or sylvopastoral systems). It is cautioned, however, that these benefits in soil and water protection do not occur automatically by virtue of having trees on the land. For instance, there can still be erosion and resulting sediment in an agroforestry system, if the crop cultivation is not carried out with good soil conservation management practices, including such things as terraces in steepland and maintenance of organic litter or live vegetation on the otherwise bare soil. Even under reforested or afforested plantations, erosion can occur on steep slopes if litter cover or understory vegetation are not present (perhaps through removal, or if harvesting the plantation products is not done with attention to watershed values).

There are many excellent reasons for maintaining forests or for planting forests or trees on watershed lands. These relate not only to the direct product benefits, to biological diversity conservation, and to landscape aesthetics, but to a bundle of very practical, though difficult to quantify, benefits having to do with erosion and hydrologic safety in a watershed management context. It is important, however, for foresters and other watershed professionals not to make unrealizable claims of mythical or questionable soil and water benefits.

A wide range of claims have been made about the miraculous benefits of trees, whether in rows, groves or forests. It is alleged that they can stop floods, make rain, provide fuelwood, yield fodder, produce resins (or saps), provide food, renew springs and wells, prevent erosion, shelter and feed wildlife, keep sediment out of rivers, lakes and reservoirs, release more water during the dry season, enhance landscape beauty, supply commercial wood products such as timber and biomass for energy, and protect gene pools of biotic diversity. When planted in conjunction with annual crops, trees are alleged to provide beneficial litter, to ameliorate microclimate, to pump up nutrients, and to fix nitrogen, thereby enhancing crop yields. Forests are a home for some primitive tribal people.

'Miracle trees' indeed, and as a forester I am happy to be associated with their protection and management, or their establishment on new or formerly forested areas. It is true that rows of trees (as in shelterbelts or lines in alley cropping systems), groves of trees (as in some agroforestry systems), or closed blocks or groups of trees (as in plantations or natural forests) can produce many, but not all of these benefits. Even those benefits that they can produce are not necessarily produced simultaneously, sequentially, or under all circumstances, although much popular literature would have you believe that this is the case.

Many foresters have tended to acquiesce, by their silence, when such impressive lists of benefits were made for tree planting or maintaining forests. Small wonder it is for foresters have had to fight to get across to the planning table when forest land allocation decisions were being made

101

by economic development planners. They have had to struggle against powerful peasant pressures for forest land occupancy, and against wealthy, politically strong cattle barons and estate owners wanting to convert more forest land and 'privatize' it. Foresters have had to labour hard to restore tree cover to denuded and degraded lands. Widespread popular support based on the many benefits of forests and trees has been necessary, and from as many publics or clients as possible. Therefore, if the benefits are somewhat exaggerated, didn't the end (forest clad uplands, for instance) justify the means?

As a forester, I suggest that we had better forego the 'trees-are-a-panacea-for-all-land-and-water-ills' stance, and become more realistic in proclaiming what forests will and will not do in providing all of the aforementioned benefits. If we do not, we face real risks from disappointed publics and clients in the future. We must maintain our credibility by clarifying what benefits can be legitimately claimed, under what circumstances, and with what trade-offs among other products or services. In this presentation, I will deal only with some of the real versus touted soil and water benefits resulting from watershed management and rehabilitation. I contend that only those benefits which can be realized should be accepted as a mandate from society in watershed forestry programmes.

FORESTS AND RAINFALL

It is being advocated that watershed forests be protected, not only from conversion to agriculture or grazing, but from wood harvesting, because such actions will result in decreased rainfall, causing droughts and creating deserts. Much of the clamour concerns not tropical dry forests, or woodland, but tropical rainforest.

Popular writing about the effects logging has on rainfall in tropical rainforests comes from a wide range of sources. The World Wildlife Fund/IUCN Tropical Forest Campaign was initiated in October 1982 in Bali, Indonesia. It suggested that following logging, the 'land of green gold' is turned into 'useless desert' and that 'take away the trees and you get withering drought in the dry season' (WWF/IUCN, 1982). Suggestive of the same thinking was the title of a fine and influential book, 'Amazon Jungle: Green Hell to Red Desert?' (Goodland and Irwin, 1975). The leader of the Tree

Hugging Movement (Chipko) in India has claimed that cutting of the forest results in drought (World Water, 1981). An article entitled 'The Desertification of Asia', claimed that 'deserts can develop with great speed even in the heart of a tropical jungle' (Sharp and Sharp, 1982).

In these cases there may be some slippery semantics in the words 'desert' and 'drought', but the popular mental picture conjured up coincides with a dictionary definition that a desert is 'arid land with insufficient precipitation to permit plant growth', and that a drought is 'lack of precipitation or moisture'. It is difficult to comprehend how a tropical rain forest area receiving upwards of 1,800 mm/year of rain can be converted into a desert by logging. Even a tropical seasonal forest or woodland does not change to desert after tree harvesting. It is true, that logging followed by fire and conversion to abusive agriculture or grazing can result in degraded, strongly eroded wasteland, but deserts do not follow logging.

What does research have to offer on this topic? Some Russian work, cited and summarized by Shpak (1968) showed approximately 10 per cent more rain in forest areas as opposed to adjacent open areas. Shpak goes on, however, to point out precipitation measuring problems that invariably allow forest gages to catch more rain. He concludes that 'the considerable increase (found by some authors) ... is usually overstated ... the problem of the effect of forest on precipitation remains open at present'. An early study in the United States following large scale 'deforestation' by smelter fume injury, showed small (14 per cent) but significantly greater precipitation in the forest area compared with the denuded area (Hursch, 1948). A subsequent analysis of those experimental procedures by Lee (1978), however, indicated that when catch differences are accounted for (mainly from wind effects), the differences were less than 0.5 per cent. In the tropics, Bernard (1953) found no evidence of any influence of forests on rainfall for the one million square kilometer Central Congo Basin. He speculated, however, that forest clearing, by increasing the heat reflectance might introduce some instability into weather patterns.

Recently, however, in the Amazon Basin it has been shown that this large forested area with its unique hydrometeorology regenerates some of its own rain (Salati et al., 1979). It is speculated that large scale and permanent deforestation (not just logging) could reduce rainfall in

103

downwind parts of the basin (Salati et al., 1983; Salati and Vose, 1984). The scientific community has not reached a consensus on this speculation and modelling studies have given somewhat conflicting results. However, it would seem prudent to consider the possibility of reduced rainfall in considering future development of the Amazon.

For most hydrometeorological situations in Asia and the Pacific, it is more likely that Pereira's (1973) summary is still valid: 'There is no corresponding evidence as to any effects of forests on the occurrence of rainfall'. Although there are many compelling, scientifically sound, and philosophically imperative reasons for trying to preserve a large amount of the remaining primary tropical rain forest, the fear of large reductions in rainfall following cutting of forests is not one of them. As a matter of fact the interception of rainfall (or snow) by a forest canopy, and the subsequent evaporation of a portion of this (called 'interception loss') means that the effective precipitation reaching the ground is less than the actual precipitation. Interception losses are generally greater for forests than for any other vegetation type on land use.

There is one exception. In certain physiographic situations, for example in coastal fog belts or at high elevations characterized by frequent or persistent clouds, forest can 'capture' and condense atmospheric moisture. This so-called 'occult' precipitation is added to the effective moisture received by the area and may represent a substantial percentage of the total. For example, in Hawaii occult precipitation represented an increase of 760 mm above a nonforested 2,600 mm of rainfall (Ekern, 1964). Cutting down these cloud or fog forests results in a loss of this precipitation, though it is restored as the forest regrows. If the area is converted to another use, however, most of this moisture is removed from the water budget of the watershed, including water outflow from the immediate watershed (Zadroga, 1981). Keeping the cloud forest and fog forests intact makes good hydrologic sense in watershed management as a source of additional water for downstream agricultural, domestic and industrial use.

Conversely, no increases in gross precipitation have been shown following programmes of reforestation or afforestation in formerly open lands. And because of increased interception losses, there may even be a decrease in effective precipitation reaching the ground. Such activity is an important part of watershed rehabilitation, but not for any alleged benefits in making rain. In persistent cloud situations, however, planting belts of trees or forests can capture occult moisture, and are therefore beneficial watershed rehabilitation practices which do increase water availability (Hamilton, 1983).

FORESTS AND EROSION

Popular wisdom insists that planting trees will prevent erosion and that removing trees, per se, results in drastic erosion leading to land degradation. Trees, and particularly trees in forest stands do indeed reduce the amount of erosion, and conventional wisdom does coincide with proven effects. Soil erosion under dense natural humid and seasonally humid forest is usually less than one ton per hectare per year (UNESCO/UNEP/FAO, 1978). However, substantial surface erosion can occur in undisturbed forest (Lal, 1983), as can landslips and debris avalanches on forested unstable slopes (Lin, 1984). Nonetheless, the undisturbed forest is excellent watershed cover from the erosion standpoint, but it is more appropriate to speak of forests as having low erosion rather than no erosion; and when putting forest back on land to talk about erosion reduction, rather than prevention. To be more precise it is also necessary to separate three classes of erosion: (a) surface (sheetwash and rills), (b) gully, and (c) mass wasting (landslips, slumps, debris flows, etc.).

Soil erosion

Surface erosion under humid tropical primary forest is generally more severe than in humid temperate forests, because of more frequent and intense rains and less litter and ground vegetation on the soil surface (Birot, 1968). In dry or seasonal forest, rates of erosion are probably comparable between tropic and temperate zones, depending on rainfall patterns. If understory vegetation in forests is not overgrazed nor the litter burned, erosion rates are still very low.

Moreover, simply putting trees or forests back on the land does not eliminate surface erosion. Bell (1973) reported significant erosion problems in pure *Tectona grandis* plantations in Trinidad, and similar problems have been

105

reported in El Salvador and Thailand (Kunkle, 1983) and in Java (Coster, 1938) where there is no understory vegetation and/or litter is removed. Brunig et al. (1975) reported annual erosion rates on moderate slope for undisturbed natural forest, teak plantation widely spaced with mixed understory, and dense teak plantations with no understory as 0.2-10, 2-10 and 20-160 tons/ha, respectively.

Advocates sometimes talk about the benefits of having a tree canopy interposed between the falling rain and the bare soil to reduce splash erosion (detachment of particles by raindrop impact, and then movement). Actually, splash erosion can be greater under trees because drop sizes are larger. Coalescing raindrops on large-leaved species (such as teak), falling from a high canopy may be more damaging to the soil than the rain itself. For instance, Albizzia falcataria with canopy height of 20 m yielded raindrops with an erosive energy 102 per cent of rain in the open, but the Anthocephalus chinensis with its large leaves at only 10 m canopy height, this figure was 147 per cent (Lembaga Ekologi, 1980). Repeated results of surface erosion studies in forests have shown that it is the leaf litter and low understory that impart erosion protection (for example, Wiersum, in press). If these are removed for fodder and/or fuel, or if livestock are turned in to graze, the presence of trees will not minimize surface erosion on slopes. Wiersum (1984) has synthesized much of the research literature on erosion under various forest and tree crop systems and presented an interesting table of averages (lumping all data, even though derived from different slopes and soils - Table 4.1). Note that as soon as the litter is removed by cultivation or weeding or burning, the erosion rate increases substantially.

Introducing trees into a cropping system, whether shifting agriculture or sedentary agriculture, has been suggested as a desirable watershed management practice. It should be recognized that from the surface erosion standpoint, the trees will only give reductions if the cropping practices maintain much leaf litter and vegetative cover on the soil. Good soil conservation farming (or grazing) must prevail if an agroforestry system is to claim erosion reduction benefits in a watershed strategy.

Another aspect concerning trees and erosion merits some attention. A hazard arises in connection with any soil disturbance associated with preparing the site for reforestation or afforestation, and with any subsequent

Table 4.1: Erosion in various tropical moist forest and tree crop systems (ton/ha/year)

	Minimal	Median	Maximal
Multistoried tree gardens (4/4)*	0.01	0.06	0.14
Natural forests (18/27)	0.03	0.30	6.16
Shifting cultivation, fallow period (6/14)	0.05	0.15	7.40
Forest plantations, undisturbed (14/20)	0.02	0.58	6.20
Tree crops with cover crop/mulch (9/17)	0.10	0.75	5.60
Shifting cultivation, cropping period (7/22)	0.40	2.78	70.50
Taungya cultivation (2/6)	0.63	5.23	17.37
Tree crops, clean-weeded (10/17)	1.20	47.60	182.90
Forest plantations, burned/litter removed (7/7)	5.92	53.40	104.80

* (x/y) x = no. locations. y = no. treatments or observations. From Wiersum (1984).

cultivation to reduce competition in the early establishment phase. In the drier parts of tropical Asia and the Pacific, competing vegetation may not be a concern and thus the hand-planting and lack of subsequent cultivation bring no erosion problems. But experience in moist areas of Queensland and Nigeria has shown that site preparation pays off in terms of increased survival and growth. Even in the Fiji dry zone, Bell and Evo (1982) suggest that the Fiji Pine Commission employ cultivation prior to and during the establishment of eucalpyt energy plantations. Cassells in Australia is currently developing a set of planting site preparation guidelines for tropical Queensland based on erosion studies conducted since 1974 (Cassells et al., 1982). Contour row-ploughing has been found most satisfactory in erodible soils (Cassells, pers. com.). Fast growing, nitrogen fixing trees would seem to offer advantages in requiring little weeding because of growth rate, and encouraging protective ground cover due to N-fixation.

An important part of watershed planning and management involves identifying areas of high surface erosion hazard. The hazard is a function of rainfall erosivity, slope (gradient and length), soil erodibility and the amount of vegetative protection on the surface. Megahan and King (in press) have presented the various methods of predicting erosion, including use of the modified Universal Soil Loss Equation (Dissmeyer and Foster, 1980). High erosion hazard forest lands might be termed 'critical' and require either total protection or special practices for wood extraction. If these high hazard areas are already cleared lands under a use that cannot be meliorated by soil conservation measures (e.g. grazing control, installation of terraces), then they might well be closed to such uses and reforested or afforested as a rehabilitation measure.

Gully erosion

Gully erosion in existing forest usually develops from surface erosion, applies to minimizing the development of gullies. Once gullies have developed, through some inappropriate land use practice, their stabilization in watershed rehabilitation is important, but difficult. In an advanced state, gullies are usually undergoing complex erosional processes of headcutting, slumping and surface erosion. The important remedial action is to protect the surface with vegetation, litter and root systems networks as rapidly as possible, and to alter the flow of water away from gully headwall. Trees have a major role to play here, especially fast-growing species, though they may be combined with grasses, herbaceous material or shrubs. Gully stabilization may even require reshaping or minor structural measures especially at the gully heads. Gully stabilization and rehabilitation with productive vegetation is a complex technical activity, and may require more than forestry expertise to do well and permanently, especially in nonhumid areas with a rainfall regime of high intensity storms and difficulties in getting vegetation established due to lack of soil moisture. Weber and Hoskins (1983) presented various structural methods that can be carried out manually with local materials in Africa, and Crouch et al. (1984) have documented techniques using small but more sophisticated weirs for gully control in Australia.

Mass erosion

In watershed planning and management, slopes which are prone to mass wasting merit special attention as 'critical areas'. Megahan and King (in press) have made suggestions for identifying areas with high hazard for mass erosion. Land use allocations and management policies for landslide-prone areas should be based on the degree of climatic, topographic and edaphic hazard. In the case of deep-seated slides this is indicated simply by whether or not slides occur in the area (i.e. 'hazardous' or 'not hazardous'). For shallow slides, the degree of hazard can be assessed, and stratified, for different levels of care. The criteria for the hazard rating are based on storm rainfall intensity and duration, and on slope gradient and shape. Megahan and King summarized the literature and suggested that shallow landslips are limited to slopes greater than 45 to 55 per cent with a maximum frequency of occurrence at about 70 per cent. Landslips also are correlated with slope concavities and convergences that concentrate water. Phillips and Pearce (in press) have illustrated terrain stability zoning in New Zealand using somewhat different criteria, more related to geologic and geomorphic factors.

Sites that are prone to shallow landslips, are given greater stability by tree roots. These roots impart shear strength to the soil. Loss of this shear strength following tree cutting or tree removal and subsequent greater incidence of slope failures has been reported by O'Loughlin and Ziemer (1982). By establishing plantations on erosion-prone sites, O'Loughlin (1984) documented that between 5 and 10 years after establishment young Pinus radiata, root development began to increase substantially the slope resistance to shallow failures. However, he found that reforestation was not generally effective in containing retrogressive slumping around headwalls of actively eroding gullies and large landslides.

If forests are to be harvested on areas prone to shallow slides, cutting alone, even without the disturbance associated with wood removal, can alter the slope stability. Where stumps coppice, so that the root systems remain alive, there is no problem. Thus in short-rotation fuelwood plantations of fast-growing coppicing species, the root system would continue their meliorating function. Where this is not the case, loss of soil shear strength depends on the rate of root decay following cutting, compared to the growth of new roots from uncut trees or forest reproduction. Because of this, in the northern Rocky Mountains of the United States, in Japan, and in Alaska, post cutting landslide hazards did not peak until from 2 to 10 years after logging (Megahan et al., 1978; Nakano, 1971; Bishop and Stevens, 1964). If the forest is cleared for conversion to grazing or cropping, the root systems of the grasses and annual crops provide much less shear strength compared to forest, and therefore may accelerate landslide activity (Trustrum et al., in press).

Where land is already cleared and under some kind of cropping or grazing regime, the introduction of trees in an agroforestry land use system can improve the stability of areas prone to shallow slips. Rows of trees on the contour with alley cropping or grazing would appear to offer the best arrangement in utilizing both the strength of tree roots, and the 'fence' function of trapping any surface wash from uphill, thus gradually creating a series of natural terraces. A good example of such a practice, developed spontaneously over time by traditional hill people may be found in Cebu in the Philippines (Vergara, pers. com.). Here on slopes ranging up to 80 per cent, rows of Leucaena leucocephala have been established as producers of stemwood for fuel, leaves for inter-row mulch and soil amendment, and nitrogen through fixation by this fast-growing legume. Soil shear strength can also be imparted by roots of many fruit trees that may be used in an agroforestry system.

While Swanston (1981) stated that deep-seated landslides are only slightly, if at all, influenced by vegetation, O'Loughlin (1984) suggested that there may be some beneficial effects. However, road construction involving embankments, excavation and changes in slope drainage often have dramatic impact on such deep-seated mass movements. Areas prone to such mass erosion should be avoided in planning and road networks in watersheds. If forested, these areas should be maintained in forest, for such vegetation tends to involve less intensive use and disturbance even under the heavy pressure in developing countries. Any forest harvesting in the sensitive areas must be done with extreme care. If timber is sufficiently valuable, logging might be accomplished by helicopter or balloon, though there is little or no experience with these 'high-tech' methods in developing countries. If fuelwood is required, transporting should be done by hand or by animal power without road construction. Minor forest product harvesting would appear acceptable. In many cases these steep areas might well be allocated to forest preserve status or to park status, if there are appropriate national patrimony values.

Human activity

The undisturbed, closed forest is unquestionably the best situation in watershed cover, for this permits the canopies, litter, soil organic layer and root systems to have the greatest roles in minimizing erosion of all kinds. A hierarchy of human uses can be considered, each with an increasing order of disturbance to this protective function. These might range from scientific study and wilderness recreation, through minor forest product harvesting, to logging and shifting cultivation. As the uses of a particular forest site increase the area's susceptibility to erosion, a greater degree of land use control would need to be instituted. For instance, performance standards (logging guidelines) have been developed for timber harvesting that are universally applicable, with specific local modifications (for instance, Gilmour, 1977a; Megahan and Schweithelm, 1983). These minimize, but do not eliminate the disturbance effects on erosion, and are effective in permitting this kind of use on all but the very high hazard areas. However, if politically, culturally or economically such control is impossible, then such a human activity would have to be confined to low erosion hazard sites, and prohibited on sites with intermediate or high erosion hazard.

Other land uses, such as grazing or agriculture may also have little erosion on low to medium hazard areas, if adequate soil conservation and animal management performance standards are instituted. The stable, terraced rice paddies on steep slopes in several parts of South and Southeast Asia are testimony to low erosion under intensive agricultural use. Unfortunately, however, much hill land under agriculture in the region is unravelling testimony to the lack of good soil and water conservation. It should also be remembered that the conversion process itself is almost invariably accompanied by serious erosion if the land is sloping. The excellent studies at the International Institute of Tropical Agriculture at Ibadan by Lal and his co-workers have documented the soil loss risks under various methods of

111

land clearing (see, for instance, Lal, 1981). Thus, even though a new use such as rubber plantations with adequate soil conversion, can replace forest with only slightly more erosion occurring once the new use is in place, a watershed planner must consider the erosion associated with the land clearing, and the subsequent erosion every time the rubber crop is replaced.

In the tropical dry forest, or even seasonal forest, fire can be a factor in watershed management. Fire is often used as a land management tool by graziers or those practicing in shifting cultivation. Fire can 'escape' into the adjacent forest, or be deliberately introduced to secure a usufructuary or tenurial advantage. The major watershed effect of fire is in the removal of the litter and low vegetative cover that protects the soil surface from surface erosion (Hamilton, 1983). Very hot and prolonged fires may also reduce the organic content of the soil, and reduce structural stability. Such a fire may also kill the trees completely, thus initiating loss of root strength. Frequent fires may keep a forested site in a continually eroding condition. In Pakistan, frequently burned stands of Pinus roxburghii were reported to exhibit as much erosion as unterraced croplands (Raeder-Roitzsch and Masur, 1968). In planted forests, particularly those consisting of conifers, eucalypts or Casuarina, fire is a major hazard. If the programme of watershed rehabilitation involves reforestation or afforestation, there may be local customary users of the land who would prefer not to find trees occupying the land. Their support must be obtained before commencing a watershed tree planting programme, or fire may be a continual problem.

Summary – forests and erosion

One mandate for forests that can be accepted by foresters and land use planners is that of erosion reduction. In this connection it must be recognized that the high degree of soil protection derives from three major characteristics of forests and groups of trees. The first is the development and maintenance of litter and understory vegetation to give soil surface protection from splash, sheet and rill erosion. The second is the additional shear strength afforded by tree roots in areas prone to mass erosion. This is perhaps augmented by the high evapotranspiration rates that reduce the frequency of soil water saturation conditions leading to slope failures. The third is that forests have traditionally been susceptible to only low intensity uses, e.g. minor forest product harvesting, long-fallow shifting agriculture, and fuelwood or timber harvesting at long intervals. This intensity of use pattern is changing. Long-fallow, stable, shifting agriculture is being rapidly replaced in much of the tropics with unstable, cash crop, shifting agriculture, accompanied by serious erosion and productivity degradation. In cooler steeplands of the tropical world, fodder lopping and fuelwood cutting have become so heavy that they have become, in essence, conversion activities accompanied with fire, grazing and sometimes cropping even on public forest land. Mechanized logging techniques using heavy equipment are also commonplace in timber harvesting, and they employ dense road and track networks plus log landings occupying from 16 per cent of Malaysian logging sites (Burgess, 1973) to 25 per cent of sites in Australia (Gilmour et al., 1982). Moreover the increasing wood fibre and energy demand is leading to the short-rotation, 'all and any tree' type of harvesting. This may result in heavy equipment returning to the same area on a short cycle. Such a situation can no longer be characterized as low-intensity, and will require great care by foresters in ensuring effective soil and water conservation practices.

FORESTS AND SEDIMENT

Increased sediment in streams, lakes and reservoirs can: harm or kill valuable aquatic life (including fisheries and mangrove resources); impair water quality for drinking, other domestic uses, and industrial processes; reduce reservoir capacity for important flood, hydropower, or irrigation storages; shorten the useful life of hydroelectric turbines and water pumps; interfere with navigation; and aggrade river channels, thus aggravating flooding. Most of these unwanted effects of sediment are in the downstream portions of watersheds where reside usually the greater part of the wealth, political power and population of a drainage basin. The link between upstream land erosion and downstream sediment problems has been recognised by these affected people, and there are increasing levels of action being called for to stop or reduce harmful sedimentation through better upland watershed management. Attention is

Figure 4.1: Erosion/sedimentation processes in a watershed (Megahan, 1981).

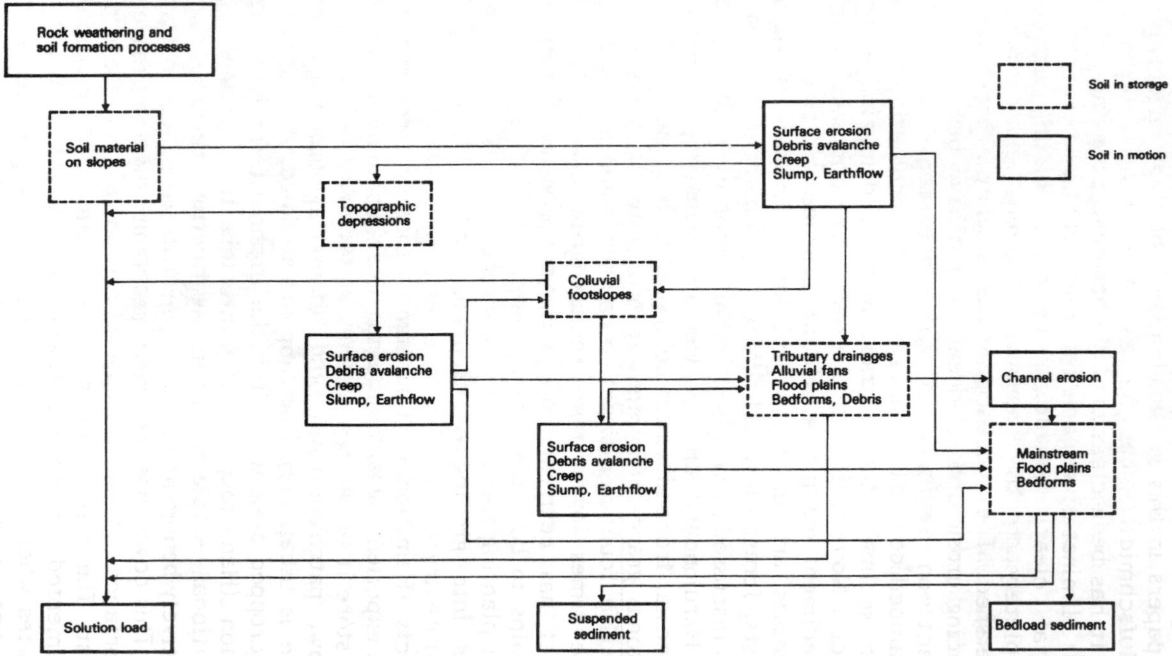

Soil in storage

Soil in motion

Rock weathering and soil formation processes

Soil material on slopes

Topographic depressions

Colluvial footslopes

Surface erosion
Debris avalanche
Creep
Slump, Earthflow

Surface erosion
Debris avalanche
Creep
Slump, Earthflow

Surface erosion
Debris avalanche
Creep
Slump, Earthflow

Tributary drainages
Alluvial fans
Flood plains
Bedforms, Debris

Channel erosion

Mainstream
Flood plains
Bedforms

Bedload sediment

Suspended sediment

Solution load

being currently given to benefit/cost assessments of the erosion/sedimentation interaction in major water resource development projects (see, for instance, Fleming, 1982, and the papers in this symposium by Brooks and Gregersen and by Hufschmidt).

It has been claimed that the presence of forests on an area eliminates stream sediment problems (waters flow crystal clear) and that restoring forest cover will completely rectify serious sediment problems in a watershed. The presence of forests, by their effects in reducing erosion, does indeed have an important beneficial impact on sediment output. Streambank erosion and streambed degradation are, however, normal processes, and much sediment that causes mischief derives from these sources. Nonetheless, land erosion contributes substantially to sediment loading of streams. The erosion/sedimentation processes are illustrated in Figure 4.1. The effects of forests, forest uses, and reforestation on erosion rates have been discussed in Section 2 of this paper.

Hardjono (1980) reported on reforestation benefits in Indonesia, from subwatersheds planted with Pinus merkusii, Tectona grandis, Swietenia macrophyla, and Eucalyptus alba. He found sediment yield from forested areas to be three times lower than an agricultural watershed. This effect has been discussed in the previous section, and pertains to both the role of maintaining forests on the site or of planting trees on erosion-prone sites. Even introducing trees into grazing or cropping land in a well-managed agroforestry system can have important sediment reduction effects (Hamilton, 1983). Having forests downslope of an area experiencing surface erosion can also trap the sediment and store it either temporarily or permanently. Under long-fallow, patchwork mosaic, shifting agricultural systems, there is usually brushland or forest downslope adjacent to the cropped area which may be experiencing some surface erosion (Hamilton, 1983). It is this feature that causes traditional stable shifting cultivation systems to be relatively benign as far as sediment in streams is concerned.

This downslope, sediment-trapping effect highlights the importance of streamside buffer strips of undisturbed forest. The effectiveness of streamside buffers has been documented for tropical Australia by Gilmour et al. (1982) on sites where substantial overland flow occurs due to an impeding layer at about 20 cm. This also has been well illustrated in work by Graynoth (1979) in New Zealand, who

115

reported mean suspended sediment concentrations for four forest watersheds that had received the following treatments: control (8 mg/l), logged with no protection (213 mg/l), logged with no protection (188 mg/l), and logged with riparian protection (27 mg/l). Observations of serious stream sediment problems in South Africa following logging led Bosch and Hewlett (1980) to develop strong recommendations and planning design aids for what they termed 'streamside management zones'. These riparian forest areas can also reduce streambank erosion by helping to stabilize banks.

The trapping and storing process suggests another major problem having to do with watershed rehabilitation measures to reduce sediment. It is extremely difficult to predict when the reduction of erosion by a practice such as reforestation, will show up as less sediment in a reservoir - capturing a benefit to which money value can be assigned. Megahan (1981) has described the storage in the erosion/sedimentation processes and depicted them as in Figure 4.1. The sediment showing up in a stream after one storm event may have come from temporary storage where eroded soil over a number of years has been deposited. Thus the full effect of soil erosion reduction measures through a practice such as reforestation, may not show up for many years, even decades, in terms of a realizable downstream benefit in sediment reduction.

Nonetheless, it has been demonstrated that appropriate forest land use practices can reduce sediment yields in streams emanating from the area treated. Conversely, careless forest land uses increase sediment discharge from the immediate catchment. Logging of a tropical catchment in North Queensland, Australia, produced a two- to three-fold increase in suspended sediment load at high flows. Sediment load increased from about 180 ppm before logging to about 320 ppm during the first year after logging, and to about 520 ppm during the second year after logging (Gilmour, 1977b). The increase in the second year was attributed to differing rainfall characteristics, for ordinarily revegetation regrowth would be expected to gradually reduce the sediment yield. At another North Queensland site involving heavy logging of virgin tropical rainforest, during high intensity rains the peak concentrations at sampling stations below the logging area increased six- to twelve-fold (Gilmour, 1971). The sediment derived from streams flowing through undisturbed forest was largely organic, in contrast with the dominantly mineral sediment in streams coming from the logged area. Gilmour reported that the principal sources of sediment were from poorly located, undrained roads and skid trails, from log landings, and from earth- and log-filled stream crossings.

Burning of forest land can result in dramatic increases in sediment. The impact of burning depends on the fire intensity, duration and frequency, on the occurrence of major storms over time following the burn, and on the rate of revegetation. One of the most dramatic reports was based on a major wildfire in Australia's temperate Snowy Mountains (Working Group on the Influence of Man on the Hydrologic Cycle, 1972). Suspended sediment content at a flow of 60-80 cumecs was increased 100 times in comparison with pre-fire conditions. It was estimated that the total sediment load in one of the creeks draining a burned catchment was 1000 times greater than it was before the fire. Under humid tropical conditions, such large increases in the sediment load have not been reported after burning because of the more rapid regrowth of vegetation. Much also depends on how soon a major storm event occurs after a fire (Boughton, 1970). One is bound to speculate about the Great Fire in Kalimantan, Indonesia, during the 1983 drought and its effect on river sedimentation when the rains finally occurred. No reports are as yet available.

In summary, there is good evidence that forests have an important beneficial role to play in reducing the downstream social and economic costs of unwanted sediment. The question of when such benefits are realizable, and their quantification even with 'ballpark' sediment delivery ratios, remains unanswered. Techniques for minimizing sediment production, even under forest land uses such as logging are known and can be implemented where control over loggers is possible. Recognizing that appropriate controls over logging practices are difficult to achieve in developing countries, policies should be oriented toward total protection forest on the higher erosion hazard sites. Streamside buffer strips are useful for sediment reduction, as well as having important wildlife habitat and aesthetic functions. Fire prevention is an important activity in watershed forest lands. The key to fire risk minimization may well lie in the sociological and community participation realms. Local involvement and support for forestry practices is the best medicine for fire malaise.

FORESTS AND FLOODS

There is a widespread belief that forest-covered upland watersheds will <u>prevent</u> floods on the mainstream, downstream, on major rivers. This belief is also translated to 'floods are <u>caused</u> by forest cutting, and flood damage can be <u>eliminated</u> by large scale reforestation or afforestation of upland catchments'. For instance, monsoonal floods in the Ganges and the Indus (which have always occurred) have been attributed to tree cutting in the uplands (World Water, 1981). Recently, the European Environmental Bureau (1982) writing about tropical forests stated that 'forests guard against flooding', and was referring to major floods on large rivers, not just on small streams emanating from the forest in the upper watershed. A statement by Openshaw (1974) that 'the principal cause of the recent floods in the Indian subcontinent was the removal of tree cover in the catchment areas for fuelwood', was repeated at the 1978 World Forestry Congress (Avery, 1978). In the Philippines following the great Agusan flood of 1981, the state minister in a newspaper interview placed '30 per cent of the blame on logging' of headwater forests, even though 'flooding is an annual event, and major floods are expected about every 20 years' (Corvera, 1981). In the same newspaper article, a top official in the Philippine Bureau of Forest Development was interviewed about the measures necessary to control logging and encourage reforestation in order to <u>avoid</u> such catastrophic flooding. Sharp and Sharp (1982) claim that 'overlogging is now officially recognized as the cause of the July 1981 severe flooding of the Yangtze' in China.

Are people looking for a scapegoat so that they do not have to consider that floods have always occurred, but that damage is truly increasing because of greater flood plain occupancy, greater channel constriction and alteration by human structures, and more roads, ditches, and nonabsorbing surfaces speeding water on its way downhill? Are they equating forest cutting to large-scale forest clearing followed by conversion to a subsequent abusive land use which denudes, degrades, compacts and gullies the area so that precipitation is largely transformed into rapid surface runoff and then into stream stormflow? Are these popular concerns about forest cutting and floods valid, or are they misinterpretations of research findings?

Findings from paired small watershed research in which

118

one watershed has been logged do indeed usually (but not always) show greater stormflow volumes, higher peakflows, and earlier peaks in streams emanating from the logged area (Douglass and Swank, 1975; Reinhart et al., 1963). Flooding may be increased close to the cutover area, but as the water is routed down a major river basin, this effect is quickly reduced to insignificance amid other processes of overriding importance, such as the nature and intensity of the precipitation, the direction the storm moves across the basin, and the size and morphometry of the basin. Hewlett (1982) has recently examined the evidence worldwide from forest watershed research and reported that there was no cause-effect relationship between forest cutting in the headwaters and floods in the lower basin. Even if a whole basin were under a forest harvesting regime, normally it would not be logged off all in one year. Those portions that are logged rather quickly return to a prelogging hydrologic regime as the forest regenerates and full canopy is restored, even though it is young growth. Moreover, a substantial part of this stormflow/peakflow effect is due to poorly located and designed roads, skid trails, and log landings, all of which speed water off-site. Thus, proper conservation logging can reduce effects on upstream flooding. Major floods occur due to too much precipitation falling in too short a time, or over too long a time (prolonged), beyond the capacity of the soil mantle to store it and the stream channel to handle it - not due to cutting of forests.

The previous discussion has referred to the impacts of forest harvesting on floods, not on the effects of forest harvesting followed by conversion to agriculture and grazing and subsequent degradation by misuse. Such degraded areas, encompassing whole river basins, may indeed aggravate flooding and be one of the causes of increased and serious flood damage. However, if converted to controlled grazing lands or agriculture under a sound soil and water conservation regime, such watershed land use should no more cause floods than careful forest harvesting does. One cannot observe the well-designed and well-maintained rice terraces on steep slopes in Java, Bali, or Nepal with their fine water control effects, and claim that disappearance of the former forest is causing floods. Yet it must be recognized that such good soil and water conservation is not commonly practiced in the current land-hungry conversion of forests to agriculture in much of the hill country of developing nations.

119

The pseudo-scientific articles that have been written showing beautiful correlation between the reduction in forest cover in a basin over time (often done with remote sensitive aids) and the increasing frequency and extent of flooding in the lower basin are <u>not</u> related to cause and effect. They are simply correlations, and similar significant correlations could be found associated with the increased mileage of roads, the increased number of children in the basin or the decrease in number of tigers.

Foresters and watershed planners must be clear about forest cutting, stormflows and downstream floods. They must also not raise false expectations about flood control being achieved through reforestation or afforestation activities. Tree planting beneficial effects may be minor in reducing major flooding from infrequent major storms or monsoonal type rainfall. It is true that local stream flood peaks are delayed, and stormflow volumes usually reduced. These are important upstream benefits. However, once the soil water storage capacity is saturated, all the water reaching the ground surface will convert to streamflow. Thus, on shallow soils, the effects of forests may be very small in any kind of prolonged rain.

There is one indirect way in which forest removal can contribute to downstream flood severity or by which reforestation could somewhat ameliorate it. Any erosion induced by poor logging or by total conversions (removing all cover) followed by poor cropping or grazing practices ultimately shows up as sediment in flood control reservoirs or in the river channel itself. By reducing the ability of dams to impound floodwater, or by raising the river bed, such sediment can aggravate normal floods. Conversely, if we can, through reforestation, slow down erosion processes, this activity reduces sediment delivery and has some flood reduction effect.

FORESTS AND WATER AVAILABILITY

There is a widespread belief that logging of tropical forest watersheds has caused wells, springs, streams, and even major rivers to cease flowing, at least during the dry season (Eckholm, 1976; Sharp and Sharp, 1982). Policies establishing protection forests which may not be cut are being advocated because of a supposed 'sponge' effect of the tree roots. It is claimed that the roots soak up water in the wet periods and release it slowly and evenly in the dry season to keep water supplies adequately restored (Spears, 1982; Myers, 1983). Roots may be more appropriately labelled a 'pump' rather than a 'sponge'. They certainly do not release water in the dry season, but rather remove it from the soil in order that the trees may transpire. Moreover, the interception losses in short or low intensity rains in the dry season may be proportionately quite large. It is difficult to reconcile such policies and statements with small watershed cutting experiments that almost universally have given increased total water yields over the year, with the greatest proportional increases usually in the low flood months. Bosch and Hewlett (1982) have reviewed 94 controlled catchment studies from many parts of the world and reinforced this relationship. They have even indicated some predictive quantification as to the amount of increase (as reported earlier by Pereira). Moreover, most cutting experiments have shown increases in groundwater levels that maintain well levels and springs, until the forest regrows (Boughton, 1970; Hamilton, 1983).

Perhaps some of the dilemma arises because of semantic problems. The catchment experiments involved forest cutting and logging, not conversion to another use such as grazing or annual cropping. The real life problem in the tropics is that forest harvesting is often the precursor to a conversion, and the term 'deforestation' (which is often used) may refer to the sequence of logging, clearing, and then agriculture or grazing without soil and water conservation. If compacted surfaces with intervening and frequent gullies are the end result (and one finds such landscapes all too commonly in the upland tropics), then it is possible that lower watertables (less reliable springs and wells) and lower dry season flows in streams may occur. There are, unfortunately, no large-scale, long-term experiments to support this intuition and professional judgment.

One problem is that most controlled watershed experiments are in the temperate zone. The few reliable tropical paired catchment experiments that do exist, however, do not indicate any different results (Hamilton, 1983).

There are valid reasons for establishing totally protected watershed forests with no forest harvesting permitted, but concern that cutting alone will result in dry wells and springs and create ephemeral streams where

121

perennial streams once prevailed, does <u>not</u> have a scientific basis. Conversion and subsequent land degradation on a large scale may be a different story. At some point in land degradation dry season flows may be lower and wells and springs may be less reliable. The total water yield will still be greater, but the distribution will be seriously skewed to the wet season.

Reforestation of upland watersheds has been advocated partially on the grounds that it will induce greater dry season stream flows and raise groundwater well levels and restore the reliability of springs (World Bank, 1978). The Chipko movement leader claims 'tree planting, particularly of broad leaved varieties creates water' (World Water, 1981). In most respects, putting forests back on open land produces the opposite hydrologic effects to cutting them down. Most well-conducted experiments have shown that reforestation reduced streamflow year-round (Banks and Kromhout, 1963; Van Lill <u>et al.</u>, 1980). For instance, Mathur <u>et al.</u> (1976) in India, reported yield decreases of 28 per cent following establishment of eucalypts. The Fiji Pine Commission planting activity in their dry zone grassland has resulted in serious reductions in total yield and especially dry season reductions of 65 per cent (Manner and Drysdale, 1981, pers. com.). Lowering of groundwater levels has usually followed reforestation (Holmes and Wronski, 1982). It is currently reported that in several parts of China, planting of <u>Populus</u> is being used to improve areas where the water table is too close to the surface for growth of annual food plants in an agroforestry situation.

The fact is that on deep soils forests use more water in evapotranspiration than other types of vegetation, so that there is less water available for streamflow. One might speculate that increased evapotranspiration loss due to tree planting would be more than compensated for on compacted and degraded areas by having their infiltration rate and capacity improved. There are no experimental results showing greater recharge benefits to wells and springs, and to the base flow that supplies dry season streamflow. We do need information from controlled, monitored, paired catchments, where, for example, eroded, badly overgrazed hills are successfully reforested and measured against a control. Popular wisdom and a great deal of professional judgment argue for recharge and increased (base) flow. While all of the research evidence so far is contrary, most of the research has been conducted in circumstances of less severely degraded land. Until supporting results are forthcoming, however, watershed project managers and foresters should carefully eschew claiming such benefits.

CONCLUSION

There are very many excellent reasons for maintaining undisturbed or 'protection' forest on watersheds. They may be habitat for endangered species that require undisturbed forest for their existence. They may represent important in situ gene banks of material for present or potential great usefulness in fields of forestry, agriculture, industry and medicine. They may be among the last wild places where a country's urban citizens can find a sane sanctuary from crowded and stressful living conditions; or where similarly stressed tourists from other countries can find similar recreation. They may be 'sacred' forests, held in reverence by local residents or an entire religious group. (For example, approximately 2 per cent of the total area of the prefecture of Xishuangbanna, China, is in forested 'holy hills', revered and protected by the Dai people (Pei, in press).

Some other good reasons pertain to the function of protected forests in connection with their influence on soil and water, though not all of these reasons, though often alleged, are in fact valid. Where there is avalanche hazard (not discussed in this paper) there is sound evidence from mountain country research that protection forests provide hazard reduction. Areas prone to mass wasting, particularly shallow landslips, are given greater stability by undisturbed forest than by any other cover or use. Undisturbed forest gives the greatest amount of protection against surface erosion. Undisturbed forest, though using more water than other types of cover, does delay peak flows, and usually reduces peak flows and stormflow volumes more than other cover or logged forest. This effect occurs primarily in the streams emanating from the forest. As stormflows are routed down the watershed, these effects become increasingly smaller as other factors come into play. Protected 'cloud' forest can capture more occult precipitation from the atmosphere, giving a net addition to the water budget.

When forests are disturbed, as in production forests and community fuelwood forests, some of the aforementioned benefits are foregone. The impacts can be minimized by

123

zoning out 'critical areas' and by careful adoption of performance standards on areas that are disturbed. Religious or cultural values usually would be an exception, for in this case, probably any human intervention would be completely destructive. Avalanche and mass wasting protective functions also have a very low threshold for disturbance.

When forests are being considered for conversion to other land uses, careful environmental impact assessment is required, because most of the forest cover benefits are totally lost.

There are many excellent reasons for reforesting or afforesting upland watershed lands, and the clarion call to embark on large-scale tree planting programmes makes good sense. As a strategy to establish 'wood factories' to meet needs for fuel, timber and other wood products, these programmes are very much needed. Such actions may relieve some of the pressures on the remaining bits of natural forest. As a rehabilitation device to make degraded, unproductive lands produce a useful crop, and to gradually rebuild productivity, tree planting is well proven (though the economics may be questionable on the poor sites).

Once a leaf-litter or understory has been established, forest plantations are normally very protective against surface erosion. Once a surface root network develops, and downward striking roots penetrate into any consolidated layer, greater resistance to mass erosion ensues. Since most plantations are established with the intent of subsequent harvest, it is important to remember that disturbance of the litter and understory ground cover and death of the roots, will reduce these protective functions.

It is important, however, in justifying or advocating reforestation or afforestation projects, that unrealizable claims of some other benefits not be made. Tree planting has not been shown to increase local rainfall (may capture occult precipitation, however, in certain locations), to prevent floods, to increase the flow of streams and springs, or to raise well levels (unless it be a cloud forest situation).

Problems in achieving sustainable development and conservation of soil and water resources in the tropics are legion enough, without being plagued by misunderstanding, myth and misinterpretation. Semantic fuzziness adds to the scene. Words or phrases such as 'deforestation', 'drought', 'flood prevention', and 'runoff' usually need to be defined or avoided in favour of more precise words or phrases. The consequences may be seen in fruitless disagreement between interest groups, propaganda instead of education, bad policymaking because of shaky scientific base, or even good policymaking but for the wrong reasons - an action that may backfire. Perhaps foresters have been guilty of acquiescing by silence in the use of some misinterpretations and misunderstandings, because the arguments or rhetoric being used were aimed at protecting forest resources or at establishing new forests - surely actions worthy of nations and statesmen. But, if we close the watershed forests to human use and reservoirs still silt up, and when we have totally reclothed the basin in planted forest and we still have floods, and if on top of that the streams still dry up or dry up even more ... then there may be a well-deserved backlash, and the credibility of foresters and other watershed professionals may be called into serious question. There are many eminently sound reasons for forest conservation and reforestation in the tropical developing countries. Let us not condone the use of unsupportable or questionable hydrologic and erosional relationships in this important policy scenario.

REFERENCES

Avery, D. (1978), Firewood in the less developed countries. Eighth World Forestry Congress, IUFRO Voluntary Paper, Agenda Item 3

Banks, C.H. and C. Kromhout (1963), The effect of afforestation with Pinus radiata on summer baseflow and total annual discharge from Jonkershoek catchments. Forestry in South Africa 3:43-65

Bell, T.I.W. (1973), Erosion in the Trinidad teak plantations. Commonwealth Forestry Review 52: 223-33

Bell, T.I.W and T. Evo (1982), Energy plantations in the Fiji dry zone. Fiji Pine Research Paper 10. Suva and Lautoka

Bernard, A.E. (1953), L'evapotranspiration annuelle de la forêt equatoriale congolaise et son influence sur la pluviosite. Comptes Rendus, IUFRO Congress, Rome pp.201-4

Birot, P. (1968), The Cycle of Erosion in Different Climates, London, B.T. Botsford

Bishop, D.M. and M.E. Stevens (1964), Landslides on logged areas in Southeast Alaska. USDA Forest Service, Res.

Paper NOR-1

Bosch, J.M. and J.D. Hewlett (1980), Sediment control in South African forests and mountain catchments. South African Forestry 115:50-5

Bosch, J.M. and J.D. Hewlett (1982), A review of catchment experiments to determine the effect of vegetation changes on water yield and evapotranspiration. Hydrology 55:3-23

Boughton, W.C. (1970), Effects of land management on quantity and quality of available water: A review. Australian Water Resources Council Research Project 68/2, Report 120. Manly Vale, University of New South Wales

Brunig, E.F., M. von Buch, J. Heuveldop and K.F. Panzer (1975), Stratification of the tropical moist forest for land use planning. Plant Research and Development 2: 21-44

Burgess, F.F. (1973), The impact of commercial forestry on the hill forests of the Malay Peninsula. Proc. Symposium on Biological Resources and National Development, Applied Geography 1:237-58

Cassells, D.S., D.A. Gilmour and P. Gordon (1982), The impact of plantation forestry on stream sedimentation in tropical and subtropical Queensland - an initial assessment. Proc. Conference on Agricultural Engineering, Inst. of Engineers, Australia

Corvera, A. (1981), What caused the great Aqusan flood? Weekend, March 1, pp.12-3

Coster, C. (1938), Surficial runoff and erosion in Java. Tectona 31:613-728

Crouch, R.J., R.A. Henry, W.J. O'Brien and V.G. Sherlock (1984), Small weirs for gully control. Jour. Soil and Water Cons. N.S.W. 40(2): 88-93

Dissmeyer, G.E. and G.R. Foster (1980), A guide for predictive sheet and rill erosion on forest land. U.S. Forest Service Tech. Publ. SA-TP11, Washington

Douglass, J.E. and W.T. Swank (1975), Effects of management practices on water quality and quantity. USDA Forest Service Gen. Tech. Report NE-13:1, Upper Darby

Eckholm, E. (1976), Losing Ground, W.W. Norton, New York

Ekern, P.C. (1964), Direct interception of cloud water on Lanaihale, Hawaii. Proc. Soil Sci. Soc. of America 28:417-21

European Environmental Bureau (1982), The environmental

importance of tropical moist forests. Deforestation and Development Newsletter, June 1982, pp.1-7

Fleming, W.M. (1982), Environmental and economic impacts of watershed conservation on a major reservoir project in Ecuador. In: Economic Approaches to Natural Resource and Environmental Quality Analysis, M. Hufschmidt and E. Hyman (eds.), pp.292-9, Tycooly, Dublin

Gilmour, D.A. (1971), The effects of logging on streamflow and sedimentation in a north Queensland rainforest catchment. Commonwealth Forestry Review (Australia) 50:38-48

Gilmour, D.A. (1977a), Logging and the environment with particular reference to soil and stream protection in tropical rainforest situations. In: Guidelines for Watershed Management, FAO Conservation Guide 1, Rome, pp.223-35

Gilmour, D.A. (1977b), Effect of rainforest logging and clearing on water yield and quality in a high rainfall zone of northeast Queensland. Hydrology Symposium, pp.156-60. Inst. of Engineers, Brisbane

Gilmour, D.A., D.S. Cassells and M. Bonell (1982), Hydrological research in the tropical rainforests of north Queensland: Some implications for land use management. Proc. First National Symp. on Forest Hydrology, pp.145-52, Melbourne

Goodland, R.J.A. and H.S. Irwin (1975), Amazon Jungle: Green Hell to Red Desert? Elsevier, New York

Graynoth, D. (1979), Effects of logging on stream environments and faunas in Nelson. N.Z. Marine and Freshwater Research 13: 70-109

Hamilton, L.S. (with P.N. King) (1983), Tropical Forested Watersheds: Hydrologic and Soils Response to Major Uses or Conversions. Westview Press, Boulder, CO

Hardjono, H.W. (1980), The effect of permanent vegetation and its distribution on streamflow of three sub-watersheds in Central Java. Paper at Seminar on Hydrology and Watershed Management, Surakarta, 5 June 1980

Hewlett, J.D. (1982), Forests and floods in the light of recent investigation. Proc. Canadian Hydrological Symp., June 14-15, pp.543-60, Frederiction

Holmes, J.W. and E.B. Wronski (1982), On the water harvest from afforested catchments. Proc. First National Symp. on Forest Hydrology, pp.1-6, Melbourne

Hursch, C.R. (1948), Local climate in the Copper Basin of Tennessee as modified by the removal of vegetation. U.S. Dept. of Agr. Circ. 774, Washington

Kunkle, S.H. (1983), Forestry support for agriculture through watershed management, windbreaks and other conservation actions. Proc. Eighth World Forestry Congress, vol. 3, pp.113-38, Indonesia Directorate of Forestry, Jakarta

Lal, R. (1981), Deforestation of tropical rainforest and hydrologic problems. In: Tropical Agricultural Hydrology, R. Lal and E.W. Russell, (eds), pp.131-40. John Wiley and Sons, New York

Lal, R. (1983), Soil erosion in the humid tropics with particular reference to agricultural land development and soil management. In: Hydrology of Humid Tropical Regions, R. Keller (ed.), pp.221-39, IAHS Publ. No. 140, Wallingford

Lee, R. (1978), Forest Microclimatology, Columbia University Press, New York

Lembaga Ekologi (1980), Report on study of vegetation and erosion in the Jatiluhur catchment, 1980. Inst. of Ecology, Bandung

Lin, Y.L. (1984), Status of forest hydrology research in Taiwan. In: Country Papers on Status of Watershed Forest Influence Research in Asia and the Pacific, L. Hamilton, M. Bonell and E. Mercer (eds.), pp.238-96. East-West Center Working Paper, Honolulu

Mathur, H.M., Rambabu, P. Joshie and B. Singh (1976), Effect of clearfelling and reforestation on runoff and peak rates in small watersheds. Indian Forester 102: 219-26

Megahan, W.F. (1981), Nonpoint source pollution from forestry activities in the western United States: Results of recent research and research needs. In: U.S. Forestry and Water Quality: What Course in the 80's? Proc. Water Pollution Control Federation Meeting, pp.92-151, Washington

Megahan, W.F. and P.N. King (in press), Identification of critical areas on forest lands for control of nonpoint sources of pollution. Accepted by Environmental Management in March 1984

Megahan, W.F. and J. Schweithelm (1983), Guidelines for reducing negative impacts of logging. In: Tropical Forested Watersheds: Hydrologic and Soils Response to Major Uses or Conversions, L.S. Hamilton (Appendix C).

Westview Press, Boulder

Lal, R. (1981), Deforestation of tropical rainforest and hydrologic problems. In: Tropical Agricultural Hydrology, R. Lal and E.W. Russell (eds.), John Wiley and Sons, New York

Megahan, W.F., N.F. Day and T.M. Bliss (1978), Landslide occurrence in the western and central Northern Rocky Mountain physiographic province in Idaho. Forest soils and land use. Proc. Fifth Northern American For. Soils Conf., Ft. Collins, CO, Aug. 1978, Chester T. Youngberg (ed.), pp.116-39. Colorado State University, Fort Collins

Myers, N. (1983), Tropical moist forests: over-exploited and under-utilized? Forest Ecology and Management 6(1):59-79

Nakano, H. (1971), Soil and water conservation functions of forest on mountainous land. Gov. For Expt. Sta. (Japan), Forest Influences Div.

O'Loughlin, C. (1984), Effectiveness of introduced forest vegetation for protection against landslides and erosion in New Zealand's steeplands. Proc. Symp. on Effects of Forest Land Use on Erosion and Slope Stability. IUFRO, East-West Center, U.S. Forest Service, N.Z. Forest Service, pp.275-80. East-West Center, Honolulu

O'Loughlin, C. and R.R. Ziemer (1982), The importance of root strength and deterioration rates upon edaphic stability in steepland forests. In: Carbon Uptake and Allocation; a Key to Management of Subalpine Ecosystems, R.H. Waring (ed.), pp.70-8, Corvallis

Openshaw, K. (1974), Woodfuels in the developing world. New Scientist, January 31, 1974, pp.271-2

Pei, Sheng-ji (in press). Some effects of the Dai people's cultural beliefs and practices upon the plant environment of Xishuangbanna, Yunnan Province, Southwest China. In: Cultural Values and Tropical Ecology, K.L. Hutterer, A.T. Rambo and G.W. Lovelace (eds.), Ann Arbor: University of Michigan Center for South and Southeast Asian Studies

Pereira, H.C. (1973), Land Use on Water Resources in Temperate and Tropical Climates, Cambridge University Press, London

Phillips, C.J. and A.J. Pearce (in press), Terrain suitability zoning of the Owhena and Mangawhero blocks of Tokomaru State Forest. N.Z. Forest Service FRI Bulletin, Christchurch

Raeder-Roitzsch, J.E. and A. Masur (1968), Some hydrologic relationships of natural vegetation in the chir pine belt of Pakistan. Proc. First Pakistan Watershed Mgmt. Conf., November 1968, pp.345-60. Pakistan Forest Institute, Peshawar

Reinhart, K.G., A.R. Eschner and G.R. Trimble, Jr. (1963), Effect on streamflow of four forest practices, in the mountains of West Virginia. U.S. Forest Service Res. Pap. NE-1, Upper Darby

Salati, E., A. Dall'Olio, E. Matsui and J.R. Gat (1979), Recycling of water in the Amazon Basin: an isotopic study. Water Resources Research 15(5): 1250-8

Salati, E., T.E. Lovejoy and P.B. Vose (1983), Precipitation and water recycling in tropical rain forests with special reference to the Amazon Basin. The Environmentalist 3(1): 67-72

Salati, E. and P.B. Vose (1984), Amazon Basin: a system in equilibrium. Science 225(4658): 129-38

Sharp, D. and T. Sharp (1982), The desertification of Asia. Asia 2000 1(4):40-2

Shpak, I.S. (1968), Effect of forest on water balance components of drainage basins. Kiev, pp.137-43. Academy of Sciences of the Ukraine SSR. (Translated from Russian, 1971. Israel Program for Scientific Translations, Jerusalem)

Spears, J. (1982), Rehabilitating watersheds. Finance and Development 19(1):30-3

Swanston, D.N. (1981), Creep and earthflow erosion from undisturbed and management impacted slopes in the Coast and Cascade ranges of the Pacific Northwest, USA. Int. Assn. Scientific Hydrology Publ. No. 132, pp.76-91

Trustrum, N.A., M.G. Lambert and V.G. Thomas (in press), The impact of soil slip erosion on hill country pasture production in New Zealand, Proc. Second Int. Conf. on Soil Erosion and Conservation, Ankeny: Soil Cons. Soc. America

UNESCO/UNEP/FAO (1978), Tropical Forest Ecosystems. Natural Resources Research XIV. UNESCO, Paris

Van Lill, W.S., F.J. Kruger and D.B. Van Wyk (1980), The effect of afforestation with Eucalyptus grandis (Hill ex maiden) and Pinus patula (Schlect. et Cham.) on streamflow from experimental catchments at Mokobulaan, Transvaal. Hydrology 48: 107-18

Weber, F. and M. Hoskins (1983), Soil Conservation

Technical Sheets, University of Idaho, Moscow
Wiersum, K.F. (in press), Effects of various vegetation
  layers on an Acacia auriculiformis forest plantation on
  surface erosion in Java, Indonesia. Proc. Second Int.
  Conf. on Soil Erosion and Conservation, Ankeny: Soil
  Cons. Soc. America
Wiersum, K.F. (1984), Surface erosion under various tropical
  agroforestry systems. Proc. Symp. on Effects of Forest
  Land Use on Erosion and Slope Stability, IUFRO, East-
  West Center, U.S. Forest Service, N.Z. Forest Service,
  pp.231-9. East-West Center, Honolulu
Working Group on the Influence of Man on the Hydrologic
  Cycle (1972), Influence of man on the hydrologic cycle:
  Guide to policies for the safe development of land and
  water resources. In: Status and Trends of Research in
  Hydrology, pp.31-70. UNESCO, Paris
World Bank (1978), Forestry Sector Policy Paper. World
  Bank, Washington
World Water (1981), How trees can combat droughts and
  floods. World Water 4(10): 18 October
WWF/IUCN (1982), Tropical forest campaign. WWF booklet,
  World Wildlife Fund, Gland
Zadroga, F. (1981), The hydrological importance of a
  montana cloud forest area of Costa Rica. In: Tropical
  Agricultural Hydrology, R. Lal and F.W. Russell (eds.),
  pp.59-73. John Wiley and Sons, New York

5

THE EXPLANATION OF LAND DEGRADATION

P. Blaikie

INTRODUCTION

The point of entry of this paper into the explanation of land degradation in Nepal is the recent work on the role of human agency in various types of erosion and degradation observed there. This link probably indicates that the most visually obvious forms of erosion are overall less due to human agency than previously thought. Mass-wasting is caused mostly by geomorphic processes; and high overall levels of erosion predate much of the recent extension of cultivation onto steeper slopes in the hills. Severely lopped secondary forest and pastures are probably the main areas which account for much of human-induced accelerated erosion.

However, much of this debate rests upon selective perception of outside observers and on notoriously inaccessible and unreliable geomorphic data. A method of explaining land degradation which starts where uncertainty about accuracy and relevance of data are least is suggested. A 'chain of explanation' starts with the farmer and the natural resources he/she uses and focusses on the decision-making process in using and managing land. It identifies an 'energy crisis' as the principal bottleneck in transforming Nepalese agriculture, where purchased forms of nutrients and energy are only available to a very few farmers, principally the larger ones with <u>khet</u> land, in valley-floors and in the <u>terai</u>. Because of a widespread and severe problem of access to resources, sustainable cropping and livestock management practices are not carried out, although many farmers know of them. Other 'exits' from the problem of falls in crop and livestock yields are sought, which in aggregate reflect the distribution of access to resources in the peasant economy as a whole. The next link in the chain of explanation is to put these aggregate decisions over land-use into a regional framework and to acknowledge that there are important spatial variations in both resources-in-use and social conditions of access to these resources, settlement histories and so forth. At the same time the social relations of production and exchange in which farmers find themselves provide a framework in which these decisions are made. Finally, these relations are put into a wider context of the political economy of Nepal and of her international relations (principally with India and international agencies). The approach as a whole can be called 'regional political ecology'.

THE ENVIRONMENTAL CRISIS

Nepal is a classic area for the study of land degradation. With an intensely varied environment, including the world's highest mountains, a strip of the Gangetic plain, and the high-altitude desert of the trans-Himalaya, Nepal is among the world's least developed countries with a high and rising density of population on its limited areas of arable land (see Figure 5.1). Rural population densities reach over 1500 per km^2 of cultivated land, or fifteen to the hectare, and there are districts in the middle hills with even higher densities. This is similar to densities in central Java and is fifty per cent higher than Bangladesh (Strout, 1983).

In the main agricultural areas of the middle hills or Pahar almost all arable land is terraced. Irrigated land (khet), whether fed by rivers or from springs, grows rice and winter crops of wheat and potato wherever possible; dry land (pakho) is also terraced, but with a slope from almost level to as much as 25° or occasionally more. These dry lands grow mostly maize, often with finger millet as a relay crop which is transplanted from a seed bed under the growing maize. Unterraced land, used mainly for pasture (charan) but with a few cultivated patches, now occupies only the steepest slopes and ridgetops, but was in former times much more extensive and the site of shifting and semi-permanent cultivation among the mixed forests (Quercus spp., Castanopsis spp., Pinus roxburghii), and Rhodedendron arboreum that used to cover these hills

Figure 5.1: Physical and political geography of Nepal

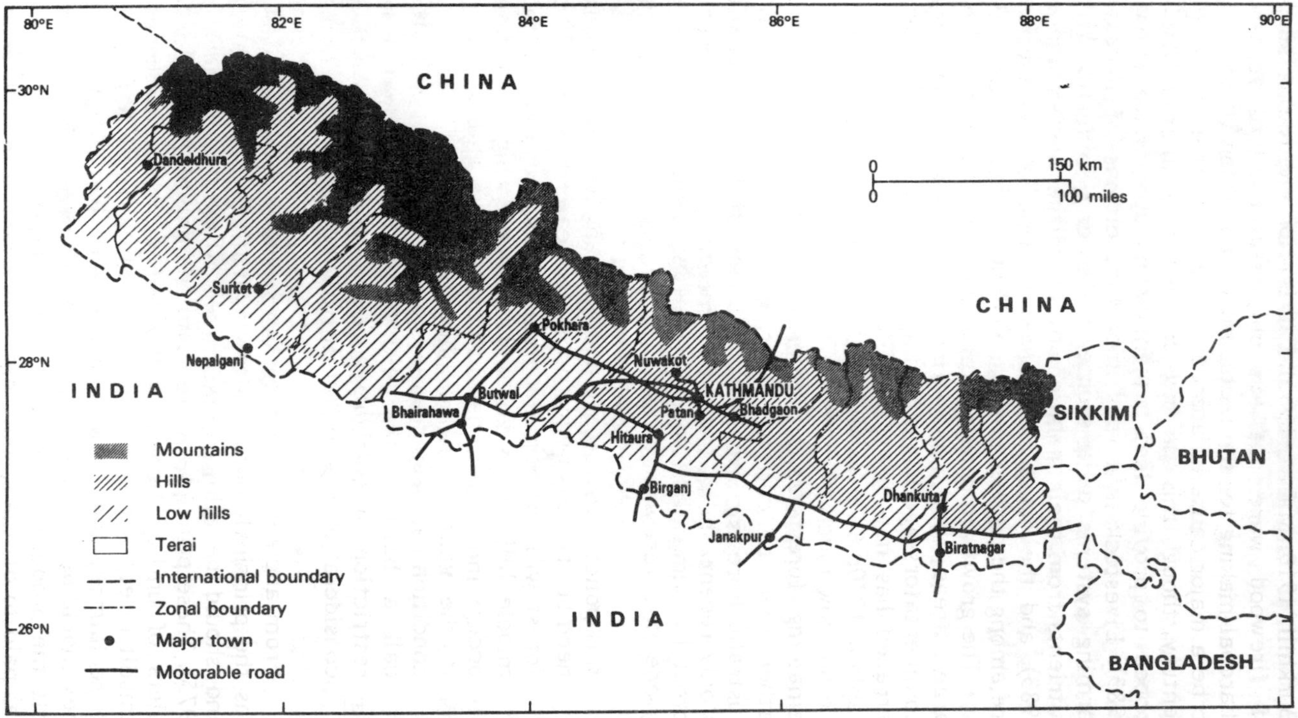

(Burkhill, 1910; Mahat, 1985). Cultivation and the collection of firewood were not the only reasons for clearance; charcoal-making for the metal industries of Nepal continued to be a major cause of depredation until early in the present century, though this has now diminished, and trees are also lopped to provide leaf-fodder for livestock (Bajracharya, 1983). Livestock is a very important element in Nepalese farming systems as a source of power for ploughing, of nutrients from their manure, and of milk (Axinn and Axinn, 1983), and the numbers of livestock per human inhabitant are among the highest in the developing world.

The growth in population has eliminated the forest from large areas and has replaced it by cultivation. Commentators agree that virtually all land capable of being terraced has now been taken up in the middle hills (e.g. Caplan, 1970: 6-7; Mahat, 1985), so that forest boundaries are not now much in retreat. The degraded condition of the remaining forests is indeed now attributed to historical rather than to current practices (Mahat, 1985; Nepal-Australia Forestry Project, 1985). Yet this relative stability is only recent. In 1928 the Government policy of replacing forest by human cultivation wherever possible was praised by one observer, who felt that

> this policy must be pursued for many years before there need be the slightest grounds for fearing that sufficient forest will not remain. For in the temperate zone (the middle hills) it is certain that cultivation can never occupy more than one third of the total area ... Perhaps in the valley of Katmandu (sic) and its vicinity a condition has been reached in which it would be wise to call a halt ... But elsewhere the day on which restriction of cultivation need become a question for consideration is still far off (Collier, 1928/1976: 253).

From ancient times the state owned all land, and as it was the principal source of revenue to rulers, no cultivable land should be allowed to lie idle (Regmi, 1976; Stiller, 1975). These principles were sustained and developed by the rulers of unified Nepal after 1768 so that the first king himself directed that all land convertible into fields should be reclaimed, and, if homesteads were built on such land they should be moved (Regmi, 1978). Peasants paid the state half the produce of the land in tax, or rent, and later this was paid to officials and others who received grants of land

135

(and its income) in lieu of salary or as reward for service. Even so, only the irrigated khet land seems to have had firm definition until modern times, and in a village near Pokhara Macfarlane (1976: 52, 87) noted that the pakho land was not shared out individually until about 1940; before that 'patches of jungle were slashed and burnt by those who had the labour'. By the late 1960s, however, only a few rocky and steep patches remained to be cleared, and 'the limits of maize cultivation had been reached'. On the other hand, there have been no significant changes in areas under agricultural use and under forest since at least 1900 in a densely-peopled area at Thokarpa, east of Kathmandu, despite large population increases (Mahat, 1985: 232). It seems that extension of the cultivated margins in recent times is variable locally, although it is likely that current extension has been slow overall, and stationary in many places.

Exposure of the slopes has serious consequences for runoff under the torrential seasonal rain, especially at the beginning of the monsoon when there is little ground cover after the long dry season. Heavy erosion of the sloping terraces is a result, especially as the risers of these terraces are cut back each dry season to add new mineral phosphorus and soil to the terraces, which are thus widened and progressively flattened through time. Each season a proportion of these terraces is rendered useless, and the land reverts to uncropped pakho; each season, however, new or reclaimed terraces are created on the pakho land. Slopewash, gullying and especially mass movement occur on all slopes, and mass movement also affects the lower-lying khet terraces, which become over-charged with water and saturated in depth. In occasional flash floods, the best valley-bottom khet is sometimes washed out by heavily-laden streams which widen their channels. As much as 50 per cent of the eroded material may be carried into the lowland, causing wide channel braiding, choking rivers and adding up to a metre of soil per 20 years to adjacent fields in the hills and certain areas of the terai. Sediment loads as high as 25,000 p.p.m. are regularly recorded in the major rivers.

The distribution and nature of erosion are, however, important. Dry terraces may lose only 0.4 - 1.6 mm/y, with corresponding losses of organic matter, nitrogen, phosphorous and potassium, and some of this is redeposited downslope, especially in irrigated terraces which can gain soil and nutrients. Much higher losses are experienced under degraded forest without surface protection from small shrubs, and also from grazing land. In one small watershed gross estimated losses ranged from only 2 t/ha/y from the irrigated terraces to 20 t/ha/y from grazing land. However, while topsoil lost from this 63 ha catchment and carried beyond its bounds totalled only 200 t (3.86 t/ha from 57 ha of the area), the total loss was 1320 t/y, the balance being derived from mass wasting on the remaining six ha (Carson, 1985). Caine and Mool (1982) calculated annual mass wasting losses to be as high as 13 t/ha from another catchment but derived from only one per cent of its area. Moreover, much of the landslip damage is repaired, and much land that appeared irreparably damaged when mapped in 1979-80 (Kienholz et al., 1983) was totally reclaimed under terraces, wet or dry, three or four years later (Ives, 1984; 1985). Brookfield (1984) using the 'geomorphic damage map' of the Ives and Messerli (1981) Mountain Hazards Mapping Project in the field, confirms that specific areas mapped as debris flow in 1979-80 were again wholly terraced in 1984. Maps and stored visual impressions of soil erosion (particularly gulleys and mass-wasting) only record at a single moment in time and cannot incorporate well the idea that much of the evidence is dynamic and temporary. These striking visual impressions can be thought of as a 'stock situation' through which they move from land which is intact, through erosion, and later (after the map is drawn and the rural tourist has written his/her report), repaired.

The importance of accelerated (human-induced) erosion in Nepal has been the subject of a great deal of uncertainty (Thompson and Warburton, 1985a and b; Ramsay, 1985). A variety of commentators have been convinced that Nepal is an ecological catastrophe. A single doom-laden quotation from a wide choice will suffice:

> Population growth in the context of a traditional agrarian technology is forcing farmers onto even steeper slopes, slopes unfit for sustained farming even with the astonishingly elaborate terracing practised there. Meanwhile, villagers must roam farther and farther from their homes to gather fodder and firewood, thus surrounding villages with a widening circle of denuded hillsides (Eckholm, 1976: 77).

However, a detailed and quantified analysis of the extent of

137

degradation has produced a more qualified interpretation. A recent FAO study stated that the results of their analysis suggest that past descriptions of conditions in Nepal have exaggerated the erosion problems, and go on to say that the three per cent figure of the total land surface classified under poor and very poor watershed conditions is not a serious erosion problem (FAO, 1980: 5). Interestingly, they attribute part of this possible misconception on the effects of road-biassed 'rural tourism' according with Chambers' (1984) apposite diagnosis of misconceptions of foreign and urban-based observers. There is an often-visited panorama which almost all visitors see as they travel west from Kathmandu by road towards Pokhara, at the point of leaving the Kathmandu Valley. From the lip of the valley westward and northward lies a rather desolate scene of considerable erosion, deforestation and degraded pastures. The higher parts of this same area were clad in heavily-lopped Q. semecarpifolia scrub when Kirkpatrick traversed it in 1793 (Burkhill, 1910). This scene finds its way into numerous articles and publications on the ecological crisis of Nepal, but it is not representative of the country as a whole. Indeed, much of the agricultural land is in surprisingly good condition (FAO, 1980: 7). The worst land erosion is on shifting cultivation land in the Mahabharat Lekh, and in the arid trans-Himalaya, where mass wasting and wind erosion carry away all soil from steep, unprotected slopes. In general, it seems that charan land including abandoned cultivation patches and pastures suffer from most serious erosion, particularly sheet erosion and loss of topsoil. Pakho land is the next most seriously affected followed by khet (Carson 1985: 7). However, mass wasting and catastrophic events such as large-scale slope failures are probably not due to human interference (Carson, 1985; Ramsay, 1985). Hence the most noticeable and dramatic forms of erosion remarked on by rural tourists, are probably little accelerated by Nepalese farmers at all.

UNCERTAINTY, COMPLEXITY AND VARIABILITY

In 1985-6 Thompson and Warburton published a series of influential articles on sustainable development in the Himalaya. One of their major theses was that there are such a variety of opinions about what is actually happening in the Himalaya, and such enormous ranges of quantified estimates of rates of erosion, fuelwood requirements or use and many other important parameters, that it is better rather than to pursue better quantification, to question the whole approach which is currently being taken. Certainly the lack of data and the problems of generalisation across an extremely heterogeneous social and environmental field of study must strike many researchers, policy-makers, or advisors there. However, these authors go on to develop this theme and suggest that we should not ask 'What are the facts?' but 'What do you like the facts to be?'. In the view of this author, this is an extreme response to uncertainty, and one that tends to be wasteful of what we can be <u>reasonably</u> certain.

For example, this author questions whether there is a crisis in Nepal at all (1985(a): 120). The word crisis is perhaps an overworked word (and indeed this writer co-authored a book entitled <u>Nepal in Crisis</u> (1980)). It has a number of uses, and each, in the case of Nepal is perhaps (unfortunately) appropriate. The word 'crisis' can be used to mobilise people to action, and undoubtedly some of the more extreme 'eco-doom' predictions, particularly of Eckholm (1976), Brown (1978, 1981), and others quoted in this paper have this objective. The word can also be used journalistically to annote merely that 'things are bad'. Certainly economic conditions in Nepal are bad, and almost every survey and every indicator makes depressing reading. Estimates of crop yields, available food, fuelwood production and requirements and so on may be imprecise in many instances, but they seldom indicate anything else but hardship and poverty.

There are two further senses in which the word 'crisis' is relevant to Nepal. The word, taken originally perhaps from medical usage, implies a point beyond which <u>either</u> the organism will return to its previous condition and steady state <u>or</u> will change fundamentally and will never return to its previous state. Two ideas exist here - the direction of development through time (is the organism heading towards a crisis point?), and secondly the distance travelled towards that point. Frequently both ideas are merged, particularly in political economic literature where structural crises are frequently identified as inevitable (and maybe over-determined) and the question of distance to crisis becomes therefore redundant. Nepalese political economy has been analysed in sufficient detail to indicate that there are important ways in which the state (and other outside institutions) is unable to intervene effectively in changing the social, economic or environmental situation; and in which the class nature of Nepalese society shows insufficient signs of transforming itself (e.g. Shaha (1975), Blaikie, Cameron and Seddon (1979 and 1980)). This paper will return to these larger issues later, but it is claimed here that there is enough known and the messages are clear and similar enough to state that (a) the direction of economic indicators and political progress in Nepal is unequivocally towards crisis (i.e. irretrievable and rapid change) and (b) the points at which crisis will occur in different and interconnected parts of Nepalese society and environment are happening right now.

To return to the more general issue of uncertainty, complexity and variability, it is certainly the case that technical and quantitative estimates in the agrarian sector of Nepal often are imprecise and sometimes wild guesses. What seems to be self-evident can fall away in the face of new (but maybe not more reliable) evidence. The case of the extent of human agency in accelerated soil erosion outlined in Section 2 ('The Environmental Crisis') is but one example.

However, this paper attempts to provide an explanation of land degradation in Nepal which acknowledges uncertainty in quantitative measurement and enormous heterogeneity in society and environment; but which tries to construct an explanation which builds in those 'facts' which we can rely upon - either because there is considerable redundancy in the information system, or because exact calibration is not vital to the explanation. While there is much to agree with in the suggestions made by Thompson and Warburton, it is wasteful of existing knowledge of Nepalese development and environment to suggest that it is the wrong sort of knowledge and scientific approach altogether. The methodology of my approach follows in the next section.

REGIONAL POLITICAL ECOLOGY

The point of entry into Nepalese development and environment at the outset of this paper was to review recent work which questions whether much of the visible evidence of soil erosion is due to human agency. Much of the evidence is certainly uncertain and contradictory, and relies upon geomorphic rather than socio-economic measurement.

An alternative framework is suggested here which forges a chain of explanation. It starts with the farmer and land-manager him(her)self, and focusses upon the ways in which decisions over land-use in general and specifically agriculture, livestock and forest are taken. On this there are a number of surveys undertaken which are quite reliable, and some of their major findings corroborate each other. The next link is to trace the social relations between these decision-makers and other land-users and others in the 'wider society'. These relations (e.g. social relations of production and exchange) are the context in which people pursue their livelihood and make decisions about the use of land. The state, and ultimately the world economy, are the last links in the chain, since both (often the latter mediated by the particular nature of the former) directly and indirectly have repercussions on the land and those who use it.

The approach as a whole can be called 'regional political ecology'. The first link are the farming households themselves, each with varying access to resources and involved in a variety of social relations of production and exchange. Some will be characterised by specific locations within the region - e.g. the more socially marginal groups involved in more marginal activities on ecologically more marginal land (e.g. the Sukhumbasi or illegal squatters). Sometimes there is a caste specificity to altitude (Brahmin-Chhetri castes living at lower altitudes, and other ethnic groups such as Magar, Gurungs, or Tamang at higher altitudes). In such co-variance between socio-economic and environmental variables there is an important locality-based specificity implied by the word 'regional'. Such important variations as altitude, orientation of slopes, soil and drainage characteristics, or the spatial variability of likelihood of hail damage are some of these physically-derived specificities. Local settlement histories and ethnic diversity (with different patterns of choice in the use and planting of trees, emphasis on livestock, preferences for different programmes, etc.) are other human-resource specificities which regionally vary in important respects.

The phrase 'political ecology' combines the concerns of ecology with political economy. This encompasses the constantly shifting dialectic between society and land-based resources, and also within classes and groups within society itself. It also involves notions of the state and the way that certain classes and functionaries of the state use natural resources (e.g. government forest policy; investment in irrigation; the various 'biasses' or emphases in state-sponsored research and development in improved or HYV seeds; and the legal superstructure plus its selective implementation regarding illegal settlement).

The implications of using this approach to explain land degradation in Nepal are as follows:

(a) it allows a choice of levels of generalisation depending upon why the research question is being asked, and who (if anyone) is listening;

(b) it starts with the farmers themselves about which the least unreliable information exists, rather than less accessible and more unreliable geomorphic measures and the processes with which Section 2 concerned itself;

(c) it avoids single themes and single conclusions about environmental degradation, but it orders and organises 'plurality of perceptions, plural problem definitions, plural expectations and plural rationalities' (Thompson and Warburton, 1985(a): 123).

In the next section this framework with its chain of explanation is used to order an explanation of land degradation in Nepal.

HOW NEPALESE FARMERS COPE - PROBLEMS OF SHORTAGES OF FUEL, SOIL NUTRIENTS AND LABOUR

At a superficial level, the Nepalese problem has appeared to many observers - local as well as foreign - to be a classic example of the effect of population pressure on resources (PPR), specifically through deforestation and the dry-terracing of steeply-sloping land in a sensitive environment. Eckholm (1976) suggests that Nepal will slide away into the Ganges by the year 2000, and has no doubt that PPR is the principal culprit. A secondary culprit, however, has been identified as the Nepalese farmer of whom the Asian Development Bank (1982, II: 34) was highly critical. The practice of building un-bunded, outward-sloping dry terraces was attacked with particular severity, and inward-sloping bench terraces were urged as a means of checking runoff. Water management was also regarded as primitive, a view shared by two local agricultural scientists (Nepali and

142

Regmi, 1981) who wrote that 'the technology of water management is scanty if not absent'. Under pressure of declining resources per-capita cattle holdings are declining, and moreover the technology of composting manure is 'primitive', so that up to 52 per cent of the nitrogen and up to 80 per cent of the phosphorous are oxidized. Over 90 per cent of the fodder consumed by the animals does no more than keep them alive, leaving only ten per cent for yield of 'economic products' (Asian Development Bank, 1982). All this is regarded as very inefficient.

Others who start from the first link in the chain of explanation (the farmer and land manager as the focus of study) differ, at least to parts of this deluge of complaint. Axinn and Axinn (1983) analyze the flows of energy within the farm system, and stress the vital significance of 'keeping the animals alive' to plough the land and manure it, both 'economic products' of their existence. Ives (1985) notes that dry terraces slope outward to avoid waterlogging of dry crops, and to prevent accumulation and penetration of water which would cause landslipping; the absence of a bund is a deliberate measure to ensure runoff. He is impressed by the skill of Nepalese levelling, terrace-construction and water management, which includes extensive systems designed to enlarge the command area of irrigation flows. Gurung (pers. comm.) argues that it is the capital needed to build irrigation systems that is 'scanty', not the known technology. Against the view of the critics is the glowing tribute paid by Cool (1983: 7):

> Personal observation suggests that it may require up to twenty years to fully transform an afforested hillside into a relatively stable irrigated terrace. The enterprise is marked with difficulty, setbacks and occasional failure. Yet what stands out is the skill and energy that goes into their design and execution and how successful the hill farmer is in maintaining and improving his terraced fields year after year, generation after generation. Flooding, landslips, goats and cattle, and occasional earthquakes are taken in stride. With only hand tools and simple bullock-drawn ploughs, but with enormous fortitude, the mountain farmer, rebuilds, reploughs, reseeds and survives.

Much greater detail concerning the manner in which farmers of the Kolpu Khola area manage the specific hazards of their environment is provided by Johnson, Olson and Manandhar (1982), who describe methods of maintenance, repair and damage-reduction, both those used by individual farmers and those known to them but beyond their means. The problems are well understood, although supernatural explanations form part of the folk-explanation of sudden and unpredictable terrace collapse. Maintenance is a regular and time-consuming task. When damage actually occurs the problem becomes one of lack of access to resources. Thus (Johnson, Olson and Manandhar, 1982: 84):

> Farmers evaluate the options and, often, must choose the less effective one which is, however, the one within their means. Timing is a crucial factor in this decision. Constraints and limited resources may lead the farmer to postpone taking preventive measures in the face of warning signs. This may result in rapid deterioration or destruction of the endangered field, or it may allow time for the accumulation of resources for complete repair.

All farmers, however, are willing to experience temporary loss, even of long duration, in order to reduce the risk of greater loss. Thus farmers may cut irrigation off from endangered khet land and use it as lower-yielding dry terrace, or even let it lie waste until consolidation is achieved. Even more drastic is the deliberate diversion of erosive flows of water onto land threatened with slumping to wash it away before new terraces are built to entrap new soil and rebuild irrigated fields, which then take some years to recover full capability. On the other hand, loose temporary terraces are sometimes made on the pakho land in order to obtain a little extra production at extreme risk. Differences in resources between farmers may lead to differences in nett damage suffered by the poor and the wealthy, so that 'the overall effect of "random" landslides and floods may result in increased disparities between rich and poor' (Johnson, Olson and Manandhar, 1982: 188).

Undoubtedly these are regional variations at various scales to the management of land as described above. A 'hill-top-valley-bottom' dichotomy was identified by Blaikie, Cameron and Seddon (1976 and 1980) in which in west-central Nepal two inter-related but distinct economies and land management problems emerged. In the valley bottoms, khet land is much more plentiful and is often marked by

Brahmin-Chhetri small landlords or 'advantaged peasants' using wage labour. Income differentials are high, but as a whole valley-bottoms exported paddi, husked rice, some wheat, and rape oil to deficit households upslope. Hill-top areas with predominantly maize-millet pakho fields, are often in deficit, and their agricultural economy is typically supported by remittances from non-agricultural activities (e.g. the Gurkha armies). However these steeper, less fertile and less resilient lands suffer from more serious erosion (see Section 2). Food shortages and the export of labour is more marked in these areas and remittances are spent on purchasing food from farmers in the valley floors (Porterage and Traffic Surveys and Rural Surveys in Blaikie, Cameron and Seddon, 1973, 1975, 1976). How far this generalisation can be extended from the study area of west central Nepal it is impossible to say. The data do not exist outside this area. One suspects that it fades away to the Far West where the valley-bottom and hill-top distinction is physiographically less distinct and where the social differentiation between Brahmin-Chhetri and other ethnic groups is less marked. Other regional variations in erosivity and resilience of soil and vegetation are also crucial but their mapping and explanation has hardly started.

If the extent of soil erosion is regionally and socially differentiated, and perhaps overall not so marked as external observers have stated, it is certainly necessary to look for other ways in which the environment may be altered by the growing pressure of population on resources under existing social and economic conditions. One of the most fundamental relationships in evaluating the impact of this pressure is upon its impact on the extension of cultivation and the productivity of land and labour. Between 1970-71 and 1980-81 the increase in population was greater than the increase in cropped area in both highlands and lowlands (Gurung, forthcoming), and in the highlands most of the increase was due to extension of double cropping (Mahat, 1985). However, inadequate data indicate that food-crop production declined by 0.5 per cent between 1970-72 and 1980-82 in the middle hills but increased by 9.6 per cent in the lowlands, against area increases of 11.6 and 15.1 per cent respectively (Gurung, forthcoming). Another set of data give a slightly less depressing picture for rice and wheat production but exhibit the decline in maize supply:

While the unreliability of the data must be emphasised, Svenjar and Thorbecke (1984) have used regression analysis

Table 5.1: Index values for yield and per-capita production of three main crops (1965-66 = 100)

	1965/6	1970/1	1975/6	1981/2
Maize				
area	100.0	98.9	99.8	107.8
production/ha	100.0	97.3	87.4	101.3
yield/caput	100.0	98.4	87.4	93.7
Padi				
area	100.0	106.4	113.1	116.7
production/ha	100.0	104.4	118.0	116.0
yield/caput	100.0	98.0	104.0	99.0
Wheat				
area	100.0	193.2	278.8	349.2
production/ha	100.0	131.3	262.6	351.0
yield/caput	100.0	68.0	94.4	100.0

Source: Nepal Agricultural Statistics 1965/6 - 1981/2

to indicate trend and strength of trend. Some of the R^2 values are low, but trends for all crops which they analysed have negative regression coefficients. Since there has been little actual extension of cultivation in the hills, most of the decline of yields of maize must be attributed to declining yields on existing land, indicating a loss of capability under pressure. Forest clearance in the terai has now reached the limits of good land, and the weakening situation of padi production probably reflects the extension of cultivation onto less fertile land.

Mahat (1985) describes the double-cropping, inter-cropping and relay-cropping systems in use in a part of the Middle Hills east of Kathmandu. Livestock manure is the basis of production, and in the hills there is one 'livestock unit' per head of population, mainly cattle and buffalo (41 and 22 per cent at weights of 1.0 and 1.5) plus goats and pigs for meat. However, in Nepal as a whole the annual increase in cattle population between 1966-67 and 1979-80 was only 0.12 per cent while the buffalo population declined by 1.3 per cent (Rajbhandari and Shah, 1981). A decline of cattle per head in the terai reported by USAID (1982, Appendix C) also seems to be quite marked. Stored-up fertility of forest soils recently cleared in the terai maintains yields for a few years until manuring (or artificial fertiliser) is required.

However, forest areas in the <u>terai</u> (as opposed to the hills), where cattle can find fodder, have been declining very fast. The consequences for production are probably better illustrated by a representative interview with a farmer than by unreliable statistics:

> some thirty years ago we still produced enough grain to allow us to exchange surplus for necessary daily goods, which we could not get from out of farming. Of the grains harvested, one third was exchanged ... While the good farmers who have enough cattle and do very intensive cultivation can still increase their yields, this is not the general trend. In a <u>khet</u> (irrigated) field where we sowed 4 <u>mana</u> of seed we used to get 1 <u>muri</u> of paddy; now we need an area with 8 <u>mana</u> of seed to get 1 <u>muri</u>. Our wheat used to have big ears and long halms and we filled six baskets a day, nowadays it is sometimes only one or two. In many houses there is no longer enough food. For some, the harvest grains are sufficient for only three to four months a year (Banister and Thapa, 1980: 90).

The small size of the corn-cobs on stacks outside the houses in the Middle Hills is a matter of observation, though whether or not any trend is present is impossible to determine except by farmers' recall.

Intensive questionnaire work undertaken by Blaikie, Cameron and Seddon in 1973-74 and 1980 (Blaikie, Cameron and Seddon, 1979 and 1980) indicated that farmers were in fact well aware of decline in yields on old-established fields, particularly <u>pakho</u> fields which support maize and millet. The main problem is one of a reduced availability of plant nutrients, which come predominantly from composting of forest products and involve a 'transference of fertility' from the forest to arable land. Cattle are stall-fed much of the time and are fed forest-litter, tree loppings and hand-cut grass all of which are gathered daily. The manure, together with leaf material from animal bedding, is then applied to fields. As population rises, the increased demand for food crops is met by heavier lopping, which thins and destroys the forest.

Fuel needs also reduce forest cover. Indeed, wood fuel demands are supposed to exceed supply by 2.3:1 in the Middle Hills and by 4:1 in the drier Far West. One source estimates that all accessible forests will be eliminated

Table 5.2: Numbers and percentages of rural survey interviews cross-tabulated by total cash farm sales, relations in employment and existence of non-agricultural income

'Class' position of households:	Labourers: (greater than ½ food grain not from own farm)		Labourers + Dom./ Peasant Producers: (at least Rs.200 from lab. but less than ½ food grain)		Dom./Peasant Producers (not more than Rs.200 given/received for labouring	
Non-agricultural income	Col.1 With	2 Without	3 With	4 Without	5 With	6 Without
Income from farm sales in a year						
A. Rs. 250	44	68	24	39	108	12
B. Rs.250–499	2	5	9	15	26	10
C. Rs.500–749	0	7	2	8	14	12
D. Rs.750–999	0	4	0	7	16	21
E. Rs.1000–1999	0	5	3	7	19	29
F. Rs.2000–4999	0	1	0	5	8	17
G. Rs.5000	0	0	0	0	0	2
Column Total	46	90	38	81	191	103
	7.2	13.5	5.7	12.1	28.6	15.4

Small Employers/ Rich Peasants (Rs.2000-Rs.1000 paid to labourers)		Large Employers/(Feudal and Capitalist): (more than Rs.1000 paid for labouring		
7	8	9	10	Row
With	Without	With	Without	Total %
9	1	6	0	311.0
				46.9%
3	1	0	0	71.0
				10.6%
3	1	1	0	48.0
				7.2%
4	4	0	0	56.0
				8.4%
7	7	3	1	83.0
				12.4%
9	20	4	9	73.0
				10.9%
4	4	4	11	25.0
				3.7%
39	38	18	21	667.0
5.8	5.7	2.7	33.3	100.0%

N.B. Rounding procedures have produced some minor discrepancies in % figures. Source: Rural Survey 1975.

Categories of households from which 1978 resurvey was sampled.

within 20 years (Asian Development Bank 1982: 12), but other information cited here sheds doubt on this estimate. Anyhow, demands for wood-fuel and agricultural land together mean that crop yields decline when the forest-to-arable ratio is upset. In principle at least, further population growth together with falling yields must speed up the clearing of the remaining forests for the maintenance of a minimum subsistence quantity of foodgrain per capita (Blaikie, 1985a and b). The inability of most Nepalese households to make good this 'energy crisis' by importing chemical fertilizers, and kerosene or other alternative fuel for cooking is an essential part of the explanation. If households were able to do this, then falling yields and deforestation might not be so clearly linked to degradation.

Therefore the next link in the explanation must be pursued. Simply, the vast majority of households lack the income to import nutrients (in the form of chemical fertiliser), supplementary feed for cattle, or fuel from outside. The reasons for these types of response to environmental degradation may at first seem quite simple to identify, although, as we shall see in subsequent discussion, the explanation is partly tautologous.

The distribution of rural households' access to land, the ability to earn cash surpluses by farm sales and to non-agricultural income has not been systematically studied. Various national estimates have been made of the proportion of non-agricultural income in rural households (e.g. only 64% of rural income is farm income according to the National Planning Commission (1978), or 15% according to the Nepal Rashtra Bank cited in Nepal-Australia Forestry Project (1985)). A survey which comprehensively classifies the rural population in this way was undertaken by Blaikie, Cameron and Seddon in 1974 for west-central Nepal. It is therefore somewhat dated and limited in coverage. However, it may be illustrative of the ability of households to allocate cash income to innovate in farming by the use of purchased inputs or wage labour.

Table 5.2 (from Blaikie, Cameron and Seddon, 1979) shows that the vast proportion of households have less than Rs 250 (c.$12) moving through their household budget, and from other survey work on household consumption, most of this is spent on food, and minor household items (Kirana). Non-agricultural income clearly acts as a substitute for agricultural sales, and further detailed household budget analysis shows that very little of this income is used to purchase improved seeds or chemical fertiliser, or investments to enhance production. For example, the average expenditure in chemical fertiliser for the 108 farmers in cell A5 (Table 5.2) is Rs.9 and on improved seeds Rs.5. It is only for the few farmers in cells F9 and 10 and G9 and 10 that cash sales of farm produce provide monetary access to fertilizers, HYV seeds, improved agricultural implements and investments in terracing, field improvement and tree planting. (Also it is interesting to note that of 28 farming households in those four cells, all except one were located in the terai or in valley bottoms with predominantly khet land.) These data, although now ten years old and of limited coverage, provide quite convincing evidence on the limited access to resources which households have in order to make good falling natural fertility due to the scarcity of, and pressure upon, local sources of nutrients and fuel, and to manage land effectively to improve or safeguard production in the future.

Figure 5.2 shows a decision-tree which indicates the responses in land use and management which farmer/land managers may make. Some of the main 'data' (Box 1) has already been discussed which are relevant to on-going land use management (Box 2). The crucial social and environmental data are increasing pressure on the forest and on privately-held land; limited resources of capital and sometimes too of labour to repair and improve land; considerable knowledge and skill (although its distribution by age, gender, caste, farm size, etc. is unknown); and a highly sensitive and variable environment which needs care for its management.

The analysis in 'The Environmental Crisis' and 'How Nepalese farmers cope' sections so far have indicated that the question posed in box 4 frequently elicits the answer 'no' (land capability is not being maintained or improved). Moving to Boxes 5 and 6, the extent of perception and diagnosis of declining yields and increasing soil erosion (wherever these occur) is another lacuna. This author's experience is decidedly mixed. One Magarni gave him a fifteen minute analysis of the problems outlined in this paper that would have stood up well in a graduate seminar. Others, particularly on newly settled lands of the Mahabharat Lekh (which have some very sensitive and easily disturbed soils and parent material), maybe have little idea of what seems to be happening (from an outsider's casual survey of visual signs and oral histories). Many undoubtedly

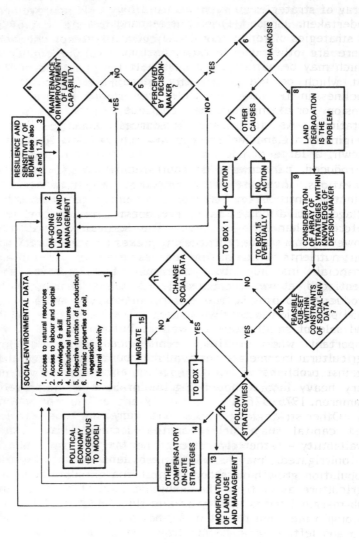

Figure 5.2: Decision-making in land management

are aware, and quotations of this awareness are frequent in written accounts, one or two of which are included in this paper. The supernatural is often invoked as an explanation for soil erosion (see Johnson, Olson and Manandhar, 1982) and is an example of 'other causes' (Box 7) being ascribed to the process of land degradation.

Then, according to this model the consideration of the array of strategies to cope with declining land capability is undertaken. Johnson, Olson and Manandhar's (1982) account of strategies of repair has already been reviewed. However, there are other on-site compensatory strategies (Box 14) which may be within the access pattern of the household, but which do not necessarily address the problems of declines in fertility and yields nor reducing future soil erosion. For example, farmers continue to intensify cropping rotations. As the Land Resources Mapping Project (originally a Canadian Project now run by HMG Nepal) has shown, a large number of new crop rotations are being introduced, particularly on south-facing slopes and lower elevations, involving relay cropping, inter-cropping, the selective introduction of quick maturing varieties, zero-tillage cultivation, allowing broadcast wheat to be sown before the harvesting of padi-rice in khet fields, and so on. However, this strategy frequently makes further demands on soil nutrients which meets the same constraints of the financial inability to purchase chemical fertilisers mentioned above. Increased levels of petty commodity production to provide the cash to make good shortfalls in food production is another strategy. The production of ghee and sale of small stock as well as buffalo is particularly important where military remittances or other non-agricultural income are not available, but these too come up against problems of available fodder and therefore require very heavy labour inputs (Blaikie in Seddon, Blaikie and Cameron, 1979: 57f).

Other strategies for those with very poor access to land and capital may simply increase their wage labour availability - rather than struggle on their own land which, if unirrigated, may reward their labour so meagrely. Population growth together with an inability to transform agriculture away from the dominant patters of small and sub-marginal farms, simply acts to shift numbers of farmers through time from the right and bottom of Table 5.2, to the top and left. A steady shift from peasant farming to part-time peasant farming and finally to proletarianisation is the nett result of this last strategy. If the local labour market is not sufficient to provide employment, then Box 15 (migration) is the only option, and one (as the 1981 census shows) which increasing numbers are taking. Thus it is not claimed that environmental degradation is directly accelerating migration from the hills to the fast-disappearing new lands of the terai, but it is claimed that it is one option given population growth and declining yields per hectare and hour worked - just as effective land management for sustainable yields is another.

How is it then that the rural population in Nepal remain so poor? There is an element of tautology in the explanation given so far, as has been mentioned already. Most are poor so they cannot respond to population growth by applications of capital on new inputs. Therefore yields stay low or further decline, keeping them poor or poorer. The 'downward spiral' effect with environmental deterioration as a vital ingredient is a common characterisation of the agrarian situation in Nepal. The extent to which this is 'true' and can be proved is open to a great deal of uncertainty, partly because time series data do not exist and secondly because other processes of impoverishment can only be expressed in terms of hypothesised alternatives. These 'other processes of impoverishment' can, according to different theories of social change, be the persistence of quasi-feudal and non-capitalist relations of production; the nature of the state; processes of underdevelopment; or the failure to move toward socialism - all of which hypothesise alternative paths of social change which have not actually taken place.

Therefore the last link in the explanation of land degradation (via the farmer, and the region) is vital, although very problematic and not reliably secured to earlier links. Nepal has had a long history of political independence, but also of quite important economic relations with British and later independent India. The independent state, however, taxed the farmers heavily and placed heavy demands on their labour for corvee work; in some areas landlordism developed as state officials were allocated areas of land and people to exploit in lieu of salary (Regmi, 1971; 1978). Until very recent times the State remained unchanged in its antique and quasi-feudal form and kept out rather than encouraged modernising reforms in education, forms of representative government as well as productive capitalism in industry and agriculture (Blaikie, Cameron and Seddon, 1980). Nepal today remains landlocked and dependent upon India, both politically and economically. Such surpluses as there are in Nepal tend to be used in merchanting, smuggling, real estate and speculative purchase of land and not so much in agricultural or industrial production. Attempts at manufacture are undermined by cheaper products from India, and the 'leaky' frontier allows subsidised fertiliser to be sold illegally to Indian middlemen, and grain from the surplus-producing terai to flow south to India rather than to the food-deficit hills. The state itself has had great difficulty in outgrowing its quasi-feudal and extractive nature to meet the daunting challenges of development at the present time (Shaha, 1975; Blaikie and Seddon, 1978). This is reflected in its limited capacity to encourage the infrastructure of all sorts to transform agriculture, such as effective and widely available credit, effective fertiliser distribution, responsive and locally relevant agricultural research and extension and so on. In more general terms, it is unable to staunch the flow of resources through the frontier to India and to harness them for national development, or to mobilise a civil service that will implement reforms effectively. Undoubtedly the problems of development in Nepal can be viewed in this critical political-economic manner, and it can provide a framework for the explanation of the creation, change and contradiction of classes in rural areas. However, to link these more general explanations with farmers' decision-making about land-use and management is to be contextural at best. As this section has demonstrated, there are so many other 'exits' from a situation of land degradation which do not involve a change in land use and management at all. The choices that people are making in aggregate undoubtedly relate to the political economy of a hard-pressed peasantry (and these choices are in turn helping to create their future), and at the level of classes or groups of farmers, the explanatory connections can be made. But at the level of the decision-making tree, and the local resource-human interface, where our degree of uncertainty is least, these last links in the chain, which deals with class, the State and international relations, remain problematic as they are essential.

REFERENCES

Asian Development Bank (1982), Nepal Agriculture Sector

Strategy, 2 vols, Manila, Asian Development Bank
Axinn, N.W. and Axinn, G.H. (1983), Small Farms in Nepal: a
    Farming System Approach to Description, Kathmandu,
    Rural Life Associates
Bajracharya, D. (1983), 'Deforestation in the food/fuel
    context: historical and political perspectives from
    Nepal', Mountain Research and Development, 3, 227-40
Banister, J. and Thapa, S. (1980), The Population Dynamics
    of Nepal, Honolulu, East-West Center
Blaikie, P.M. (1985a), The Political Economy of Soil Erosion
    in Developing Countries, London, Longman
Blaikie, P.M. (1985b), 'Soil slides south', Inside Asia, 2,
    Feb/March, 45-7
Blaikie, P.M., Cameron, J. and Seddon, J.D. (1976), The
    Effects of Roads in West-central Nepal, 3 vols, Report
    to ODA, London
Blaikie, P.M. and Seddon, J.D. (1978), 'A map of the
    Nepalese Political Economy', Area, 10, 1:30-1
Blaikie, P.M., Cameron, J. and Seddon, J.D. (1979), The
    Struggle for Basic Needs in Nepal, Paris, Development
    Centre of the Organisation for Economic Cooperation
    and Development
Blaikie, P.M., Cameron, J. and Seddon, D. (1980), Nepal in
    Crisis: Growth and Stagnation of the Periphery, New
    Delhi, London, Oxford University Press
Blaikie, P.M. and Brookfield, H.C. (1987), Land Degradation
    and Society, London, Methuen
Brookfield, H.C. (1984), 'Report on a mission to advise the
    Nepal National Committee for Man and the Biosphere,
    28 December 1983 - 21 January 1984', Kathmandu,
    National Commission for Unesco, mimeo
Brown, L.R. (1978), The Worldwide Loss of Cropland,
    Worldwatch Paper 24, Washington, D.C., Worldwatch
    Institute
Brown, L.R. (1981), 'Eroding the base of civilisation', Journal
    of Soil and Water Conservation, October, 36, 255-60
Burkill, I.H. (1910), 'Notes from a journey to Nepal', Records
    of the Botanical Survey of India, 4, Calcutta,
    Superintendent of Government Printing, 59-140
    (separately issued)
Caine, N. and Mool, P.K. (1982), 'Landslides in the Kolpu
    Khola drainage, middle mountains, Nepal, Mountain
    Research and Development, 2, 157-73
Caplan, L. (1970), Land and Social Change in East Nepal,
    London, Routledge and Kegan Paul

Carson, B. (1985), Erosion and Sedimentation Processes in the Nepalese Himalaya, ICIMOD occasional paper no. 1, Kathmandu, International Centre for Integrated Mountain Development (ICIMOD)

Chambers, R. (1984), Rural Development: Putting the Last First, London, Longman

Collier, J.V. (1928/1976) 'Forestry in Nepal', in Landon, P. (ed.), Nepal, reprinted in Kuloy, H.K. (ed.), Bibliotheca Himalayica, series 1, vol. 16, Kathmandu, Ratna Pustak Bhandar, 251-55 (first printed, 1928)

Cool, J.C. (1983), Factors Affecting Pressure on Mountain Resource Systems, First International Symposium and Inauguration; Mountain Development 2000, Challenges and Opportunities, Kathmandu, International Centre for Integrated Mountain Development, mimeo

Eckholm, E.P. (1976), Losing Ground: Environmental Stress and World Foods Prospects, New York, Norton

FAO (Food and Agriculture Organization of the United Nations) (1980), Natural Resources and the Human Environment for Food and Agriculture, environment paper no. 1, Rome, FAO

Ives, J.D. (1984), 'Does deforestation cause soil erosion?', International Union for the Conservation of Nature Bulletin, Suppl. 2, 4-5

Ives, J.D. (1985), 'Mountain environments', Progress in Physical Geography, 9, 425-33

Ives, J.D. and Messerli, B. (1981), 'Mountain hazards mapping in Nepal: introduction to an applied mountain research project', Mountain Research and Development, 1, 223-30

Johnson, K., Olson, E.A. and Manandhar, S. (1982), 'Environmental knowledge and response to natural hazards in mountainous Nepal', Mountain Research and Development, 2, 2:175-88

Kienholz, H., Hafner, H., Schneider, G. and Tamraker, R. (1983), 'Mountain hazards mapping in Nepal's middle mountains: maps of land use and geomorphic damages (Kathmandu - Kakani area)', Mountain Research and Development, 3, 195-220

Macfarlane, A. (1976), Resources and Population: a Study of the Gurungs of Nepal, Cambridge, Cambridge University Press

Mahat, T.B.S. (1985), 'Human impact on forests in the middle hills of Nepal', PhD thesis in Forestry, Canberra, Australian National University

National Planning Commission (Nepal) (1978), A Survey of Employment, Income Distribution and Consumption Patterns of Nepal, Kathmandu, National Planning Commission

Nepal-Australia Forestry Project (1985), Project Document: Phase Three, Canberra, Nepal-Australia Forestry Project

Nepali, S.B. and Regmi, I.R. (1981), 'Technological innovations for hill agricultural development' in Ong, S.E. (ed.), Nepal's Experience in Hill Agricultural Development, Kathmandu, Ministry of Food and Agriculture

Ramsay, W.J.H. (1985) 'Erosion in the Middle Himalaya, Nepal, with a case study of the Phewa Valley', MSc dissertation at the Department of Forest Resources Management, University of British Columbia

Rajbhandari, H.B. and Shah, S.B. (1981), 'Trends and projections of livestock production in the hills', in Ong, S.E. (ed.), Nepal's Experience in Hill Agricultural Development, Kathmandu, Ministry of Food and Agriculture, 43-58

Regmi, M.C. (1971), A Study of Nepali Economic History 1768-1845, New Delhi, Manjusri

Regmi, M.C. (1976), Land Ownership in Nepal, Berkeley, University of California Press

Regmi, M.C. (1978), Land Tenure and Taxation in Nepal, vols I-IV, Kathmandu, Ratna Pustak Bhandar

Seddon, J.D. (ed.) with Blaikie, P.M. and Cameron, J. (1979), Peasants and Workers in Nepal, Warminster, Aris and Phillips

Shaha, R. (1975), Nepali Politics: Retrospect and Prospect, New Delhi, Oxford University Press

Stiller, L.F. (1975), The Rise of the House of Gorkha 1786-1816, Kathmandu, Ratna Pustak Bhandar

Strout, A.N. (1983), 'How productive are soils of Java?', Bulletin of Indonesian Economic Studies, 19/1, 32-52

Thompson, M. and Warburton, M. (1985a), 'Uncertainty on a Himalayan scale', Mountain Research and Development, 5, 2, 115-35

Thomson, M. and Warburton, M. (1985b), 'Knowing where to hit it: a conceptual framework for the sustainable development of the Himalayas', Mountain Research and Development, 5,3, 203-20

USAID (1982), Food Grain Technology: Agricultural Research in Nepal, Project Impact Evaluation No. 33, May 1982

6

ALTERNATIVE SOCIAL FORESTRY
DEVELOPMENT STRATEGIES

M. Cernea

In the everyday jargon of development practitioners the term 'social' is almost never used to describe agricultural programmes. The one conspicuous exception is 'social forestry development project'. Who introduced the term 'social'? And why this unexpected exception? In other words, what is social in forestry?

My attempts to trace this term to its first and innovative user have not been successful. But a large, if imprecise, consensus has developed as to its meaning. The many references to social forestry programmes explicitly recognise that these projects are designed to trigger cultural change in the behaviour of large numbers of people with respect to the planting and protection of trees. In other words, these programmes are deliberately directed (or are assumed to be directed) not merely toward the ultimate end of growing more trees, but also toward influencing an intervening variable: people's behaviour toward trees and people's interaction with respect to trees.

However, successful social forestry development cannot result only from behavioural change and individual initiatives. Social and behavioural aspects should be understood in a broader sense, including group-collective action, institutional development, and the establishment of enduring social structures which will activate and organise the behaviour of individual actors. The present paper addresses institutional and socio-structural issues in social forestry development, arguing that alternative forestry development strategies need to be based on specifically tailored institutional/socio-structural arrangements and alternative units of social organisation. A clear sociological understanding of the type of unit of social organisation that can act as the social actor sustaining one or another specific sylvicultural strategy is mandatory. Sometimes such social structures or units already exist and need to be strengthened and mobilised; other times they must be established and organised.

In discussing these variables in their practical embodiments rather than exclusively in conceptual terms, the first part of this paper will analyse the anatomy of a real case - its objectives and its defeats, particularly in relation with land institutional arrangements and the potential for community action. The second part of the paper will resume the conceptual discussion of some structural/institutional variables in forestry strategies. In particular, it will analyse collective versus individual innovation, and a range of various units of social organisation capable of being the social actors in forestry management and development programmes.

A SOCIAL INNOVATION AND ITS UNDERLYING PREMISES

Although commercial and industrial forestry projects are not a recent invention, social forestry projects are. In the conventional type of forestry development, large corporations or government agencies hire workers to establish or expand plantations on large tracts of land the businesses and agencies control; the wood is harvested for use in industry or construction. The new approach, social forestry, is to induce a large number of small farmers systematically to plant fuelwood trees on their own lands.

The social innovation aimed at through these new programmes appears formidable indeed in the light of the long history of the traditional, patterned behaviour it is supposed to change. Generally, farmers across meridians have always counted on natural regeneration of trees to meet their firewood and construction needs, without systematically planting trees for fuelwood. The major exception was fruit trees, which have long been planted as part of various production strategies.

That large-scale behavioural and cultural change is needed to intensify reforestation, has gradually come to be recognised. Several factors underscore the urgency of the problem: (a) the world's general energy crisis has suddenly turned the spotlight on the old fact that the majority of

160

humankind still uses firewood as the main cheap source of everyday energy; (b) fuelwood shortages of almost crisis proportions have already struck many countries or extended regions of them, particularly in Asia and Africa. There is a growing awareness that the current use of forest resources, and people's behaviour toward firewood trees, without new planting, could lead ultimately to more massive deforestation and possibly a worldwide fuelwood scarcity, with dramatic human and environmental consequences in the not too distant future.

One of the responses to that increasingly ominous threat was the advent of what are called social forestry programmes and policies. Such programmes were proposed in the Forestry Policy Paper issued by the World Bank in 1978, as well as in several recent statements and policies by other development agencies in different countries. The social forestry projects already launched along the lines of these policies are, in essence, financially induced programmes for the massive planting of fuel-trees.

The social innovations fostered through such policies are two-pronged. They attempt both to change the patterns of managing existing forestry resources, by involving large groups of people in conservation and management activities, and to stimulate the adoption of a 'new' productive activity on a large scale: the systematic planting and cultivation of trees for fuel, as opposed to the age-sanctioned simple gathering of naturally grown firewood.

Several social conditions are necessary if these innovations are to succeed. This paper discusses a few of the substantive social prerequisites for every social forestry programme, whether they are explicitly identified or ignored. Financial investments alone cannot make the programme a success. These prerequisites often go beyond the dynamics of individual adoption of innovations regarding tree-growing to the more complex processes of collective adoption. Although adoption of innovations by individuals has been the subject of an entire stream of sociological research, spearheaded by Rogers and others, (1) the collective adoption of innovation, as correctly pointed out by West, has received far less attention. (2) Yet processes such as reforestation, environmental protection, watershed rehabilitation, and in general the group management of natural resources require sociologists to be more concerned with the dynamics of collective behaviour and with the prerequisites for the systematic diffusion of collective innovations.

Central among these social prerequisites is the existence of a unit of social organisation, or a structure, capable of sustaining an innovation. Financial inducements alone, however important, are not sufficient to promote innovative behaviour. Other social factors whose functions must be understood include: purposeful patterns of social organisation for conserving natural resources or for producing new resources; existing land tenure systems, that may be either conducive or restrictive for the given innovation; ownership rights and distributive arrangements regarding the newly developed resources; authority mechanisms for collective decision making and enforcing, and for mobilising group (or individual) action; social perceptions and attitudes; political power that affects the distribution of generated benefits; and the influence of external change agents.

It is often not properly realised in the planning of financially induced social forestry programmes that consideration of these factors has to be woven into the very fabric of such programmes. The penalty for ignoring them is failure. This is not to say that the recipe for how to incorporate them is readily available. It has yet to be produced. Both practitioners and action-oriented social researches have to cooperate, search, test, predict, verify, monitor, learn, redesign and retest. But this does not mean that there is no knowledge whatsoever about these factors or processes and that everything is still to be discovered. Much of existing sociological know-how can be mobilised and used as stepping stones to action, to testing, and to new knowledge. Therefore, there is no justification for sociologically illiterate social forestry programmes.

THE CASE OF A SOCIAL FORESTRY PROGRAMME

Illustrating these issues, the specific project described below is a case in which good social intentions proved to be no substitute for the missing social knowledge; a case which demonstrates that sociological factors are salient and work tenaciously under the thin layer of the 'new' reality temporarily constructed with the financial inducements of the programme. Such factors were, in this case, the existing land tenure system, the usufruct system, the local power and authority system, and the absence of social structures for collective action.

The specific case is the pilot forestry programme under the Azad Kashmir Hill Farming Technical Development Project in Pakistan, co-financed by the World Bank between 1978 and 1983. The lack of a sociological analysis when this project was appraised paved the way for false assumptions about land tenure. The strategy predicated on these assumptions backfired. The sociological analysis at project midpoint revealed the array of unanticipated consequences that had built up during the implementation process. By contrasting the complexity of the local social context with the uninformed and simplistic approach of the project, the following summary of that analysis suggests why seeing the people behind the trees should be the first commandment in social forestry. (3)

The Hill Farming Technical Development Project was started in 1978 in Azad Kashmir, Pakistan, with assistance from the World Bank, as a pilot exercise to test several new approaches, with a view to replicate the successful ones in a subsequent, large-scale project. The forestry component financed fuelwood plantations, testing of new tree species under local conditions, and the establishment of nurseries for supplying seedlings. This component was included in view of the alarming prospects of rapid deforestation, a fuelwood crisis, and environmental deterioration. Indeed, both the demographically and culturally driven fuelwood shortage in Azad Kashmir and the answer devised through the project were rather typical for circumstances in many other places. They warrant a brief description.

Increasing demand for fuelwood and timber has caused large-scale deforestation in Azad Kashmir over the past 25 years. In 1972 about 1.5 million residents, or 300,000 families, relied entirely on fuelwood for cooking and heating. At a current high rate of growth (3% annually) the population will almost double by the year 2000, and pressure on government forests is increasing as people cut wood both for fuel and to clear land for farming (through illegal encroachments). Under customary rules, area inhabitants are entitled to remove deadwood, branches, and non-commercial species from reserved forests without payment, primarily for personal consumption. In practice, however, this customary right is liberally interpreted and abused. Within a radius of several miles from habitations, virtually all trees are debranched beyond the limits set by sylvicultural recommendations. In many locations only the top 10 to 20 per cent of the crown of trees remains. Outright topping has also occurred and prematurely killed the trees. In the Chir pine areas, long thin vertical slices of the bole of the tree are removed at stump level for home lighting. Roadside trees are similarily molested. Forest resources are also devastated by local livestock that graze without adequate controls. The situation is aggravated by the transhumant livestock of semi-nomadic populations who enter from Punjab and North-West Frontier Province to use the Azad Kashmir alpine rangeland during summer.

The result is that the Forestry Department needed the cooperation and support of the area population to stop and reverse deforestation, but instead it was in open conflict with a high proportion of the local inhabitants. At the time of the project appraisal more than 50,000 cases of forest offences were pending in the courts. This amounted to about one family in six being involved in a reported forest offence, and many farmers were, therefore, reluctant to participate in reforestation schemes and were suspicious of the Forest Department.

Under the circumstances, far-reaching changes were required, both to improve the management of existing forests and to reforest depleted areas, if the need for fuelwood was to be met. In preparing the forestry component the technicians estimated the current average yearly consumption of firewood at 2 to 4 tons per family, amount to some 800,000 tons in total. The scale of reforestation needed to produce this supply was estimated at 330,000 to 400,000 fully planted and well-managed acres. At the current cost of establishing fuelwood plantations (about 2,000 rupees an acre), such a programme would incur expenditures far beyond the available government resources. The government therefore needed to examine the extent to which the private users of fuelwood should contribute to these costs.

When the pilot project was prepared, it was thought that social support for the programme (contributions from private users) could be blended with public support (government financing). Accordingly, the strategy was designed to experiment with both the technical and the social aspects of developing forestry and to involve local people in planting and maintaining the reforested areas. Community acceptance of the obligations of replanting and protecting the new tree blocks was regarded as crucial for the project's success. The government was to finance the

164

establishment of four nurseries at Patika, Kotli, Hajira, and Bagh, to produce seedlings for sale at a low price to the area farmers. Initially the government was also prepared to finance the costs of planting trees on community-owned lands in order to experiment with a model that could be replicated by farmers themselves and to provide benefits primarily to the small farmers, who make up the majority of these communities.

ANATOMY OF A FAILURE

The project design was based on a set of sociological assumptions about the tenure of the land to be reforested, about community processes, and about farmers' willingness to participate. In hindsight, these assumptions appear rather naive and surprisingly uninformed. A sociological assessment of the area's land tenure system was not made during the project's preparation.

In the absence of a sociological field analysis, the appraisal report relied on the explanations given by local officials and identified shamilat land as 'land generally left uncultivated, owned jointly by a number of families'. It was considered to be community land, for which villagers had decision-making authority as well as rights to share in its usage. The appraisal report assessed the shamilat area as a major resource of approximately 325,000 acres. This was equivalent to more than half the total cultivated farm area in Azad Kashmir, which was about 500,000 acres.

The project planned to finance the planting of 3,000 acres of fuelwood mainly on shamilat land (only a small proportion was expected to be planted on government or private land). The basic assumption was that the community would be the social unit which would stand behind the programme. It was expected that community consent would be necessary to make shamilat land available and that the project would elicit direct community participation in planting and protecting the tree plantations and would eventually generate tangible benefits for the communities involved. The small farmers in Azad Kashmir, who had less access to firewood, were expected to be the primary beneficiaries of project-financed planting on communal land. An implicit assumption was that the community structures would mobilise community support for fuelwood planting, in the form of labour, payments for seedlings, or other contributions toward reforestation costs. The same social structures were assumed to be strong enough to enforce the temporary closing of reforested areas to protect the tree seedlings and prevent indiscriminate grazing.

The features of 'social forestry' were obvious in the design of the project. The communities were to be the social units supporting the reforestation of community woodlots, and the farmers' use for non-arable areas was to be changed by converting some non-arable and grazing lands to fuelwood plantations. (Other project components were to compensate for the loss of grazing land by intensifying fodder production.) In sum, the project was setting objectives that required a modified productive behaviour. The question was: would the target communities and individual farmers respond as expected?

Given the experimental nature of this project, during the implementation process that started in 1978, more attention was paid to its socio-cultural aspects than was usual in comparable projects. The physical accomplishments of the forestry component were initially quite satisfactory. The reforestation target of the first project year was met: fuelwood trees were planted on 500 acres and the first nurseries were established successfully. During its first months the project identified 100 acres of community and private land, in addition to the 400 acres of government land. As reported by the project staff, the owners and users of the private and community land agreed to allocate the land for fuelwood plantation, although no formal contract was signed.

In the second year, the project had an increased planting target of 1,250 acres. Other landowners came forward and volunteered their non-arable lands for tree plantations, and the project staff tentatively identified for planting about 750 acres of community and private land and 500 acres of government land. This was a larger proportion of non-government land than the optimistic assumption at appraisal stage. The farmers' positive response appeared to suggest that significant tracts of private and community (shamilat) land could be incorporated into the fuelwood production circuit. A social analysis of the implementation of the forestry component was undertaken in 1979 and 1980 by the author, to ascertain whether the land identified for fuelwood plantation was consistent with the initial social and technical assumptions, and whether the expected distributional benefits were still likely.

It is noteworthy that the social analysis was not triggered by a crisis situation or a lack of progress, but was initiated to examine what seemed to be the successful advancement of the project. The analysis ascertained the socio-economic status of the farmers reached by the reforestation component of the project; determined the tenurial status of the lands involved in the project in the first two years and estimated the likely beneficiaries; assessed the social procedures used in project implementation, particularly the communication patterns between the project staff and the farmers; and assessed the adequacy of the experimental community strategy of the pitlot project for reforestation and promoting changes in the patterns of land use. Given the critical importance of the land tenure for reforestation, special attention was also paid to the social mechanism of community decision making and the procedures for sharing the expected profits from the forestry investments.

The analysis of the tenure system in Azad Kashmir identified three basic categories of forest land and land potentially usable for reforestation:

(i) Khalsa, or Crown land, is government-owned and consists of demarcated and undemarcated forests. (4)

(ii) Shamilat land itself derives its name from the concept of 'getting together' and belongs to the communities. These lands are used as grazing areas, forests, sites for village public buildings, village graveyards, and so on.

(iii) Malkiat land is privately owned and ownership rights are recorded in the revenue register and are validated by it.

As a rule of thumb, the demarcated forests areas are of higher density and better quality than the undemarcated forests, which are often located between the demarcated forests and the cultivated lands. Two other categories of forests in Azad Kashmir are forests under the management and control of the Revenue Department and private forests.

The social assessment identified significant differences between the legal or formal status of the land and the de facto situation. Contrary to expectations, shamilat land appeared to be, for the most part, not truly community land. Significant changes over time in most of Azad Kashmir had caused a dual divergent status to evolve. Although shamilat continues to be considered in principle community land, in real life it is often operated and used as private land and the usufruct benefits from this land now accrue to certain individuals, rather than to the whole community. The sociological analysis thus invalidated several assumptions made when the planting of shamilat was initially planned and revealed that unanticipated consequences of the planting programme were likely to distort the intended flow of benefits to various social groups.

How did this major change in the tenure system come about? Essentially, it occurred over a long period of time and is not yet fully complete. Reconstructing the history of social and political process that led to this change, it appears that shamilat land was indeed once set apart and allocated to villages for common use as pasture, graveyard, woodlot, or a source for drinking water for people and cattle. Subsequently, there was a long period of social and political change, still ongoing, that occurred in roughly three stages:

(a) Informal partitioning. Village facilities whose lands adjoined the shamilat areas began to divide the shamilat among themselves and numerous small and remote farms were left out of this informal partitioning.

(b) Incremental appropriation. These village families began to take over the land and even to cultivate it. (5) Rights to shamilat became transferable through inheritance or sale of fractions of the privately owned areas, which carry with them rights to proportionate fractions of the shamilat plots. While this de facto appropriation advanced, shamilat kept its formal status as community land and was not entered in the revenue records as belonging to private families. As a result, the families concerned did not have to pay land taxes on 'their' shamilat plots.

(c) Gradual privatisation. Since 1974, when the tax on land was abolished in Pakistan, the pressure has increased to have shamilat plots entered in revenue records in the names of the families who appropriated them and thus have them validated as privately owned lands. The interested families use various means to change the registration of their land, contrary to existing legal regulations.

The cycle of partitioning, appropriating and privatising of community land has progressed at different speeds in various districts of Azad Kashmir. It is reported that the system of land registration and tenure in Mirpur district, for instance, differs from that in Poonch district. Some areas and communities still maintain pieces of shamilat as truly community possessions. In general, however, the historical cycle described above seems to be continuing. For instance, current regulations continue to permit, under certain circumstances, the transfer of areas of khalsa (Crown) land to villages so that it becomes community land. Sooner or later, yesterday's piece of khalsa land thus becomes, through transfer or through encroachment, today's shamilat land, which in turn is likely to become tomorrow's malkiat land.

This being the real system of land tenure in the area, it is understandable that the project staff was not able to find genuine community land for project-financed reforestation. On close inspection, I found that the planting reported on shamilat turned out to be on individually controlled land. The social analysis of project implementation revealed that the tracts of shamilat land that had been offered for planting - and assumed by the project staff to benefit the communities - had surreptitiously changed their tenurial status. The de facto owners hoped to get 'their' shamilat lands planted at government expense, without making any repayment commitments. No community decision making was involved, and no community woodlot was established. Wherever there were still some genuine communally used plots of land, the communities did not come forward to offer them in support of reforestation, but preferred to save them for other uses.

The community forestry component, based on inaccurate assumptions and lacking from the outset a social structure to sustain it, failed in the early stages of the project.

Further analysis of the farmers who offered their private (malkiat) land for project reforestation and of the farmers who were in control of the nominally shamilat plots revealed that the larger landholders tended to take advantage of the project. The wealthiest landowners, who have the resources to contribute the costs of establishing and protecting tree stands, had not done so - nor did they intend to do so in the future. (6) At one of the reforestation sites, for instance, the main part of the 100 acres planted in the first project year belonged to one influential family of six brothers, only one of whom was 'almost' a full-time farmer, while the others were absentee landlords operating shops and small enterprises in Muzaffarabad. Another landowner, who offered about 125 acres of land for planting in the second project year, flatly refused to contribute any payment, arguing that the government of an Islamic country should provide for the citizens. A third large farmer, who wanted his 56 acres planted in the second project year, requested government-paid guards to protect the plantation and to restrict the access and customary rights of smaller farmers to collect grass, tree branches, and the like.

On the other hand, the smaller farmers hesitated to accept project planting on their lands. They were fearful of losing possession or control over their land to the government once it was planted by the Forest Department, or of being deprived of rights to collect fodder and graze their cattle. Most of the smaller farmers interviewed indicated that they might offer small plots for project planting, provided they could be convinced that the Forest Department would not alienate their lands and that they would be able to cut grass for their cattle.

In contrast, the larger landowners, being confident of their political power, did not regard tree-planting by the Forest Department as a threat to their ownership of land and trees, and tended to manipulate available project opportunities and resources to their own benefit. This attempt was facilitated by the absence of a legal framework that defined the obligations, not merely the rights, of the large farmers whose land was being reforested through government contribution. The absence of a contract left a huge loophole that enabled the large landowners to avoid making contributions. (7)

LESSONS FROM THE SOCIAL ANALYSIS

The findings of the sociological analysis led to immediate changes in the project and generated several lessons of broader validity. The project's management was asked to reconsider the areas identified for fuelwood planting and to limit immediately the planting on shamilat land. During the following year the project re-examined the 800 acres of alleged community land and private lands, identified initially for planting, and instead of the entire area retained only 400 acres, of which only 25 acres was shamilat land. The intent was to prevent turning the pilot project into a full 'giveaway' programme, until a cost-sharing system could be designed. The funds that remained available were redirected in the short run to planting on Khalsa land, so

170

that the total pilot area was increased from 400 to 850 acres. The project's selection of private (malkiat) plots for experimental planting with fast-growing species was more emphatically orientated toward the smaller farms.

More important than these short-run adjustments were other benefits of the sociological analysis. It prevented the extrapolation of the pilot approach on a much larger scale, as initially intended. The failure proved more convincingly than other arguments that the social analysis should have been carried out at the time of preparation and appraisal, when it could have steered the pilot project on a different path, consistent with the local social landscape. Though done relatively late, it was instrumental and consequential.

When the follow-up development project in Azad Kashmir was appraised in 1983, the earlier errors with regard to forestry could be avoided. The new orientation was toward overcoming the social constraints to a systematic hill development programme. Most hillsides are a mix of various social tenure systems, and each hillside is a separate eco-system that must be treated as such. It is of little use to design production and conservation measures on one part of the hill when run-off from another part is not checked at the same time. Consequently, the new project was orientated towards integrated hill management plans, based on agreement between the individual owners in each catchment area, the communities where relevant, and the government, with envisaged cost-sharing and benefit-sharing arrangements. Since strong sustaining structures within the farming communities were neither identified nor established in the available time, these hill development programmes were to be implemented mainly by government departments in a rather paternalistic top-down manner. At the same time, however, a different approach to forestry development received prominence in this follow-up project: 'farm forestry' (discussed in the next section).

Substantively, the sociological analysis described above brought three sets of social variables into the limelight: (a) the complex land tenure system and the processes affecting it at deep structural levels; (b) the community unit with its internal interactions, non-homogenous groups, and inability to act consensually; and (c) the behavioural patterns of individual farmers. It hardly needs repeating that no social forestry project can be conceived and prepared without in-depth and timely treatment of at least these social variables.

ALTERNATIVE UNITS OF SOCIAL ORGANISATIONS

The three clusters of variables discussed above, which were crucial to the failure of that particular forestry project, have in fact a more general relevance, since such variables are intrinsic to many forestry projects. Therefore, I would argue that sociologists and foresters together should turn around such findings and translate them into methodologies for future action. Information about past social processes should be distilled into forward looking strategies. This is the substance of social engineering at its best. For the call of sociological analysis is not only to analyse and explain, but also to assist in transforming the status quo. Speedy feedback from sociological analysis for the sake of short-run corrections, important as it is, should therefore be further enhanced through formulating sociologically substantiated operational strategies.

Perhaps the most important factor in designing the social strategy of forestry programmes is the adequate identification of the unit of social organisation likely to undertake the programme and able to do so successfully. For a while, various forestry projects have lumped together, under the broad umbrella of social or community forestry, various objectives and different approaches. This resulted (as in the Azad Kashmir project) in an unclear or mistaken identification of the social unit which could perform the intended activities.

Contributing to this insufficient clarity was the fact that the concept of community forestry was at a certain point loosely defined by some major agencies as 'including any situation which intimately involves local people in forestry situation' (emphasis added). (8) Contrary to this overly encompassing definition, the operational challenge is to disentangle the broad term 'people' and to identify precisely who and how: what social units of organisation among 'the people' can and will do afforestation, and which social units and definable groups can act as sustaining social structures for long-term production activities.

Such social units of organisation can be either natural (existing) social groupings, like the family household, or purposively organised grouping, specifically for performing the activity of planting and protecting trees. Such purposively created groups, as will be discussed further, can be, for instance, tree growers associations or women's groups. Creating such social units, organising them, is,

172

however, a task which requires both correct social understanding of what is to be done and appropriate methods for social organisation. The need to establish them introduces a clear sociological dimension in forestry development projects and/or in the work of forestry departments.

Establishing a functional social group means, of course, much more than simply lumping together a set of individuals into an artificial entity labelled group. It implies a process of selection and self-selection of the members, a willingness for association and participation, a perception of both self-advantage and co-responsibility, and the establishment of an enduring social structure with well defined functions. This will in turn help mould patterned behaviour among members and is the essence of grassroot, purposive institution building. Forming enduring units of social organisation is particularly important in the case of tree growing, given the long time dimension of the production cycle which requires structured support over an extended period. Such small scale organisations are capacity enhancers; building them maximizes the cumulative impact of the contributions of the group's individual members, enabling them to perform activities and achieve objectives that otherwise might not be attained.

The social arrangements which need to be designed and established for social forestry will have to vary also depending on the different technologies envisaged for reforestation in one or another ecological areas. There is a need for compatibility between the technical/physical characteristics of a forestry programme, on the one hand, and the socio-structural characteristics of the unit that is its social actor, on the other hand.

When forestry programmes are designed, it is essential to realise not only that there are a number of different potential 'social actors', but also that they are not equally fit for different technical (sylvicultural) approaches to forestry. The appropriateness of various tree planting technologies to one or another local situation is not neutral to social structure. Such technologies refer to species selection, nursery development, planting technology and configurations, plantation managing, protection, marketing, etc. For instance, to determine which one of three basic alternative types of tree arrangements - block planting, linear planting or mixed associations of trees and crops - is most adequate in a particular case would require to identify

173

the socio-economic characteristics of the farmers themselves, and to assess the local land tenure systems and land availability. Therefore, finding the proper fit between the technical elements of afforestation (from species selection to harvesting) and the attributes of the unit(s) of social organisation around which an afforestation strategy can be built is at the core of the cooperation between forestry experts, sociologists and planners.

The range of structurally different social actors in forestry development projects is quite broad: communities, villages, village governing bodies, farm families, groups of farmers, cooperatives, schools, private companies, and public institutions. Some of these 'actors', together with their sociological characteristics relevant to forestry work, are examined below.

Community woodlots

Until recently, the community woodlot has been widely accepted as the dominant model in social forestry.

Many experts considered that massive fuelwood planting can be best induced if large areas of communal lands would be used and large numbers of people would become co-interested in planting and protection. It, therefore, seemed natural to introduce this innovation through the community as a natural social grouping. Planting for social forestry was implicitly conceived and treated operationally, as a collective innovation. Much emphasis was put on establishing woodlots on communally owned land. The apparently plausible sociological assumptions were that communities would influence their members to plant, would mobilise labour and promote self-help and would collectively protect the young plantations on 'their' land. It was also assumed that they could ensure the wide distribution of benefits among the small farmers who make up the majority of the community. Successful village woodlots in countries such as China and Korea, which had been supported authoritatively by the government, lent credibility to this approach and were assumed as valid models for other social contexts.

When replicated in other countries, however, many community woodlots fared much worse than expected. Azad Kashmir is but one example, but results in Gujarat and other Indian States, in Niger and other African countries and elsewhere were similarly disappointing. The review of actual experiences, some of them in Bank-assisted projects, revealed that in most of these failures the village community was not effective as a social unit, for several reasons:

- Communities are generally large, not homogeneous, often split and stratified, and thus not able to sustain long-term projects which require efforts today for uncertain and delayed benefits in the future.
- The interests of community members often differ to such an extent that unified action is impossible. The 'commons' syndrome (9) is particularly intractable since it runs contrary to the need for community members to cooperate in establishing woodlots, in abstaining from premature cuttings, and in protecting against animals. What is advantageous for one subgroup is not necessarily advantageous for another or for separate individuals. Local community leaders appear often reluctant, or not strong enough, to enforce restrictions to protect the trees.
- When available community land is limited and block sites are small, costs are high.
- The tenure status of communal lands is often uncertain; it is similarly unclear what social body has jurisdiction over the allocation of communal lands. (10)
- The elaborate distributional arrangements to ensure that produce from village woodlots is given to those needing it most have not worked out in practice. Usufruct is often blurred and clear rules for distribution are absent. The long production cycle for trees weakens the confidence of those planting today, that they will get wood eight years down the road and it engenders the suspicion that the communal authorities will appropriate the wood in any case.
- Last but not least, communities are not necessarily organised as joint producers in any other respect. Externally designed programmes seldom bother to establish grass-roots organisations and institutional structures within communities to achieve the goals of these programmes. The close interdependence of members required by community schemes cannot be fostered by decree.

Because of such factors, poor results were obtained in

many places. In the 'bois de village' (village forests) in West Africa the community system was found 'ill-suited ... to serve as a vehicle for reforestation' (11) and in Asian countries its adequacy was questioned as well. (12) Often the forestry department had eventually to take over responsibility for the village woodlots to maintain the plantation.

Family forestry

The growing perception of the ineffectiveness of the community-centred approach led to a substantial shift in thinking and strategies among foresters and planners. They began to focus on the <u>individual</u> farmer and family farm unit, as opposed to the community unit, in social forestry programmes. This approach is being given various names - farm forestry, family woodlots or agroforestry - but the common denominator behind the semantic variability is that the family farm/household is the social nucleus around which reforestation is planned and financed. The technological package is different from the one proposed for community woodlots and is designed to suit the opportunities available to the individual small farmer.

This is not to say, of course, that there is no longer concern with village plantings or that previously there was no interest in supporting tree planting on individual farms. What I want to underscore is a shift in emphasis, a refinement of social forestry strategies, a reallocation of priorities, and a change in the sociological underpinnings of certain forestry programmes. This new type of programme implies a demand for sociologists to refine the social strategy for this approach.

Recent Bank-assisted forestry projects - in Karnataka, Kerala, Haryana, and other Indian states, as well as in Nepal, Mali, Haiti and elsewhere - provide strong support and incentives for tree planting on individual farms. Farm forestry is now a substantial part of the follow-up project in Azad Kashmir, for instance, where about 12 million seedlings will be distributed to farmers. In the Jammu and Kashmir India social forestry project, village woodlots will represent only 11.3 per cent of the total planting programme, while farm forestry will represent about 43 per cent, supported by a distribution of about 47 million seedlings without cost to individual farmers.

Sociologically, the significance of the family forestry strategy is multifold; first, it replaces the joint (community) responsibility for planting with individual (family) responsibility. It replaces joint ownership of trees with individual ownership. It also vests the management authority over the tree plantation in a real person rather than in a diffuse, amorphous entity. Further, the simplification of the distributional implications is obvious and enormous. For the farmer, the correlation between his inputs (labour or cash) and the output becomes direct, understandable, proportionate, and less risky.

Technically, trees can be grown on individual land not just as small blocks (family woodlots) - more effectively in the aggregate - along linear landscape features such as farm boundaries, internal field borders, watercourses, etc. From a socio-economic viewpoint, tree planting technologies which will maximise the use of interstitial locations and other marginal lands are particularly suitable to individual small farmers because they are not competing with existing land uses. Even small farmers who cannot afford to set aside an arable plot for a tree block can use their hedgerows for planting. Thus, opportunities for expanding tree planting are indeed enormous. Foresters have concluded that, since farmers secure most of their fuelwood by lopping branches, homestead boundary trees can produce several times more volume than calculations based on clear felling from plantations. This has clear implications for mitigating the fuelwood shortages, since it is easier to persuade a farm family to plant on farm boundaries than to persuade communities to provide scarce land for block plantations. Current projections of increases in fuelwood planting until the year 2000, therefore, expect family forestry to contribute the central share, with community woodlots and state forests accounting for the rest. (13)

The sylvicultural technology recommended for family forestry programmes differs, in certain significant aspects, from the one recommended for tree-block planting. These differences are linked to the sociological underpinnings of farm forestry. Under this approach, tree planting is incorporated into the farmer's own farming system, rather than remaining parallel to it on a remote communal lot. Technologically, this integration may entail the use of multipurpose species of trees, since these will satisfy farmers' needs not only for fuelwood, but also for shade, fodder, construction poles, and so on. Species suitable to meet farmers' needs for animal fodder, with fuelwood as a subsidiary rather than primary benefit, often integrate more organically into their overall farming systems than species like eucalyptus, that have been promoted widely by many programmes. If appropriate species are selected, trees can become a cash crop, not merely a dual-purpose product for home consumption. Forestry can be complementary to, not competitive with, agriculture. In favourable ecological circumstances, with reasonable rainfall, an average rural family needs comparatively few mature trees (according to some estimates), which when correctly spaced can help increase agricultural crop yields, and it appears that land availability need not be a constraint to increased afforestation, provided that family forestry indeed becomes widespread.

Since family forestry is essentially an innovation to be individually adopted, through decision making at the family/household level, the spread process is free from the difficulties that community forestry presents, such as factionalism impending collective adoption processes. However, adopting family forestry does mean a change in behaviour, inasmuch as farmers did not previously plant fuelwood systematically. In India, for instance, it was estimated that in 1984 only a small fraction (no more than 10 per cent) of all farmers plant fuelwood trees. Sociological studies in Yemen, Malawi, Zimbabwe, India, Haiti and other countries confirm that farmers are primarily interested in planting trees for multipurpose uses - fruit, poles, fodder, fuelwood, etc. and potentially as a cash crop for generating income.

Through the understanding of the spread mechanisms of this innovation, the sociology of forestry development can make it clear to forestry workers that such behavioural change has to be actively elicited, motivated, and supported as part of the social strategy for reforestation. External factors may play a potent role in facilitating farmers' decisions to plant and protect trees. Adequate social strategies need to incorporate: (1) extension efforts focused on forestry, based on communicating information to farmers and influencing their perception of impending threats and existing opportunities; (2) incentives and inputs, such as low-cost or free seedlings, fertilizers, and seeds; and (3) sometimes water supply and credits. Several successful forestry programmes (in West Bengal, Haryana, Jammu and Kashmir) use special change agents (extension agents called 'motivators' or 'social forestry workers') who were established as new positions in the staffing patterns of Forestry Departments, with the explicit function of persuading farmers to plant trees and giving them technical assistance in doing so.

Because of the long time lag between planting and harvesting trees and because small farmers often cannot afford to wait several years for income, special incentive systems will be needed in certain situations to give financial support for inducing change in behaviour. Economic incentives, though sometimes necessary, are difficult to provide when government funds are scarce or where there are not cash markets for fuelwood, poles, and other forest products. Alternative incentives, perceivable to the farmer, should therefore be sought. The appropriate use and combination of incentives are an important aspect of social engineering, and sociologists can contribute a great deal to their design.

Imaginative incentive systems can be developed with sociological knowledge of the local culture and value-systems. Farm forestry can be linked to various other activities or events, which stimulate the farmers' interest. For instance, in projects to regularise land tenure, large numbers of farmers, who have only customary right to land, get a formal legal title to it. Since titles are very important to farmers, granting them can be used as an incentive for farm forestry. Farmers can be asked to plant trees along the boundaries of their demarcated plots to facilitate the process. Farm forestry can also be linked to irrigation and settlement projects and to the construction of infra-structure. In general terms, tree planting can be linked to many events in the farm family's life that are imbued with positive values, thus facilitating the successful adoption of the behaviour.

As an enduring social unit able to sustain forestry development programmes, the farm family is thus an excellent social resource. Tapping its potential requires a deftly tailored integration of technical, sociological and economic elements, as well as operational cooperation between foresters and sociologists in designing and implementing this strategy.

Small groups

The often spectacular success of family-centred forestry may obscure the fact that group-centred approaches have development potential which is sometimes overlooked because of the ineffectiveness of the community approach. The community-centred strategy should not be dismissed altogether, however, because in certain socio-political and institutional contexts it can produce results. It would be throwing out the baby with the bath water if the de-emphasis of community woodlots were interpreted as renouncing all group-centred approaches.

Sociologists are best equipped for pointing out to planners and foresters that communities are just one type of group and that the community forestry approach is only one of many possible group-centred strategies. Foresters, in turn, must ask the sociologist: are there social formations in between the entire community and the individual farmer, which are capable of acting as supporting structures for the development of forestry or other natural resources? Is it possible to avoid the weaknesses of the community approach, yet preserve the advantages and social synergy of group-powered efforts in forestry?

The sociologist's answer to this question has to be affirmative. Sociologically, alternative types of groups can definitely be organised and some have already been formed as a result of local social invention under favourable circumstances. The problem is to have a group that is free from the limitations of large sized, community-wide groups, yet able to generate the synergy that makes groups more effective than the sum of their members.

The limitations of communities as social units are traceable to their large size and internal stratification. Other groups of a more manageable size could prove fully functional. Their smallness would not create problems of system maintenance that are more complex than those the group is originally called on to solve. Small groups are likely to be less diverse and stratified, more homogeneous. A common interest, pursued more effectively by joint action than by individuals, links the members together. A simple rule for the distribution of benefits (for example, equal share for all) would eliminate actual disadvantages or misperceptions of advantages. A small group can also enforce rules about contributions through peer pressure, so as to eliminate free riders. Small groups often manage other natural resources (such as a water users' association formed around a small branch of the irrigation system) and could operate a woodlot often without the conflicts that surround community woodlots.

One successful example is a group farm forestry scheme developed in West Bengal. A group of landless or marginal farmers is given a block of marginal public land for tree planting. The members are not granted title to the land, but have usufruct to the land and ownership of the trees they are expected to plant and protect. Under this system there is no possibility to change land use or mortgage the land. The area allotted and the number of trees to be planted guarantee enough wood from lops, tops, dead trees, and branches to meet a family's domestic requirement. The stem volume is then available for sale, and the total output ensures participant interest.

The protection of land parcels can be organised jointly by the group. The group strategy thus not only maximises land use for forestry, but also encourages and facilitates consensual action for tasks that would be performed less effectively if carried out individually.

The target group of this West Bengal scheme is highly dependent on the income generated by their labour and cannot be expected to work without remuneration. Incentive payments have therefore been made to help meet consumption requirements of the families during the early stages of the plantation. Incentives are also given for each surviving tree to encourage maximum survival rates. This type of group farm forestry is feasible only if land is available for planting close to the beneficiaries' residence. Tailoring this approach to particular sites and social strata also increases the role of land-use surveys in area population survey data, as baseline for targeting.

The operational principle is to create a clear link between a well-defined small group and well-defined piece of land that is converted into a woodlot. In addition, there needs to be a clear correlation between contributions and returns, and authority and benefits must be restricted to the members of the group, not left open to the community at large.

The potential for such groups is substantial, but a methodic socio-organisational effort is required to establish and validate these small groups. The advantage, however, is that they will then supply the social structure necessary to put to productive use certain natural resources that would otherwise remain under-utilised or completely neglected. Several states in India envisaged considerable expansion of group farm forestry on public lands. It has been estimated that up to 2,500 seedlings given free to each participant, would enable the family to gather its domestic fuelwood from lops, tops, and fallen wood and to sell the main stem volume for cash income. This innovation is a socially significant instance of partial 'privatisation' of the usufruct (not ownership) of public (waste) lands, under which landless people are enabled and encouraged to raise trees as a cash crop. Where surplus labour is available and private land is scarce, this option offers the additional possibility of generating some effects that will alleviate poverty.

Associations

Even when tree planting is done by individual farmers, some form of group or association may be economically and socially beneficial. In several Indian states, where family farm forestry is being implemented faster and more successfully than anticipated, the forestry departments help establish 'tree growers associations' or similar organisations to assist farmers in the marketing of the wood produced from family forestry.

One such organisational structure that could support reforestation with the direct involvement of farmers is the forestry cooperative. With a clearly defined and not too large membership, cooperatives might be a more coherent and effective organisation than the village community as a whole. In the North-West Frontier Province of Pakistan a pilot programme to revive forestry cooperatives among Guzara forest owners envisaged the establishment of some 15 cooperatives, each with a minimum of 500 acres of forest land. Each cooperative has responsibility for managing the forests of its members in accordance with a plan approved by the Forest Department. The cooperatives receive technical assistance in preparing the management plan and the services of field foresters, both paid for by the Provincial Government. No other subsidies are given, and all other forestry costs (replanting felled areas, maintenance, extraction, and so on) are borne by the cooperatives. Funding for the cooperatives comes from the revenue from sale of existing trees. For this purpose, cooperatives are authorised to retain at least 40 per cent of the revenue from the sale of trees, and receive credit if needed. The cooperatives are registered under the Cooperatives Law. This experiment has its roots in the system practiced for Guzara forest owners in NWFP under the Hazara Forestry Act, but it allows more initiative and responsibility to the farmers. A sociological study among Guzara forest owners found that farmers strongly value the contribution cooperatives can make towards protecting their ownership rights on the forests, but see government interference and party politics in such cooperatives as a mortal threat to such organisations. (14)

Age groups

Many traditional societies, particularly in Africa, entrust to subgroups certain maintenance functions in the society. Some of these groups are defined by age and gender and are accountable to appointed group leaders as well as to the overall authority structure. Similar groups could sometimes be used for certain activities in forestry development.

One of the notable successes in recent years has been the involvement of school-age youths in small social forestry projects (in Kenya, Malawi, Gujarat and Haiti), particularly in establishing tree-nurseries. Schoolchildren are a homogeneous age group, concentrated, organised by virtue of their main activity - going to school - and with a built-in leadership system. Although the nature of this age group limits its use for activities of long duration, it is perfectly suitable for short-term technical processes in forestry, such as the establishment of nurseries and the production of seedlings.

The example of Gujarat is impressive: at the outset of a social forestry programme in 1980 there were less than 20 schools with tree nurseries. The Forestry Department decided to encourage schools and private farmers to raise seedlings, rather than to expand its own state nurseries. The programme proved to be a big success, and in three years about 600 schools opened nurseries in which school children, with guidance from foresters and teachers, produced several million seedlings a year. The only incentive provided was a guaranteed price for seedlings; when they are ready for transplanting, the state forest service buys them for distribution to local farmers. This economic incentive was backed up by technical advice from extension workers on how to construct and operate small tree nurseries. In practice, many of the seedlings have been taken home by the school children and planted around their family homesteads. The programme has thus stimulated a genuine interest in the planting, ownership and protection of trees. (15)

Women's groups

Experience with women's groups in forestry seems much more limited. Since women are responsible in many cultures for collecting fuelwood, they would appear to be the ones most directly interested in producing it. Women often possess an exceptionally good knowledge of the qualities of various tree species. (16) Evidence from a few social forestry programmes points out the contribution women could make to them. (17)

However, although women have been organised for different productive or household-related activities in various countries, little has been done to involve them in taking group responsibility for the cultivation of woodlots. Even in a country such as Kenya, where women's groups are widespread and effective, a sociological field study reports that out of 100 women's groups active in one district (Mbere), none was directly involved with tree planting. (18)

Women's groups could probably perform a role more or less similar to that of group farm forestry, described above, if adjustments were made for their other productive and household roles. Given the inelasticity of poor rural women's time, purposively organising group-based fuelwood production activities may maximise the output for women without creating additional time constraints on them. (19) In many places women and children are compelled to make enormous efforts to collect wood for cooking and heating, often travelling long distances. In certain areas of Nepal, for instance, the time a woman spends collecting fuel is estimated to between 20 and 40 days per year. It may, therefore, save both time and energy, under certain circumstances, to produce, rather than collect, the fuelwood.

A small group of women, offering mutual help and cooperation, is likely to be a more effective social device than if each woman spends the same amount of time and labour in individual farm forestry. This is certainly an area acquiring social-organisational efforts, an area for action-oriented research and sociological experimentation, which will enable sociologists to make useful contributions of a social-engineering nature to the current efforts of foresters.

Watershed forestry

Foresters, planners, environmentalists and policy-makers alike are increasingly concerned with the rehabilitation of watersheds. A legitimate question which developmental sociologists would, therefore, have to answer is: What social unit can sustain watershed rehabilitation and management?

A watershed is a physical unit, not a social one. But watersheds are inhabited by people: their resources are used in people's productive activities and are often deteriorated and degraded by them. This is why land use planning or an erosion control programme cannot be effective, and cannot be sustained, unless it is designed to incorporate watershed inhabitants into rehabilitation work.

The need for a sociological dimension in such programmes is being increasingly realised. A forward-looking strategy proposal for rehabilitating about 150 million hectares of degraded watersheds in developing countries strongly urges the recognition of this sociological dimension:

> Watershed projects deal with people. The key to securing people's participation in such programmes will lie in designing broad strategies based on a better understanding of their perceived needs and priorities and in particular of local land tenure ... This implies that enough time will have to be spent at the outset of project development on sociological studies in order to define the type of incentives needed to elicit farmers' cooperation. (20)

The challenges for sociology contained in such strategies, and the call for specific answers and implementable social engineering, are pressing. Watersheds vary enormously both in physical size as well as in population density or settlement patterns, and the general absence of organised group structures compounds the complexity of the problems.

Indeed, the first question to be asked from a

sociological angle is: if a watershed can be treated in physical planning as an ecological system, can the people who are making use of it be treated as a social system? Do they constitute a structurally coherent social unit? The answer to the last question is, in general, negative (with some exceptions). A single watershed may contain a broad diversity of tenurial arrangements, stratified social groups, and various farming systems and land use patterns. Moreover, the rehabilitation of deforested watershed demands much more than watershed forestry and massive planting of trees. It involves flood control and soil conservation; often bench terraces need to be built with massive excavation and refill work; farming systems need to be adjusted to the ecological characteristics; and there may be changes in the land rights systems, in the rules of land transmittal, in settlement patterns and the number of inhabitants.

Therefore, the work required is usually beyond the scope of what individual farmers can do on their own. Again, group action is required, as well as support from technical agencies. Coordinated social action for the group management of watersheds is probably one of the most complex types of collective adoption of innovation, particularly in the absence of structured groups.

The operational sociologist is faced here with a task probably more difficult than any of those previously discussed: to organise structures for social action and to engineer the formation of a group out of discrete and not necessarily organically interactive farmers. Watersheds and micro-watersheds may be the physical subdivisions in which farmers' activities can be aggregated into coherent group efforts. The social groups should participate in the design of a land use plan for the watershed and gain the strength to sustain it through convergent, organised behaviour based on commonly perceived objectives and jointly enforced rules. The sociologist is, therefore, called upon not only to design a watershed strategy, but to implement it and organise consensual social action, hand in hand with the land use planner, the forestry agent, and others in the field.

The textbooks for training such sociologists have not yet been written. They must be, and the sooner the better. But the actual sociological practice - albeit by trial and error, but with commitment and creativity - of such applied, operational sociology should certainly not wait for the textbooks to be written.

Continuing the same line of analysis, other types of units of social organisation will come into the limelight. Forestry enterprises, established for the industrial exploitation of forestry plantations, are also, in fact, forms of social organisation, but with a different structure and functions.

The alternative types of social units examined above are in no way an exhaustive list. The point is that such alternative social forms can be conceived and actually organised in real life. They are, in William Roote Whyte's terms, 'social inventions' (21) or purposive social arrangements for the performance of definite productive and distributional functions. A continuous learning process should accompany the process of organising such units and improving their structure and operation. There is no single 'best' social strategy available as a universal key to all development approaches in forestry; such strategies span over a broad spectrum, and alternatives are available or can be devised. Sociological perceptiveness and knowledge are therefore instrumental and indispensable for conceiving, designing and implementing any effectivity such as forestry development approach.

NOTES AND REFERENCES

1.   See E. Rogers and F. Shoemaker, Communication of Innovations: A Cross-Cultural Approach, N.Y.: Free Press, 1971. See also E. Rogers, Diffusion of Innovations, 3rd ed., N.Y.: Free Press, 1983.

2.   Patrick C. West, 'Collective Adoptions of Natural Resource Practices in Developing Nations', Rural Sociology, vol. 48, no. 1 (1983); and Patrick C. West and S. Light, 'Community Level Change Strategies for the Management of Fragile Environments'. In Science and Technology for Managing Fragile Environments in Developing Nations, K. Shapiro (ed.), Ann Arbor: University of Michigan Press, 1978.

3.   A more detailed description of this sociological analysis was given in Michael M. Cernea, Land Tenure and the Social Implications of Forestry Development Programs, World Bank Staff Working Paper No. 452. Washington, D.C.: The World Bank, 1981.

4.   The official definitions in the 1930 Jammu and Kashmir Forest Regulation Act, No. 2 are:

Demarcated Forest means forest land or waste land under the control of the Forest Department, of which boundaries have already been demarcated by means of pillars of stone or masonry or by any other conspicuous mark, or which may hereafter be constituted as a demarcated forest.

Undemarcated Forest means and includes all forest land and waste land (other than demarcated forest and much waste land as is under the management and control of the Revenue Department), which is the property of the Government and is not appropriated for any specific purpose.

5.   When a co-sharer of shamilat encroaches upon it and includes it in his cultivated area, he can be legally ejected by the Tehsildar at the request of another co-sharer (Land Revenue Act, section 150 A). However, such grievances, and particularly their enforcement have been rather infrequent.

6.   The wealthier farmers benefited most from the government's financing of all the costs of the fuelwood planting, which included seedlings and the establishment of nurseries, labour for planting and filling in, transport of plants, and protection (wages for guards) for several years. The cost for planting was estimated to be Rp.1,300 per acre, which excludes the costs of annual maintenance and protection between planting and harvesting, estimated at an additional Rp.600-700 per acre per tree-crop rotation.

7.   An interesting example of such legislation is the 1936 Hazara Forestry Act, in the North-West Frontier Province of Pakistan, which protects the ownership rights of the farmers while vesting the right to manage their forests in the Forest Department. It also institutionalises a mechanism of cost recovery, whereby government costs for forestry management and commercial exploitation are covered by a fraction of the proceeds from sold timber.

8.   See Y.S. Rao, 'Community Forestry: Requisites and Constraints'. In Community Forestry: Some Aspects. Bangkok: United Nations Development Program, East-West Centre, and RAPA/Food and Agriculture Organization, 1984.

9.   See Garrett Hardin, 'The Tragedy of the Commons', Science, p.162, December 1968.

10.   Michael Horowitz, analysing rural afforestation

alternatives in Zimbabwe, pointed out that 'the important issue where communal lands are involved is correctly identifying the locus of authority over land use allocation.' See Michael M. Horowitz, Zimbabwe Rural Afforestation Project, Social Analysis Working Paper, p.51. Binghamton, N.Y.: Institute for Development Anthropology, 1982.

11. See J.T. Thomson, Bois de Villages (Niger): Report of an Investigation Concerning Socio-Cultural and Political-Economic Aspects of the First Phase of the Project and Design Recommendations for a Possible Second Phase. Montreal: Canadian International Development Agency, February 1980.

12. See Rao, Community Forestry: Some Aspects. See also Raymond Noronha, Village Woodlots: Are They a Solution? Paper prepared for the Panel on the Introduction and Diffusion of Renewable Energy Technologies. Washington, D.C.: National Aeronautics and Space Administration, November, 1980.

13. Outlining such a global projection, John Spears and Edward Ayensu wrote:

> In order to guarantee a supply of fuelwood equivalent to the need of the 1 billion people who are already experiencing fuelwood scarcity ... current fuelwood planting rates would have to be increased at least five-fold between now and the year 2000, implying average annual planting of about 5 billion trees during that period. At least 75 per cent of this will need to be individual tree or woodlot planting on farmlands and wastelands outside government forest reserves and about 25 per cent sited close to urban townships, part of which would provide raw material for wood burning processing plants ... The main thrust of this program should be directed towards encouraging the spontaneous interest of farmers and local communities in multipurpose tree planting. The role of government agencies should be to ensure the availability of necessary inputs. (John Spears and Edward S. Ayensu, Resource Development and the New Century: Sectoral Paper on Forestry, World Resource Institute, Global Possible Conference, 1984)

14. Mohammad A. Rauf, Sociological Perspectives of Forestry Development in Pakistan, Report of Guzara Forest Owners Task Force, Islamabad, processed, p.101-4

15. See John Spears, 'Appropriate Technology in

Social Forestry'. Paper presented at the Interregional Workshop on Appropriate Technology, Kathmandu, Nepal, November, 1983.

16. See Marilyn W. Hoskins, Women in Forestry for Community Development, Washington, D.C.: U.S. Agency for International Development, 1979.

17. Gloria Scott, Forestry Projects and Women, Draft paper, World Bank, Projects Policy Department, 1980.

18. David, W. Brokensha, B.W. Riley and A.P. Cartro, Fuelwood Use in Rural Kenya: Impact of Deforestation, p.9. Binghamton, N.Y.: Institute for Development Anthropology, 1983.

19. An interesting analysis of the issues of human energy and women's work, including the implications for women's gathering, using and producing firewood, is contained in The Real Rural Energy Crisis: Women's Time. Washington, D.C.: EPOC, 1984, processed; see also Irene Tinker, Women, Energy and Development, Vienna, 1982.

20. Spears and Ayensu, Resource Development and the New Century.

21. William F. Whyte, 'Social Inventions for Solving Human Problems', American Sociological Review, vol. 47, 1982.

7

POVERTY, WOMEN AND YOUNG PEOPLE

D.C. Pitt

The purpose of this paper is to review recently published materials which discuss the relationships between population, resources, environment and development in the Himalaya. Much of the literature (Pitt, 1985) indicates that there is an environmental and developmental crisis characterised by erosion, deforestation and poverty caused in major part by population pressure. Some researchers have seen the crisis approaching catastrophic proportions as in the Sahel, though others have claimed that the crisis may be more apparent than real, and there is much argument about the relative weight of causal and consequential factors. Our tasks are to try to answer the question of whether the situation in the Himalaya is one of crisis, supercrisis, or pseudocrisis and also to identify the most affected groups and to evaluate the different top-down/bottom-up solutions.

POVERTY IN THE HIMALAYA

The first question concerns the level of poverty. Nepal and Bhutan have for a long time tailed the list of the Least Developed Countries (LDCs) and were rated fifth-to-last and last in the 1981 World Bank Atlas. This ranking is by GNP per capita. Afghanistan and the Himalayan Indian States may not be far behind, though comparisons are difficult. The last five states in the LDC list are either Himalayan or acknowledged 'supercrisis' states (that is, Bangladesh, Ethiopia, and Chad). The most recent figures from the newly produced World Development Report of 1984 (World Bank, 1984a:218) show little relative change from the

1981 figures. Indeed, Bhutan has dropped off the list completely, and Nepal, after showing an increase in annual growth rates of GNP per capita in the 1981 Atlas, is now registered as showing an annual decline rate of 0.1 per cent for the period 1960-82 - a rate only exceeded by Chad among the last five LDCs.

Most of the new poverty related data, however, as did most of the old data, refer to Nepal. It has become very fashionable to study Nepal, for both academics and agencies. This, of course, is in part due to the beauty, romance and general attractions of the country, and the hospitality of its people. But it is also due, at least in the case of some agencies, to the fact that doors have closed elsewhere. The favourite spots for technical aid in the 1960s have turned sour. The United Nations was even evicted at one point from the South Seas paradise, Western Samoa. In many African countries military coups and dictatorships have made life very difficult, and on one occasion a top level mission on model rural development projects was detained in a hotel for several weeks. Of course, the openness of Nepal may be as illusory as the the welcome to those outsiders who thought they had grasped the Samoan situation. The Samoans say the truth about them is like a live fish underwater that slips from your hand as you try to hold it - something with which followers of the current Freeman-Mead controversy will surely agree. The waters of Nepal may be even more muddy and the cultural mosaic even more intricate. Elsewhere in the Himalaya there is much that is a closed book, and even the new UN reports on Bhutan are not very informative.

It is necessary also to make the usual caveats about the unreliability of data. There are those who regard Himalayan statistics as inherently unreliable. This is because of the wildly differing sets of statistics or estimates (for example, the fuelwood estimates that varied by a factor of 67: Thompson and Warburton, 1985a:117). The indicators of poverty that are normally used, notably GNP per capita, or social indicators, such as infant mortality rates, do not vary significantly in different sources or over time, but this may be only because these sources are all quoting the same or similar sources. However, even if all figures need to be taken with skepticism, some relative points can be made and there is no alternative but to use available statistics, if only to be able to argue against those who habitually do use them.

There are two groups of comparative indicators which are widely used, the one economic, the other social (notably health and education). In the 1984 World Development Report, two economic indicators are called 'basic': GNP per capita and inflation rates. The Nepal score in the first is US$170 per capita (1982). This shows an increase of US$40 over the 1981 World Bank Atlas figure (1979). That this is regarded as a decline by the economic wizards is apparently not sleight-of-hand but a product of the method of calculation of GNP (World Bank, 1984a:274), and the fluctuating rate and purchasing power of the dollar.

As is well known, there are many things wrong with GNP as an indicator of poverty, or indeed development. GNP measures the total domestic and foreign output claimed by residents without any deduction for depreciation, and this is divided simply by the total population. No distinction is made for distribution of income. It is difficult to include the so-called 'black economy' or the activities of many big, especially multi-national companies, or the extent of foreign exchange transactions. Only quantified, quantifiable elements are included so that the whole of the subsistence economy is virtually excluded. In Bhutan, the 1981 World Bank Atlas claimed a GNP of US$80 per capita (1979). This may be quite meaningless because it is estimated that traditional subsistence agriculture accounts for no less than 90 per cent of total production in 1980-81 (World Bank, 1984b:18).

To be fair, the World Bank itself has admitted that such figures should be used with extreme caution and, in general, GNP figures are supplemented by a battery of other economic and social indicators. For example, the 1981 Conference on Least Developed Countries (UNCTAD, 1981) omitted GNP per capita completely and put more weight on agricultural indicators (that is, percentage of labour force in production, agricultural production growth rates, output per worker, and so on). Agricultural production growth rates for Nepal in 1960-79 showed a 1 per cent per capita decline, while the Bhutan rate was steady at 0.0 per cent, though this is better than the rate for all LDCs which showed a decline of 0.8 per cent.

One indicator, however, is quite remarkable for Nepal and that is the 1976-77 income distribution figure quoted in the World Development Report for 1984 (World Bank, 1984a:272). According to this, the highest 10 per cent of households had 46.5 per cent of the total income. This is very nearly a world record, being exceeded in the World Bank table only by Brazil (50.6 per cent). What this means is that the distribution of wealth in Nepal is highly stratified and that poverty is highly concentrated in lower income groups.

Inflation is a much more difficult indicator to use in the Himalayan situation although there are certainly figures available. For example, the World Bank 1984 Report for Nepal gives a rate of 8.9 per cent p.a. for the period 1970-82, compared to 7.7 per cent for 1960-79 and 11.7 per cent for the 32 low income countries (excluding India and China). However, the rate for Nepal had exceeded 10 per cent by the end of 1983 (ESCAP, 1984). The 1984 World Bank Bhutan country report suggests a rate of about 11 per cent for consumer prices. The proportions are relatively low compared to some African countries where inflation is running away at 30 per cent or more.

But inflation may not indicate very much about purchasing power or, more precisely, the ability of an ordinary young family to feed itself and provide for basic needs. The lowest average inflation reported by the Bank for any country in the world in the period 1970-83 was Ethiopia. The inflation rates quoted refer to quantified elements in the commercial and not in the subsistence economy. In the case of Bhutan over 90 per cent of the economy is estimated to be subsistence, so there the inflation rate is simply a mirror image of the Indian rate for imports. The subsistence sector in Nepal is probably around 70-80 per cent although declining (Acharya and Bennett, 1983, Table 2). Inflation, of course, can take place under subsistence conditions, as anthropologists have shown in discussing the Kwakiutl potlatch and similar situations. But here there are ritualised means of stopping an upward spiral and mitigating any effects, notably through gift exchanges. The Nepalese situation is quite different. A basic problem is that people cannot transfer their subsistence incomes into cash (or obtain cash) and the inflation rate is then effectively increasing the difficulties of obtaining any cash, and also enhancing the processes which divorce them from their land, livelihood, and means of self-reliance. If it could be calculated, this inflation rate would be very high indeed.

The difficulties with income, and other economic indicators generally, have encouraged the emphasis on social, or the so-called physical quality of life, indices (PQLI). For example, some countries which fare badly in the

GNP per capita table (for example, Western Samoa, Sri Lanka, the state of Kerala, India) fare much better when the indicators are infant mortality rates, literacy (notably female literacy), and expectation of life. Health without wealth has been seen as a desirable goal for development and a situation where poverty is not necessarily a problem. Such a circumstance (Defence for Children, 1982) has been variously explained. The status of women and a relatively egalitarian structure seem important prerequisites. For example, in income distribution tables, Sri Lanka scores very well (28.2 per cent of the household income being obtained by the highest 10 per cent of households, an egalitarian rate compared to other Least Developed Countries).

The PQLI figures are also suspect, of course, especially infant mortality rates, since many people do not register births and certainly not the infant deaths, discussion of which is often taboo. Without these figures expectation of life can only be a guess. Literacy is an ethno-centric concept, based on criteria obtained by written cultures. Most people, especially in poor countries, are part of the world of oral cultures.

With all these reservations, PQLI for Nepal and Bhutan are still not good, though not apparently worsening. For example, infant mortality rates in Nepal in 1980 were given at 150 per thousand (UNCTAD, 1981:32ff) (the WHO goal is 50; the average of low income countries, 87 per thousand). The 1982 figure was 145 per thousand (World Bank, 1984a:262). For Bhutan it was given as 147 for 1982 (World Bank, 1984b:18). The adult literacy rate in Nepal in 1975 was 19 per cent, though the most recent government figures (1981) claim about 24 per cent (Ministry of Education, 1984), which is the Least Developed Country average. The adult literacy rate in Bhutan in 1982 was 10 per cent (World Bank, 1984b:18).

Access to safe water has been a major problem, probably underlying the high infant mortality rates. In Nepal (1975) only 9 per cent of the population had access to safe water (UNCTAD, 1981:32); in Bhutan it was possibly less, as only 6 per cent of the rural population in 1982 had safe water (World Bank, 1984b:18) compared to 35 per cent in all Least Developed Countries. On the other hand, both Nepal and Bhutan had a higher than average daily calorie intake (1977) as a proportion of minimum requirement (91 per cent and 88 per cent, respectively, compared to 86 per cent for all Least Developed Countries) (UNCTAD, 1981:32). In all indicators there does seem to be some improvement.

The conclusion may be drawn that, by present measuring standards, Nepal and Bhutan are very poor countries though in some areas (for example, energy) there is much potential (World Bank, 1979). This does not necessarily imply that they will become supercrisis states like Ethiopia or Chad. It could be argued that in those latter two countries there are additional catastrophic elements that are not present in the Himalaya at the moment, even if there is the potential for them. In Ethiopia, supercrisis triggered by the rapid rise in mortality is due, in major part, to political unrest and conflict, which not only takes its own toll of lives but also prevents food aid from being distributed effectively. The environmental problem is a contributing factor but, since it has been continuous over the last few years, it may not be the single critical factor in the present situation.

In order to understand better the relationships between the environmental problems in the Himalaya and poverty, and the effects of recent changes, it may be necessary to disaggregate, to look in greater detail at the poorest groups within the country and at changes over time. Here the statistics are not overly helpful, partly because they consistently aggregate and partly because quantitative figures may be lacking on certain areas and for time series, and statistics do not tell much about causes and dynamics. Much more reliance, therefore, has to be placed on field studies including, where available, anthropological work, even if this work is scanty and may not be at all statistically representative.

What then can be said about recent changes in the poverty situation and the links to the broader environmental problems? What light is thrown on the key causal patterns? The simple explanation proposed by outside agencies has been population pressure, and indeed indicators based on per capita estimations, suggest that poverty increases with increased population. It seems, however, that women, at least, have not responded to this situation. The World Bank's 1984 report (p.256) says that in Nepal only 7 per cent of married women of child-bearing age are practising contraception. The population appears to be growing at an unexpectedly rapid rate. Nor is everyone blaming overly fecund peasants. One recent ILO study has boldly stated that 'the conclusion often drawn - that it is population growth that is <u>largely responsible</u> (their underlining) for the growing poverty of the mass of the Nepalese people - is a gross over-simplification and ignores the crucial fact that demographic change, like material deprivation or poverty, is a social product, conditioned and determined in the last analysis by the economic and social structures of the state' (Seddon, 1983). Population growth, then, may be regarded as one of the symptoms, not one of the causes, itself to be explained by what is happening in other sectors.

The Seddon (1983) study is of exceptional interest since it is based on detailed fieldwork of household behaviour and economic status. A major emphasis is food production, not the overall quantities but the access that households have to food supplies. The conclusion is that grain availability for Nepal had moved from surplus in 1971 to deficit in 1981 (from +66,921 to -108,278 metric tons) (Seddon, 1983:32). In 1981 the only region with a surplus was the Terai and it was predicted that this would be eliminated by 1987. At present the Terai surplus is earning foreign currency rather than being used to maintain minimal nutritional standards. The situation in the Middle Mountains is very much worse, and the 70,697 metric tons deficit in 1971 increased to 123,755 metric tons in 1981. In the Terai both production and yield, according to the Ministry of Food, Agriculture and Irrigation, seem to have declined between 1974 and 1978, despite the increase in land under cultivation (60,000 ha) through irrigation, the rise in fertiliser use of about 40 per cent, and the enormous increase in area under high-yielding varieties (Seddon, 1983:34). The reasons given are poor weather, failure to further extend irrigation, and inability to apply new agricultural technology. All crops seem to be in decline, except possibly rice.

As a result not only did foreign earnings from export crops decline, but international food aid was required. A special committee was established in 1980 and agreements were signed with the World Food Programme, India, U.S.A. and others. Nevertheless, food export continued and new agreements were reached with China for the export of flour, beans and pulses. Only some mountain regions maintained a grain surplus, but even here there was food aid and subsidisation.

The implications of this combination of local food deficit and increased aid are considerable. It has been shown that the effects of such aid in Africa, where there have been many negative development effects such as corruption and internal distribution problems, have resulted in a dramatic decline in subsistent, self-reliant agriculture and a decline in maternal and child health (Defence for Children, 1982). A similar scenario seems to be building up in Nepal.

The aid-giving agencies, however, have fought vigorously against the notion that top-down aid is counterproductive. The crisis of food production in Nepal has been blamed on the Nepalese farmers who, the agencies state, have not accepted quickly enough the top-down technology, but have preferred to stay with what is called their 'archaic' and 'traditional' agriculture. Such a stereotype needs careful examination. Recent studies (Seddon, 1983) have shown that the larger farmers with more land (especially in the Terai), more financial resources and capacity, did invest in the new technology. Tractor-owning farms were an average size of 17.7 ha compared to a general average 3.0 ha according to one study in Parsa and Chitwan. But even here, investment was modest by international standards. One can argue, however, that machines have limited use on steep slopes.

Fertiliser use is limited, according to Seddon (1983), not because of lack of financial stability, access, nor the weak development of extension services, but by farmers' choice. Wheat, however, is an exception and both areas and yields increased during the early 1970s, though there has recently been some decline, especially in the Middle Mountains.

The lessons from the comparative history of agricultural production are relatively simple. The retention of traditional technology has not only a long-term logic in the sense of preserving a fragile ecosystem, but is probably the only available course of action when incomes, notably from the agricultural sector, fall below a certain level (Pitt, 1970, 1976; McNeely and Pitt, 1985). At this point, population increases because traditional agriculture methods are relatively labour intensive. It is human hands and energy that provide the capital. There appears to be a striking difference between Nepal and Bhutan, the Himalaya poor states, and the supercrisis states of Africa. Traditional African agriculture and pastoralism have been virtually destroyed, in some cases by deliberate government policies which have discriminated against marginal social groups and have, in the interests of centralised political control, insisted on sedentarisation. The traditional Himalayan social ecosystem cannot be broken so easily in this way, though one might hypothesise that governments have a vested

198

interest in encouraging, or at least in not discouraging, the recent urban drift, because it provides a reserve army of labour and may facilitate political control.

It is already obvious that any simple label of poverty does not adequately define a situation where there are very considerable sociological differences in the degree of poverty. What are these sociological dimensions in Nepal? There are some interesting recent materials from which a more detailed mosaic can be constructed.

A first factor is land ownership. Generally speaking, those who own land (and their households) are better off than those who do not, and the larger the landholding the higher the standard of living. The World Bank Development Report (1984a), as mentioned earlier, indicates a high degree of concentration in the distribution of Nepalese wealth. In 1980-81 in the rural sector 2 per cent of all rural households were said to cultivate about 27 per cent of the land (Seddon, 1983:93). The land reform measures had obviously not worked, partly because the official ceiling for landholdings was quite high, 25 bighas (about 18 ha). Inequalities in size were most marked in the Terai, but in the Middle Mountains the problems continued to relate to the small, often uneconomic size of holdings. However, the proportions of landless households (continuing at about 8-10 per cent) is not high by Asian standards. Most of the rural poor have too little land on which to eke out a viable living and need, therefore, to rent additional land, to practise sharecropping on larger estates, or to seek wage labour. These options may be precluded, at least locally, by the high rentals, and the scarcity of employment opportunities. As a result, according to Seddon (1983:93), 63 per cent of family labour days were underemployed. This has led to a further stimulation of migration.

The size of landholdings also relates directly to nutrition and calorie intake. A 1978 survey of households showed that farms of less than 1 ha had an average calorie intake of 1,500 or less per person, compared to those over 1.5 ha which had 2,250 calories, or more. This depends to some degree on types of crops and the annual yield, but overall, according to Colin and Falk (KHARDEP, 1979), small farms are deficient, and farms under 1 ha produce only 60-70 per cent of household requirements while those over 1.01 ha supply 86 per cent.

APROSC (1978) report that annual per capita food consumption (in kg) varies significantly between regions (297

199

in the Far West, 480 in the Centre, and an average of 373 for all Nepal). In the Far Western region 59.2 per cent of households were considered to be below the poverty line. What is not clear from these admittedly inconsistent figures is how quickly the situation may be deteriorating. A decline is not necessarily corroborated by the steeply rising migration rate because there are many reasons, other than the economic, for migration (Pitt, 1983).

The recent figures on landlessness may even suggest that fewer people proportionately are landless in rural areas because of land abandoned by outmigration. Landholding, in certain circumstances, may be a sign of poverty. Since there is no base-line it may be that the numbers of those below the poverty line (which is somewhat of an ethnocentric concept rather variously applied from outside) have not changed greatly.

What is more interesting perhaps in the most recent figures is the indication of the concentration of poverty. But it is significant that the figures do not pinpoint the social groups who are most deprived nor explain why. Individual regions contain many ethnic and caste groups, households vary in sex and age structures, and the size of the landholding becomes irrelevant when the vital extra income has to be earned by other means. Seddon (1983) did not find an answer in any feudal-type obligations since, presumably, even the larger landowners had few resources. More significant may be the differential access which different castes and ethnic groups had to wage-earning possibilities: for example, Gurungs, Magars, Limbus and Rais are noted in military service, high caste Brahmins and Chhetris are preferred by employers and untouchables encounter employment barriers by virtue of their low or outcaste status.

Studies have indicated, however, that there is a relatively steep recent fall in standards of living because of the declining purchasing power (for rice or maize particularly) of rural people. There has been, according to one study (ARTEP, 1982), an actual fall in real wages in the last ten years.

This fall in real wages seems to have had a number of major effects in terms of the satisfaction of basic needs. First, nutrition: in the Middle Mountains and high Himalaya total available calories per person per day dropped from 1,569 in 1976-77 to 1,426 in 1983-84, and were projected to drop to 1,299 by 1989-90 (Seddon, 1983:124). Though the situation in the Terai was better than this in terms of average calories, more people had less money, especially the smallest farmers and the landless. Nutritional problems were accentuated amongst certain ethnic and caste groups, because of food taboos. The fact that demand concentrated on certain foods raised the price for these foods, although caste and ethnicity may be less important in some areas. Sacherer (1979) has shown clearly in her studies in Dolakha District how this factor affects food sufficiency. Here Brahmins had from 7.0 to 9.0 months of food sufficiency whilst 'low castes' had 4.6 to 5.0 (other figures were Chhetris: 5.9 to 6.9; Newars: 6.8; Tamangs: 8.4; Sherpas: 4.8).

This example indicates how the problem of malnutrition, at least, is the result of a deleterious change from traditional customs where taboos were in many senses related to seasonal supply and demand, and the 'modern' system which has superseded it, where supply and demand are manipulated or otherwise work against the consumer. Therefore, by denigrating traditional society, outside agencies may have accentuated the problems.

The unwise change from traditional management also applies in time as well as space. The months prior to the monsoon are months of hunger. To bridge the food gap people such as the Magar, for example, have traditionally taken forest products at this time: yams, berries, taros and suchlike, and sometimes they hunt and fish. The shrinking of the forests and the difficulties of common-land rights have curtailed these possibilities. People may even eat the next year's seeds at this time. More significantly, this is the time they fall into debt.

There are, in fact, estimates (Seddon, 1983:132) that 90 per cent of all debt in Nepal is for consumption items. As much as 80 per cent of land (especially irrigated land) may be pledged (Caplan, 1970). Interest rates may be as high as 32 per cent. In the Middle Mountains the problem is particularly acute where there are reports that 35 per cent of households are in debt. On the other hand, the debts are usually rolling ones, where the principal is not repaid and foreclosure rare. Debt, of course, also occurs in the traditional sector, notably for life-cycle ceremonies. Here, however, it was a redistributive mechanism, part of the Maussian gift-exchange structure of reciprocity, where giving (and lending) was a prerogative of rank. This traditional ethos may have carried over into the modern situation, so that debt may not be the enormous problem it appears to be from the figures.

The effects of malnutrition are cumulative. For example, there is a vicious circle between decreases in production and increasing malnutrition. An outcome is ill-health, particularly the incidence of debilitating disease and, notably in Nepal, diarrhea. Blindness caused by malnutrition, which may affect literacy rates, is also part of this complex. On the other hand, most health indicators, from infant mortality rates on, show a gradual improvement, as the number of physicians per capita has more than doubled in the period 1960-80 (World Bank, 1984:264). However, this may be mainly an artifact of collected statistics, such as the number of hospital admissions which refers mainly to the Kathmandu region. There is much less information for other regions, or social groups, and what is available is often contradictory.

The available evidence suggests that any discussion of poverty and basic needs in relation to wealth, income and land, needs careful interpretation. For example, Sacherer (1979), in her studies in Namdu, Kabre, has pointed out that whilst wealth may increase as one ascends the caste ladder, health, or at least nutrition, may decline. The main reasons are that 'the higher the caste group, the greater the number of restrictions on diet' (Sacherer, 1979:31). These restrictions constrain what is eaten by which member of the family, what is eaten at what age, by women or men at what time of the month, year and so on. Moreover, the more able and ambitious people, who wish to acquire wealth and status, will restrict their diet to move up the social scale. High-caste children, Sacherer concludes, may therefore suffer the greatest malnutrition. Brahmin food prohibitions, for example, include beef, buffalo, pigs, chicken and eggs. Children eat after adults in high-caste families (and also amongst untouchables) and girls after boys. If there is a shortage of food the child at the end of the line suffers most. It is possible then to have wealth without health as well as health without wealth.

But even these social correlations should be handled with care. For example, many young Brahmins told Sacherer that they did not believe in caste rules, restrictions, and privileges. They had travelled to Kathmandu and, indeed, often to India and, whilst orthodox in their home villages, wanted changes especially for their children. The situation was complicated by inter-caste and inter-ethnic marriage (for example, a Brahmin married to two wives, one Brahmin and one Chhetri). It is uncertain, however, whether social distance affects intermarriage; in other words, do proximate caste people intermarry more readily, and how often is caste intermarriage part of wider Maussian gift exchange where things cancel each other out. Nor is there an adequate explanation of the 'success stories' that Sacherer (1980) encountered among the mid-ranking Sherpas, Jirels and Newars. Finally, Sacherer's study is of only two panchayats and it is not known how representative these are.

Some speculation is in order here. As an example, there is the curious paradox in Sacherer's figures that the groups who made the greatest use of the health posts - the Brahmins, Tamangs, and Chhetris - had the highest rate of child malnutrition, although the relationship to mortality and morbidity rates is unknown. It is surmised that lower caste/ethnic groups avoided the health post for ritual and cultural reasons, notably the way the dead were handled. The hypothesis proposed elsewhere (Defence for Children, 1982) that health posts may do more harm than good (for example, by distributing inappropriate baby foods) should be carefully examined in Nepal. Another interesting point is that female child malnutrition rates were higher than male in all caste and ethnic groups except the Sherpas and the Jirels, where the rate for males was higher. This would seem to indicate that females are not prejudiced against amongst the Sherpas and Jirels as they appear to be in many caste and ethnic groups. This raises several questions. Once again, is the traditional context important in improving health and nutrition? Is the introduced system of health, in some senses, counterproductive?

Discussion of other basic needs, such as education, housing and water, is very constrained by lack of evidence. Sacherer's (1980:18) studies indicate that Brahmins (23 per cent) in one panchayat were considerably more literate than Chhetris (12 per cent), or Newars (9 per cent), but not than Tamangs (22 per cent). But in the other panchayat Brahmin literacy was both low (8 per cent) and not significantly different from that of Sherpas and Jirels (7 per cent). Overall in the Dolakha District males were much more literate (18.3 per cent) than females (2.3 per cent). The national averages at that time (presumably 1977) were 23.6 per cent and 3.9 per cent, though the most recent survey of education (Ministry of Education and Culture, 1984) gives males 34 per cent (6 years and over) and females 12 per cent. Brahmins and Tamangs were also over-represented in the primary school population of the two panchayats, whilst Sherpa males (though not Sherpa females) were underrepresented.

The data raise additional questions. How much do literacy rates reflect local abilities or central inabilities? For example, it has been suggested that teachers are not of a high quality and that both teachers and students often play truant. Dropping out is common. How important is literacy? In an age of cassette-recorders, oral cultures may have a new importance and greater relevance to poverty problems.

Literacy has been linked especially to health, through family planning. Again, the Sacherer (1980:43) evidence shows that Brahmins were more likely to practise contraception than, for example, Sherpas, who did not. But the overall level of use was so low that these figures may not be important. Nor is the evidence on numbers of living children necessarily indicative even though, in one panchayat, it is the untouchables and former slaves who have the greatest number of living children (5.5) compared to Brahmins (3.3).

None the less, some inferences are warranted. The tentative suggestion proposed here is that one contributing cause of poverty is the decline of traditional culture whilst introduced institutions are working against diminishing poverty and may even be exacerbating it. This helps explain phenomena such as relative health without wealth amongst some ethnic groups. The higher the caste position, the greater exposure to introduced institutions, the greater may be the problems. In health and nutrition matters, in education, in family life and so on, some caste and ethnic groups may insulate themselves against outside intrusion. As suggested elsewhere, independence and identity are not correlates of poverty, but rather an alternative means of achieving significant life values, wants, and aspirations (Pitt, 1983). Ultimately a firm base of self-reliance may become the vehicle for promoting economic development. When the independence and identity of a social group is broken down, severe problems may result - not simply the breakdown of social rules and order, but also a continuing dependence, which may or may not be the intention of those newly introduced institutions. At certain times traditional societies are more exposed to intrusions, and perhaps less able to resist, at least in certain sectors. Famines, epidemics and related disasters, or military disorder, have been the classic examples of outside 'intrusion', notably on the food or health front. Once involved, it seems difficult for outside forces to disengage. The saving grace of Nepal, in contrast to sub-Saharan Africa, may be the ability to prevent the label of disaster being attached so often and so widely.

Outside intrusions, however, have been most noticeable and traditional resistance least effective in the environmental field, especially in terms of forest management. Here the excuse was certainly not the designation of a crisis or disaster. In some views there has been rather a creeping exploitation in which commercial or government interests have played a major part (Bajracharya, 1983; Mahat, 1985), both in tree-cutting and road building. It might be suggested that, because in the traditional tenure patterns, forests formed an area where rights and controls were less clearly marked (that is, an approximation to Western concepts of common lands) it was very much easier for outsiders to develop control. This does not necessarily imply that deforestation is not due to local population pressure (cf. Mahat, 1985). There is no doubt that, as population has increased, there has been a noticeable increase in the use of fuelwood. However, some of the areas of deforestation are areas of outmigration or livestock decline, whilst many forest products, such as medicines and berries, have decreased dramatically.

This, however, is not necessarily because of shrinking forests. In Sacherer's studies the uses of forest declined for a variety of reasons; for example, the import of cheap Indian textiles over 30 years ago replaced 'forest' cloth; the use of traditional herbal medicine declined; livestock grazing gave way to cultivation of pakho type maize and millett. The fundamental reason why the forest is currently being abused is not the population pressure per se, but rather that the traditional eco-philosophy, in which the forest was important, has now long been abandoned. The Tamang and Sherpas of Namdu, Kabre today rarely talk of, or know about, the traditional botanic lore. The economic changes particularly coming from outside, or from the central government, triggered the switch away from forest conservation. Local conservation taboos and controls declined. The increased use of the forests for fuelwood then becomes a result, not a cause of a changing forest situation.

The forest problem and the economic situation, as a

whole, demonstrate the important point that there is really no turning back. It may be possible for caste and ethnic groups to keep the condom merchants and pill pushers at bay through the privacy of their own domestic rituals, but much less can be done when cheap cloth is imported, or when money is needed even for the essentials of life. The Rousseau-like romantics, who endorse the retention of pristine and pure mountain communities, are hardly realistic even if self-reliance in the form of subsistence may be a major answer to the poverty problem.

Fieldwork so far has provided very little reliable information on the problem of erosion or deforestation (Ives, 1985; Mahat, 1985; Byers, 1986). One gets the impression that this is not very important in the people's own minds. Sacherer (1980:5) writes, 'Erosion is alternately viewed by the villagers as either a natural process (too much rain this year) or a supernatural one (the gods must have been angry for some reason). It is not an activity over which man has control, even if the reasons for erosion, and solutions to the problems are understood'. This apparent fatalism is very suggestive. Is erosion something of a red herring? Are there benefits in some forms of erosion (for example, the broken-up detritus)? How important are people's ideas? Are there, as the French social scientists say, 'mentalites collectives'? What effect do they have on poverty, now and in the future? How much is 'poverty' in the mind? Whose mind? Who forms public opinion? What form does it take?

WOMEN AND YOUNG PEOPLE

Since the mid-1970s many UN reports about women, children and youth appeared, and are appearing, including reports from Nepal, even if the UN has never defined (or recognised other definitions of) what is a child and has accepted a purely chronological limit for youth (up to 26 years!). There have also been UN International Years for Women, Children and Youth. The argument is being developed that women, in the past, to use the World Bank's phrase, have been 'invisible', and that all three groups are the most deprived in poverty, especially in extreme poverty, situations.

How does this fit in Nepal? Are women/children/youth 'problem' groups? What part do they play in the 'crisis'? What roles do they, can they, play in the dynamics (top-down and/or bottom-up) of development?

At first glance women seem to have received the worst of the poverty situation. Female infant mortality (1976) rates are higher, women's incomes, life expectancies, literacy rates, and so on, are lower for Nepal, though, as has been indicated, this does not hold true across all caste and ethnic divisions, nor in life expectancy, which at least for 1982, is nearly balanced (45 for females, 46 for males).

The World Bank, also, in its latest report (1984a:198) has a battery of indicators showing the 'low' international status of Nepalese women. They had (1980) a ratio of adult male/adult female literacy worse than any other country in the world except the Yemen Arab Republic. They had (1980) the fourth lowest percentage in the world enrolled in a primary school (just ahead of Somalia, Upper Volta, and Mauritania, and equal with Ethiopia). They had (1977) the lowest mean age at marriage (17) sharing lowest place with the Yemen Arab Republic.

The Child Welfare Coordination Committee (CWCC, 1980) and UNICEF have also collected very interesting documentation on the deprived status of the child in Nepal. The death rate of children, 1 to 4 years old, was high (35.3 per cent) and this was highest in rural areas. Morbidity rates were high, especially illnesses, where the CWCC gives a rate of 23.2 per cent for intestinal infections, the most common illness, with pneumonia second (16.7 per cent). One survey (CWCC, 1980:15) reports a high incidence of stunting (48.1 per cent) amongst rural children, especially males. Dr Bagchi, of WHO, reports that 70 per cent of pre-school children are malnourished (WHO, n.d.). Primary school enrollment has risen (Ministry of Education, 1984:14) although it is much lower in remote regions, and the wastage rate (Grade I) has been put at 53.3 per cent, mainly due to examination failures. In 1977, 68.8 per cent of girls, but less than 10 per cent of boys, had no access to education. Many children are working, a figure of 13.5 per cent (for the late 1970s) of the total work force has been officially given, which is very high when compared with the global average (for example, Bangladesh, 10.2 per cent). Unofficially as many as 75 per cent of children of school age may be working or are what the ILO euphemistically calls 'unemployed'. The effects of child labour on health and life opportunities are enormous.

But again, many of these figures need to be broken down into ethnic, caste, or regional components. Infant mortality rates are much lower in urban areas, for instance; fewer children in the Terai (CWCC, 1980:46) are below height for age (45.5 per cent) than in the Middle Mountains (55.5 per cent). Rates for Terai Brahmins were lower (35.9 per cent) than for Terai Chhetri (43.3 per cent) and both were lower than those of their hill-caste mates.

Women and children certainly suffer from many forms of deprivation or exploitation. First, they work relatively long hours. The women's sphere in Nepal is still mainly in the household; there are exceptions: for example, Thakali women are involved in the hotel and catering businesses, educated Gurung and Chhetri women are employed in clerical positions in the private and public sectors, women from occupational castes may work as labourers or porters (Seddon, 1983:139). But even women who are in the household sector have a major role in subsistence work. Acharya and Bennett (1983) estimate that women account for 57 per cent of adult input time into subsistence agriculture and contribute half of household income (compared to 44 per cent for men and 6 per cent for children). These patterns varied to some degree in different communities, but always the women put in more hours than the men. For example, Acharya and Bennett report in Parbatiya Bakundel that the women work 12.5 hours per day as opposed to 8.16 hours for men. The lowest number of hours worked by women was among the Tamang, 8.46 hours, compared to Tamang men, 7.65. In several groups men did more work in what Acharya and Bennett (1983) call sphere one (including cooking, serving, cleaning, shopping and child care); notably the Tharu-Sukraware men worked 7.29 hours per day, the women, 4.97.

These long hours worked by women were not well rewarded in monetary terms, even if the value of the subsistence sector was relatively high, up to 80.8 per cent in the Acharya and Bennett (1983) studies, and even if women's work was more valuable than men's in the cash and subsistence sector combined. Nor did women have a major voice in the important decision-making processes, certainly not concerning labour allocation, though they did help to decide technical matters such as what crop to plant, what seed to use, and the amount and kind of fertiliser.

These studies, however, provide data which may challenge ideas of what women do spend their time on in some areas at least. The classic version of the deforestation-crisis theory has women walking farther and farther to the shrinking forests for fuelwood, or for water, as aquifers, wells, and water supplies dry up on eroded terrain. As a result they are worn out, and they and their babies' health suffers. World Bank figures show that the most time any women spent on fuel collection was 0.69 hours per day (Newar women), or about 6 to 7 per cent of their time. In a number of other cases men spent more time than women collecting fuelwood, but this never exceeded 0.58 hours per day. Water collection involved more time in some communities, although the average was about the same as fuelwood collecting. The most time recorded was 1.12 hours per day in Pangma, which was still less than 10 per cent of the time spent on all activities. The biggest single activity involved agricultural work. However, in Ehrich's (1980) fieldwork in Kungra District, India, fuelwood and water collecting did account for 55 per cent of the total women's time, again raising the danger of extrapolating conclusions drawn from one Himalayan region to another.

There is also now documentation showing the low status and oppression of many women within this domestic subsistence sector (CEDA, 1979). Seddon (1983) cites a strong tendency in 'high-caste' Hindu families, and particularly amongst Brahmins, for women to be treated more unequally and to be socially more oppressed than among the tribal groups, such as the Limbus, Magars, Gurungs, or even the untouchables. These restrictions result in severely reduced access to education and health facilities. Women, especially young women, had in many areas few rights with regard to choosing marriage partners or the age of marriage, and the early arranged marriages may be part of the explanation for the population explosion.

Poor health and nutrition amongst women was reflected in the health and welfare of infants and young children, according to recent materials published on the child care programme in Dhankuta, a 'Save the Children' UK project, and in the Kosi Hill Area Rural Development Programme (Ministry of Local Development and Britain's Overseas Development Administration; Nabarro, 1984). These figures show both time and space variations and raise important issues. For example, wasting amongst children was highest at the end of the monsoon (Nepalese month of Bhadra - August/September) and lowest in Mangsir (November/December), three months after the maize harvest. Food shortage was a reason for this and also for the prevalence of diseases, notably diarrhea. Nabarro speculates that the incidence of diarrhea is related to outbreaks of measles. But the causes of the wasting are multiple: food shortage; a moist environment which favoured oral faecial transmission; parents who could not afford time to go to a health post or to provide the child with extra ghee or sugar; and measles, which may often have been, as studies have shown elsewhere, the catastrophic straw which breaks the camel's back. But there were also many hidden factors: the time it takes to try to raise extra income or to negotiate loans, or to persuade children without appetites to eat when they are sick. An interesting point to emerge is that, although the research team could show that wasting or stunting vary with the amount of land a family held, it was less easy to explain morbidity and mortality. Much depends on the mother's behaviour and ability to cope. Some mothers 'innovate' because of superior education or wealth; other, poorer mothers out of desperation.

The status of older children seems to be bad also, and is compounded in the case of females. Child labour is apparently far more prevalent in Nepal (in the official figures anyway) than in India or Bangladesh. In the Acharya and Bennett studies (1983:43) girls contributed more than twice as much as boys to household production. The effects and consequences of child labour are not well understood, partly because in some sectors, notably the urban, it is a relatively new activity and the long-term effects (for instance, on health) may not be apparent for some years. The UN, ILO and some NGOs (Pitt and Shah, 1982) have recently put together a catalogue of major health and other exploitative consequences which may contribute much to low life expectancy and high morbidity. The CWCC/UNICEF investigation (1980) has provided case studies of child labour in Nepal. This includes work in restaurants, domestic service and newspaper stalls. Working children are to be found also in the so-called informal 'black economy', and in criminal and related activities, especially in Kathmandu. However, most working children (well over 90 per cent) recorded in the censuses are in the agricultural sector and this proportion has not changed much since the 1952 census. Some authorities have pointed out that the figures on health hazards are somewhat speculative and, in any case, if children did not work in the agricultural sector, families would starve. The force of this argument is somewhat diminished by the fact that families are starving anyway and that the causes of this starvation are related to external factors, notably prices.

None the less, a distinction should be made, as Bouhdiba (1982) has done, between exploitative child labour and that labour which contributes to the child's education and his family's income and well being. Certainly the growth of child labour is a major reason for a continuing high population growth.

One of the most serious consequences of child labour is simply that children, especially female children, do not receive even primary school education. In 1977, for example, in a number of districts, notably in the Far West, over 90 per cent of female children had no access to primary school education (CWCC, 1980).

Little is known about the social dynamics of child labour, and even less about the 15-25 year-old group which is generally called 'youth' in the UN nomenclature. This group certainly has a high rate of unemployment or underemployment. Many in this group are married with children. In the 1971 Census, 7 per cent of the population between 6 and 14 years old in Central and Western Development Regions were already married. Many of the group are in the van of migration to the cities, notably Kathmandu. Sacherer's studies (1979, 1980), for example, showed that young people were much more ready to change their attitudes and behaviour in response to outside cultural influences.

Nevertheless, it should not be assumed that Nepalese youth are simply a component of the global mass-culture youth model. For example, in Nepal migration has been regarded as a 'final' option for those in the most desperate category. According to a study quoted by Seddon (1983), there has been a change in the basic reasons for migration over the last 25 years. In the early period, migration of households (and this should be distinguished from individual migration) was largely the result of natural calamities, particularly the loss of hill land through erosion. It is argued that more recently the increasing pressure of debt has become the main cause. Both reasons involved loss of, or greatly reduced access to, land. Young people were carried along on this tide with their families, but until recently such migration was to other farmland and primarily involved movement from the Middle Mountains to the Terai. In recent years, however, this option has gradually been closed by the government move to control resettlement, as conflicts have developed with officials and other land-hungry people in the Terai, and as the stock of available land has decreased.

Desire for land remained the fundamental motive, and when a sample of Middle Mountain people were asked why they wanted to migrate, most (over 60 per cent) gave reasons relating to the difficulties of producing enough on land in the hills and the prospects of more land elsewhere. A similar proportion of those who had already migrated to the Terai gave similar reasons. It is interesting to note that only a relatively small proportion (about 5 per cent) of both samples gave the loss of land through foreclosure of debt problems as the reason, or indeed, loss of land through erosion and natural calamities (3.9 per cent of the Terai sample).

New strategies for households to cope with this situation seem to be emerging and in these young people play a major role. First, since there are, or are thought to be, wage earning opportunities in the cities, permanent migration of households may be giving way to individual migration of young people who are remitting wages back to support older and younger members of the family. As the debt problem is one of structural relationships, however unequal, between lenders and borrowers other forms of exchange may be taking place across this divide. For instance, Sacherer has referred to the marriage of low-caste young women to higher caste men. However, the situation may not be stable since the higher caste men are also, or have been, migrants. All this may help to explain the sudden upsurge in urban population numbers in the 1981 Nepal census (Goldstein et al., 1983).

Overall, therefore, there appears to be a worsening situation in the status of Nepalese women and children in the general context of deepening poverty. This is not the place to analyse the efforts of government and the various agencies who are trying to improve the situation. The literature that is available paints a picture in the 1960s and 1970s of a centralised monarchy which had introduced the so-called panchayat democracy in order to preserve the traditional structure. There was much rhetoric about decentralisation and 'back to the village' slogans, but popular participation was, according to most reports, limited. Shrestha and Mosin (1970), in their survey of village panchayats in the late 1960s, report that most people were confused about, or had little knowledge of, the panchayat system though a popular vote in 1981 confirmed its continuation.

Since the beginning of the 1980s there have been changes stimulated by unrest amongst the students and intelligentsia and by pressure from leaders of the banned political parties, if not from the grass roots. The Royal Palace is still central, perhaps more so, but here, and in the government and the bureaucracy, there is what Seddon (1983) has called 'a new cast of thinking'. The essence of this new thinking, which can be seen clearly in the Sixth Five Year Plan (1980-85), is the so-called Basic Needs Strategy. This strategy, according to Seddon, owed much initially to the work of the international agencies and foreign donors. But it has been taken up by local politicians, bureaucrats, and the intelligentsia and has already produced some concrete results, including specific legislation on decentralisation and increased participation. What was seen by most observers as a bottom-up rhetoric early in the 1970s may become a part of the dynamic structure of the society.

Notwithstanding the impacts of the new thinking, some doubts have been expressed. First, in recent interviews the King himself has favoured free market economy forces: this is contradictory to the Basic Needs philosophy. The top ranks of the bureaucracy (including the military) are dominated by three castes, Brahmins, Chhetris and Newars, and this has been true for over 100 years (Beenhakker, 1973). Most come from Kathmandu Valley (in one estimate, nearly half of the entire civil service comes from this region which has only 5 per cent of the total national population). However, increasingly a meritocracy is emerging of what Blaikie et al. (1980) call 'modern bureaucrats' - those who have taken advantage of the new educational openings, including study abroad. These 'key' personnel have 'radical' new ideas which are already showing, for instance, in the Nepal Planning Commission. There remain many obstacles to this new thinking and action, notably inter-departmental rivalries, lack of vertical co-ordination, the poor quality and training of the middle level bureaucrat, the existence of a parallel foreign-manned bureaucracy in some sectors disguised as a 'counterpart system', and so on.

As important as any new directions at the centre may be, the new decentralisation process which put district-level officials in much closer contact with the panchayats and created new district organisations which group together workers, women, young people, and ex-servicemen. There are many problems, too, with the new decentralisation measures; for instance, continuing feuds and corruption in the panchayats and the continuing influence of a rural elite. Most influential panchayat positions (for example, Chairmen) were held by the larger upper-caste landowners in the 1960s and 1970s, except in those villages which are all low-caste. This power structure continues and has been cited as a major factor in inhibiting recent food distribution schemes in drought areas.

In terms of meeting basic needs the greatest difficulties can be expected in the health and education fields. There have been significant improvements but Nepal still spends much less (as a proportion of total expenditure) on such sectors as education, health, housing, community amenities, and social welfare, than many other countries. According to the 1984 World Bank Development Report (p.268) in 1981, 9.7 per cent of the total expenditure was devoted to education (11.5 per cent was the average for low-income countries), 4.1 per cent to health (a decline from 1972 when 4.4 per cent was the low-income country average), 1.5 per cent to housing and community amenities, social security, and welfare (6.1 per cent for all low-income countries). It is too early to predict whether these figures will improve after the new legislation and whether there will be many effects, but it must be an uphill struggle.

Most central government expenditure during the 1970s and 1980s (about 57 per cent) has gone into the economic sector, particularly agriculture, and in many observers' views, this has favoured the wealthier rural classes. Some Nepalese by the mid-1970s, however, were calling for 'an integrated rural development' and this idea was supported by a number of international agencies and foreign donors. The Agricultural Project Services Centre (APROSC) acquired a central role, and many programmes were directed toward the small farmer. There was a national 'Back to the Village' campaign and the co-operative movement (Sajha) took on new momentum. Blaikie et al. (1980) have claimed that the more general campaigns were largely rhetoric but specific programmes may have been more successful.

There has been particular criticism of the failure of decentralisation in the control of forests and common mountain land. In the 1970s the FAO had called for the vesting of ownership of forest lands in the village and for entrusting the village panchayats with their management in a context of land reform. Seddon (1983:193) has concluded that 'in the last ten years no such measures have been adopted, land reform has not been implemented, and what forms of cooperative and collective control over common resources were established have been systematically eroded rather than supported or encouraged'. A Sherpa may now have to walk four days to obtain permission to cut a tree. The traditional taboos, local consensus for conservation of forest resources, and local management practices have all probably declined in the face of a system with the panchayat as its centrepiece, which is not egalitarian. Some have blamed excess exploitation of the forests on the absence of enough 'people participation' in the panchayat system, and on the Nepalese process generally. The people themselves individually may have destroyed the forest, but this is because there is not an alternative means of ensuring collective (and with it, individual) well being.

Put another way, bottom-up processes cannot proceed if individuals take the law into their own hands, or behave selfishly; anarchy is no basis for development. The existing system, even when it purports to promote bottom-up development, does not do so unless local collective forms can emerge, and until there is an adequate communication process.

But are there no indigenous collective social forms? What place do women and young people have in this structure and process? What roles can they play?

The role and potential of traditional co-operatives have been described elsewhere (Pitt, 1970). These may remain outside the official ambit but despite, or because of, this may have a significant, if unrecognised potential. In Nepal co-operative groups become increasingly important in any switch from herding to cropping, where there may be more need for co-operative labour inputs. In such 'non-conventional' co-operative forms both women and young people play an important role. And women play a much greater role in health activities. Here, and in the analysis of the role of young people, there is a lack of data. There is certainly a growing literature on women in Nepal, both from expatriate researchers and local scholars. But the foreign works, at least in anthropology, reflect the biases of Western scholarship. For example, there is the obsession with kinship, originally mainly male but now concerned with the analysis of topics such as 'mother's milk and mother's blood', that is, with women's symbolic roles (Bennett, 1973).

None the less, there is a literature on women's roles in agriculture (Schroeder and Schroeder, 1979), and also in

215

maternal and child health (CWCC, 1980). The CWCC study has produced interesting materials on the role of women in child rearing in a number of castes and ethnic groups. For example, in the Sherpa community studied (Rolwaling) there was no diarrhea, partly, it seems, because nobody defecates or urinates near the water sources, and parents take pains to clean up the children's defecations. Nutrition in this community depends a good deal on potatoes, which are also fed at an early age to children. Infant and child mortality rates appear from both this and Sacherer's (1979, 1980) studies amongst this group to be low, and there is a high level of nutrition. Other factors may be the relatively later age at which women marry, the spacing of children, and breast-feeding.

In the Rolwaling village the role of women is important, but it should be noted it is not particularly collective. Women perform many tasks, even child-birth, without others. Much of what they do is based on the traditional oral knowledge system. Twenty per cent of the people, in fact, had learned to read and write from the lamas, but none of these were women, except for two anis (nuns). However, since 1972 there has been a school established by Sir Edmund Hillary's Himalaya Foundation and this has been enthusiastically received, and girls, who have apparently been impressed by the superiority of lady tourists, are going to school.

The role of women and young people in agricultural cooperatives shows how this kind of organisation may form the base for an upward internal generation of development, and even more interestingly, as a mechanism for crossing horizontal ethnic and caste lines. The official cooperative movement in Nepal has been described as a failure in one sense or another (Meserschmidt, 1981). Compulsory savings were the problem in the 1960s, 'faltering' administration in the 1970s, and outright official hostility in the 1980s, as the economic situation worsened. But most cooperatives in Nepal were neither officially inspired nor directed. They existed before, during and after the official programmes and in them women and young people were prominent, if not principal participants. Most commentators from Western societies have discussed co-operatives in terms of spheres of male influence and power. But it is hardly surprising that women and youth should be most active in the co-operatives since most of the work in Nepal is done by them. There are certainly some male-dominanted co-operatives in Nepal,

216

apart from the official ones; they include, for example, the temple associations (Greenwold, 1974).

Labour cooperatives are rather different. A well-described and typical example is the Gurung Nogar (Messerschmidt, 1981), which is a temporary village-level association of Gurung youth. Nogar, in fact, are occasionally all female, but the shortage of males has been explained by their absence on military service with the Gurkhas. Most Nogar members are in their teens and twenties, usually drawn from the rodi communal house. Rodi girls, in fact, invite boys to work with them. Rodis, it should be noted also, act as a means of uniting people from different villages. They also play an important role in courtship, focusing on the rodi-ghar (girls' sleeping dormitories). Nogars may also move across ethnic and caste lines. There are examples in the literature of non-Gurung blacksmiths (Kani) joining. There are records of exclusively untouchable Nogars (Pignede, 1966), and Tamang membership (Macfarlane, 1976). The fact that there are not more records, according to Messerschmidt (1981), is because scholars have never really looked at this phenomenon and because of the fact that caste groups live at some distance from each other. The poorest families have their own smaller co-operative activities.

Nogars seem to be very successful with great morale and bursts of energy. This positive, productive attitude, what Pignede (1966) calls the 'esprit de nogar' is a major driving force in the subsistence economy. Because Nogars are 'part of life', especially part of the marriage cycle, they encourage motivation. All this is part of the Gurung success. Other groups, however, may be less likely to co-operate successfully. An example is described in Doherty's (1975) study of the Brahmin and Chhetri castes where the woman's role is much less dominant.

CONCLUSIONS

Despite all the complexity, it is possible to draw several general conclusions. Some of these raise doubts about much of the accepted wisdom on the Himalayan crisis.

1. The environmental problem itself (erosion, deforestation) may seem to be slipping in importance, certainly in the views of local people.

2. The problems of subsistence and access to land

are becoming more pressing, though the role of debt in this may be a less disadvantageous factor (for local people) than burdens which are imposed from above and outside.

3. Women, children and young people do suffer most in a situation where wealth, power and prestige are to some degree male preserves and are assets which are distributed through top-down mechanisms.

4. This low status of women and children varies across different subcultural groups and in different situations. Some caste/ethnic groups are more egalitarian, and some young people are achieving mobility. Both women and young people are involved in co-operative, bottom-up activities.

5. It may be that the more traditional, in some cases lower, caste groups are faring better, despite, or possibly because of, their traditionality.

6. There is some evidence in Nepal, as in the Indian Himalaya, that women are the heralds and foot soldiers of the bottom-up movement, in which environment and health are major sectors. Hugging the trees is not only to be found in the Chipko movement (cf. Shiva and Bandyopadhyay, Chapter 8, pp.224-41). But in the Nepalese setting, the woman's role may be rather in health, especially child health, which remains quite traditional and sometimes very effective, especially amongst the sub-cultures of the high mountains. The recent improvements in infant mortality rates, therefore, may well be a sign of this growing role, as it has been in countries such as Western Samoa.

7. If women are a force in bottom-up developments, young people are more involved in linkages between top-down and bottom-up processes: what is here called the 'ping-pong model' process - because they are the migrants in body, and mind, and because they are prepared to change their attitudes and behaviours.

Some of these characteristics can be found in other parts of the Himalaya. For example, in Bhutan (World Bank, 1984b), though data are still very scanty, the traditional way still seems to be very strong. Urban development has been much slower than in Nepal, partly because of a government policy making sure that each district has its town. Subsistence agriculture dominates, is labour intensive (so that population increases are absorbed), and also is more of a male preserve. Land is apparently temporarily re-assigned to equalise the land-labour ratio. Labour is also exchanged within a matrilineal kinship system. According to FAO, there is no significant pressure on fuelwood sources. The absence of labour and forest problems has been partly due to government controls through compulsory employment practices and severe restrictions on commercial felling (from 1979), amounting to nationalisation. Tourism, too, has been greatly restricted, partly because there is a relatively small need for hard currency. Very little is known about the status of women and young people in Bhutan although, even compared to Nepal, a very small proportion are in school.

Certainly the World Bank report paints a relatively glowing picture of Bhutan and expresses surprise at finding a 'well-managed' economy and a much higher than expected overall standard of living, despite the retention of the traditional way of life. Not all indicators are so positive, of course - for instance, the infant mortality rate. But this rate itself may require closer scrutiny. If the total population of Bhutan is not known, it is unlikely that a far more socially sensitive figure, such as infant mortality, will be accurate. In any case, such rates are themselves partly a matter of cultural practices, as for example, in attitudes to handicapped babies. More important perhaps, infant mortality rates can be lowered dramatically (as the Samoan material shows) when women (through village committees) have more power. Bhutan, though matrilineal, is still patriarchal, particularly through the role of the monasteries.

In the Indian Himalayan region, women's movements of the Chipko kind have been a marked and well-publicised feature of recent history. This, however, has been less a sub-cultural social fact, in the sense of the preservation of tradition, rather than an assertion of power at the grass roots. It is populism rather than traditionalism with many political ramifications, notably a strategy to remain in the hill regions and confront the outside/top-down forces (Shiva and Bandyopadhyay, Chapter 8).

What are the implications of all this for policies which are designed to solve the Himalayan crisis? These can be quickly summarised or suggested.

1. The situation is extremely complex and may be becoming rapidly more complex. This may require more study, but since there is a flood of material now being produced, a much closer scrutiny of the information already available should be fed back into the general discussion and policy-making process.

2. Whatever action is taken an emphasis should be

directed at the possible future emergence of a supercrisis situation (food-wise) of the Ethiopian/Chad kind, especially in parts of Nepal, and other areas where there is a high risk of political instability. An early warning system is called for.

3.   Women and young people should receive more attention, not only to their plight but to their essential role in bottom-up development and in the 'ping-pong model'.

If it is not shortage of information, nor perceived lack of urgency, that is restraining research and action, what is? The sociology of the international agencies may be as important as the sociology of the Himalaya. Bitter conflicts and internecine manoeuvres have certainly slowed the process as international agencies jockey for power and funds in the Himalaya. A rumoured trust fund of several millions makes Himalayan research a sort of Eldorado. Some of the coyness is related (or so the agencies say) to the respect for local national governments and a desire not to offend anyone, though the credibility of this reason shrinks when one considers the foreign, counterpart, development empire, in Nepal at least. In any case, government opposition is not a problem. And there remains a huge arena of international population, environment, and development issues for which country experiences are illustrations and springboards for the new ideas that are needed to explain, and therefore to mitigate, the world-wide crisis of poverty.

REFERENCES

Acharya, M. and Bennett, L. (1983), Women and the Subsistence Sector, World Bank Staff Working Papers, no. 526, Washington, 140pp

APROSC (Agricultural Project Services Centre) (1978), Agrarian Reform and Rural Development in Nepal, Kathmandu, Nepal

ARTEP (1982), A Challenge to Nepal, ARTEP, Bangkok

Bajracharya, D. (1983), Deforestation in the food/fuel context: historical and political perspectives from Nepal, Mountain Research and Development, 3(3):227-40

Beenhakker, A. (1973), A Kaleidoscopic Circumspection of Development, Rotterdam University Press, Rotterdam

Bennett, L. (1973), Mother's Milk and Mother's Blood, PhD thesis, Columbia University

Blaikie, P., Cameron, J. and Seddon, D. (1980), Nepal in Crisis: Growth and Stagnation on the Periphery, Clarendon Press, Oxford, 311 pp.

Bouhdiba, A. (1982), Exploitation of Child Labour, United Nations, New York, 44pp.

Byers, A. (1986), A geomorphic study of man-induced soil erosion in the Sagarmatha (Mount Everest) National Park, Khumbu, Nepal, Mountain Research and Development, 6(1):83-7

Caplan, P. (1970), Land and Social Change in East Nepal, Routledge, Kegan Paul, London

CEDA (Centre for Economic Development and Administration) (1979), The Status of Women in Nepal, vol. 1, Kathmandu

CWCC (Child Welfare Coordinating Committee) and UNICEF (1980), Status of Children in Nepal, UNICEF, Kathmandu, 300pp.

Defence for Children (1982), Self Reliance, Defence for Children, Geneva, 251pp.

Doherty, V. (1975), Kinship and Economic Choice, PhD thesis, University of Wisconsin, Madison

Ehrich, R. (1980), Living Conditions and Potential Economic Activities of Women, German Agency for Technical Cooperation (GTZ) Ltd., Palampur

ESCAP (1984), Statistical Indicators (June), ESCAP, Bangkok

Goldstein, M.C., Ross, J.L. and Schuler, S. (1983), From a mountain-rural to a plains-urban society: implications of the 1981 Nepal census, Mountain Research and Development, 3(1):61-4

Greenwold, S. (1974), Monkhood versus priesthood in Newar Buddhism, in von Furer-Haimendorf, C. (ed.), Contributions to the Anthropology of Nepal, Aris and Phillips, pp.129-49

Ives, J.D. (1985), Yulongxue Shan, Northwest Yunnan, People's Republic of China: a geoecological expedition, Mountain Research and Development, 5(4):382-5

KHARDEP (1979), A Study of the Socioeconomy of the Kosi Hills, Surbiton, England

Macfarlane, A. (1976), Resources and Population, Cambridge University Press, 364 pp.

McNeely, J.A. and Pitt, D. (eds.) (1985), Culture and Conservation, Croom Helm, London, 308pp.

Mahat, T.B.S. (1985), Human Impact on Forests in the Middle Hills of Nepal, unpublished doctoral dissertation,

2 vols. Australian National University, Canberra

Messerschmidt, D. (1981), Nogar, Human Organization, 40(1): 40-7

Ministry of Education and Culture (Kathmandu) (1984), Recent Educational Development in Nepal, Kathmandu

Nabarro, D. (1984), Social, economic, health and environmental determinants of nutritional status, Food and Nutrition Bulletin, 6(1):18-32

Pignede, B. (1966), Les Gurungs, Mouton, Paris

Pitt, D.C. (1970), Tradition and Economic Progress, Clarendon Press, Oxford, 295 pp.

------ (1972), Identity, tradition and development, Civilisations, 23-4 (1/2):65-75

------ (1976), Social Dynamics of Development, Pergamon, Oxford, 162pp.

------ (1983), The socioeconomic context of migrants and minorities, Journal of Biosocial Science, Supplement 8:111-28

------ (1985), People, Resources, Environment and Development, UNEP/WG 134/3, Nairobi

Pitt, D. and Shah, A.A. (eds.) (1982), Child Labour, Defence for Children, Geneva, 86pp.

Sacherer, J. (1979), Practical Problems of Development in Two Panchayats of North-Central Nepal, SATA/IHDP, Kathmandu (mimeo), 113pp.

------ (1980), Health, Education, Nutrition and Family Planning Surveys, SATA/IHDP, Kathmandu, 43pp.

Schroeder, R. and Schroeder, E. (1979), Women in Nepali agriculture, Journal of Development and Administrative Studies, 1(2):178-92

Seddon, D. (1983), Nepal: a State of Poverty, Report to the ILO, Geneva, 198pp.

Shiva, V. and Bandyopadhyay, J. (1986), The evolution, structure and impact of the Chipko movement, Mountain Research and Development, 6(2):133-42

Shrestha, B.P. and Mosin, M. (1970), A Study in the Working of Gaon Panchayats, H.M.G. Panchayat Study Series, Volume II, Kathmandu, Nepal

Thompson, M. and Warburton, M. (1985a), Uncertainty on a Himalayan scale, Mountain Research and Development, 5(2):115-35

------ (1985b), Knowing where to hit it: a conceptual framework for sustainable development in the Himalaya, Mountain Research and Development, 5(3):203-20

UNCTAD (1981), <u>Preparatory Committee for the UN Conference on Least Developed Countries</u>, A/Conf/104/PC15

World Bank (1984a), <u>World Development Report</u>, World Bank, Washington, D.C. 286pp.

------ (1984b), <u>Bhutan</u>, World Bank, Washington, D.C. 177pp.

8

THE CHIPKO MOVEMENT

V. Shiva and J. Bandyopadhyay

Conflicts over forest resources in India are mainly a product of the opposing demands on these resources. They are generated by the requirements of conservation and the need to satisfy the basic living requirements of the marginalised majority, on the one hand, and the demands of commerce and industry, on the other. During the past century, there has been a progressive encroachment by the State on the rights and privileges of the people to forest resources. The people have resisted this encroachment in various parts of India mainly through the Gandhian non-cooperation method of protest, well known as 'Forest Satyagraha'. In the forest areas of the Garhwal Himalaya this style of protest was revived in independent India as the 'Chipko' or 'Embrace-the-Tree' movement to protect trees marked for felling. Although Chipko was first practised in the Garhwal Himalaya, it has now spread to most of the country, especially the hilly regions.

This paper will examine the philosophical and organisational continuity of the Chipko Movement with the Indian tradition of resolving conflicts through non-violent non-cooperation, a political strategy revived by Mahatma Gandhi and adopted by the Gandhian workers in all parts of the country. The Chipko Movement, however, is unique in a fundamental way. Although it had its roots in a movement based on the politics of the distribution of the benefits of resources, it soon became an ecological movement rooted in the politics of the distribution of ecological costs. Further, though the visible leaders of the movement are men, the strength of the movement lies in the support from women.

The paper will analyse the subjective and objective

factors that account for the rapid spread of the movement. Finally, an assessment of its impact at the national and global levels will be made. Chipko, as a model for the resolution of conflicts over natural resources in general, will be examined.

CONFLICTS OVER FOREST RESOURCES AND THE EVOLUTION OF THE CHIPKO MOVEMENT

The conflicts and tension from which the famous Chipko Movement has emerged can be traced historically to the drastic changes in forest management and utilisation introduced into India during the colonial period. Forests, like other vital resources, were managed traditionally as common resources with strict, though informal, social mechanisms for controlling their exploitation to ensure sustained productivity. In addition to the large tracts of natural forests that were maintained through this careful husbanding, village forests and woodlots were also developed and maintained through the deliberate selection of appropriate tree species. Remnants of commonly managed natural forests and village commons still exist in pockets and these provide insights into the scientific basis underlying traditional land management (Moench and Bandyopadhyay, 1985; Shiva and Bandyopadhyay, 1985).

Colonial impact on forest management undermined these conservation strategies in two ways. First, changes in land tenure, such as the introduction of the zamindari system, transformed common village resources into the private property of newly created landlords and this led to their destruction. The pressure of domestic needs, no longer satisfied by village forests and grasslands, were, therefore, diverted to natural forests. Second, large-scale fellings in natural forests to satisfy non-local commercial needs, such as shipbuilding for the British Royal Navy and sleepers (railroad ties) for the expanding railway network in India, created an extraordinary force for destruction. After about half a century of uncontrolled exploitation the need for control slowly became apparent. The formation of the forest bureaucracy and the reservation of forest areas was the colonial response to ensure control of commercial forest exploitation as a means to maintain revenues. Forest conservancy was directed at the conservation of forest revenues and not at the forests themselves. This narrow

225

interpretation of conservation generated severe conflicts at two levels. At the level of utilisation, the new management system catered only to commercial demands and ignored local basic needs. People were denied their traditional rights which, in some cases, were re-introduced as concessions and privileges after prolonged struggles (Bandyopadhyay et al., 1984). At the conservation level, since the new forest management was only concerned with stable forest revenues and not with the stability of forest ecosystems, ecologically unsound silviculture practices were introduced. This undermined biological productivity of forest areas and transformed renewable resources into non-renewable ones (Nair, 1985).

The reservation of forests and the denial of the villagers' right of access led to the creation of resistance movements in all parts of the country. The Forest Act of 1927 intensified the conflicts and the 1930s witnessed widespread forest satyagrahas as a mode of non-violent resistance to the new forest laws and policies.

SATYAGRAHA AS A NON-VIOLENT MODE OF CONFLICT RESOLUTION

Satyagraha, in the Gandhian view, was the use of non-violent resistance as a political weapon in place of the force of arms. Unlike many other well-known political philosophies, Gandhian philosophy has never been claimed to be strictly materialist. In the absence of such overt categorisation, Gandhian philosophy usually has been assumed to be based on subjective, idealist, or moral forces, rather than objective or materialist ones. Accordingly, the most important political weapon used in the Gandhian movements, the satyagraha, has always been mystified as an emotional force without any materialist base. A closer socio-historical evaluation is needed to de-mystify the image of Gandhian satyagrahas and to establish the materialist basis of Gandhian movements such as Chipko.

The power of satyagraha in the form of non-cooperation, has been a traditional mode of protest against exploitative authority in India. In Hind Swaraj, Gandhi wrote that through satyagraha he was merely carrying forward an ancient tradition: 'In India the nation at large had generally used passive resistance in all departments of life. We cease to cooperate with our rulers when they displease us'.

The dominance of the use of moral force was not, however, an indicator of their non-material objectives of these movements. The strong material basis of the Gandhian movements becomes visible after a detailed analysis of the concrete issues and contradictions for the settlements of which the satyagrahas were taken up. Satyagrahas were used by Gandhiji against systems of material exploitation which were the main tools for profit-making of the British, and in which was rooted the material under-development of the Indian masses. It was used in Champaran to save Indian peasants from the compulsory cultivation of indigo in place of foodcrops. It was used in Dandi and in other parts of the country to protest against the exploitative Salt Law. It was used to safeguard the interests of the Indian weavers who were pauperised by the unequal competition with mill-made cloth from Europe. It was used by forest movements to resist the denial of traditional rights. Unfortunately, in spite of the fact that Gandhian satyagrahas were used to oppose the economic system that created material poverty and underdevelopment, usually they have been described and understood as non-material and spiritual transformations without any materialist base. This common perception of Gandhian movements as unrelated to the material contradictions in society is completely fallacious. The subjective and spiritual nature of the force of satyagraha has systematically been confused with the material and objective contradictions in society against which the force was used.

The classical view of the contradiction between the working class and the capitalists has dominated the attempts at analysing the class relations in contemporary Indian society. The deeper and more severe contradictions that touch upon the lives of the vast number of people, based on the contradiction between the economics of sustainable development and capitalist production for profit-making and economic growth, is hardly perceived or recognised. Gandhiji had focused his attention on these more fundamental and severe material contradictions in Indian society since he understood the problem of the invisible and marginalised majority in India. The material basis for survival of this marginalised majority was threatened by the resource demands of the capitalist production system introduced into India by the British. In this manner, without making any claims about being materialistic, Gandhiji

227

politicised the most severe material contradictions of his time.

FROM FOREST SATYAGRAHA TO THE CHIPKO MOVEMENT

The years 1930-31 witnessed the spread of forest satyagrahas throughout India as a protest against the reservation of forests for exclusive exploitation by British commercial interests and its concomitant transformation of a common resource into a commodity. Villagers ceremonially removed forest products from the reserved forests to assert their right to satisfy their basic needs. The forest satyagrahas were especially successful in regions where survival of the local population was intimately linked with access to the forests, as in the Himalaya, the Western Ghats, and the Central Indian hills. These non-violent protests were suppressed by the British rulers. In Central India, Gond tribals were gunned down for participating in the satyagraha. On 30 May 1930 dozens of unarmed villagers were killed and hundreds injured in Tilari village, Tehri Garhwal, when they gathered to protest the Forest Laws.

After enormous loss of life, the satyagrahas were successful in reviving some of the traditional rights of the village communities to various forest products.

This, however, did not mean that satisfaction of the basic requirements of the people, or the ecological role of the forests, replaced the revenue maximising objectives as the guiding principle of British forest management in India. Furthermore, the objective of growth in financial terms continues to direct contemporary forest management in post-Independence India with even greater ruthlessness, since it is now carried out in the name of 'national interest' and 'economic growth'. The cost of achieving this growth has been the destruction of forest ecosystems and huge losses through floods and droughts. In ecologically sensitive regions, such as the Himalaya, this destruction has threatened the survival of the forest-dwelling communities. The people's response to this deepening crisis has emerged as non-violent Gandhian resistance: the Chipko Movement. Beginning in the early 1970s in the Garhwal region of Uttar Pradesh, the methodology and philosophy of Chipko has now spread to Himachal Pradesh in the north, to Karnataka in the south, to Rajasthan in the west, to Bihar in the east, and to the Vindhyas in Central India.

LEGACY OF FOREST MOVEMENTS IN GARHWAL HIMALAYA

Forest resources are the critical ecological elements in the vulnerable Himalayan ecosystem. The natural broad-leaved and mixed forests have been central in maintaining water and soil stability under conditions of heavy seasonal rainfall. They have also provided the most significant input for sustainable agriculture and animal husbandry in the hills. Undoubtedly, the forests provide the material basis for the whole agro-pastoral economy of the hill villages.

Green leaves and grass satisfy the fodder requirement of the farm animals whose dung provides the only source of nutrients for food crops. Dry twigs and branches are the only source of domestic cooking fuel. Agricultural implements and house frames require forest timber. The forests also provide large amounts of fruit, edible nuts, fibres and herbs for local consumption.

During the nineteenth century a third demand was put on these forest resources of Garhwal. In 1850 an Englishman, Mr Wilson, obtained a lease to exploit all the forests of the Kingdom of Tehri-Garhwal for the small annual rental of 400 rupees. Under his axe several valuable Deodar and Chir forests were clear-felled and completely destroyed (Raturi, 1932). In 1864, inspired by Mr Wilson's flourishing timber business, the British rulers of the northwestern provinces took a lease for 20 years and engaged Wilson to exploit the forests for them. European settlements, such as Mussoorie, created new pressures for the cultivation of food crops, leading to large-scale felling of oak forests. Conservation of the forests was not considered. In his report on the forests of the state, E.A. Courthope, IFS, remarked: 'It seems possible that it was not mainly with the idea of preserving the forests that government entered into this contract' (Raturi, 1932). In 1895 the Tehri State took the management of forests in its own hands when they realised their great economic importance from the example of Mr Wilson and the government. Between 1897 and 1899 forest areas were reserved and restrictions were placed on village use. These restrictions were much disliked and utterly disregarded by the villagers, and led to cases of organised resistance

Figure 8.1: The evolution of the Chipko Movement

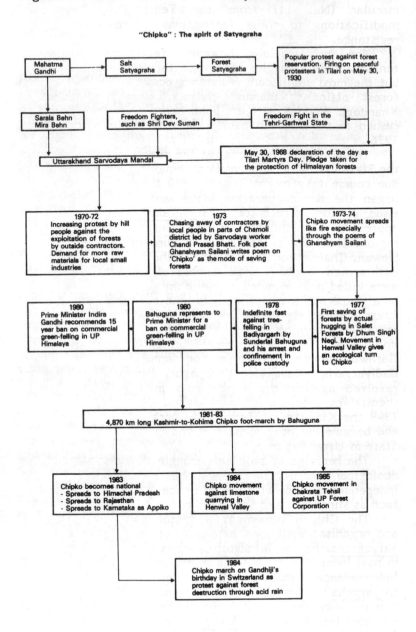

"Chipko" : The spirit of Satyagraha

against authority (Raturi, 1932). On 31 March 1905 a Durbar circular (No. 11) from the Tehri King announced modifications to these restrictions in response to the resistance.

The modifications, however, failed to diffuse the tension. Small struggles took place throughout the kingdom, but the most significant resistance occurred in 1907 when a forest officer, Sadanand Gairola, was manhandled in Khandogi. When King Kirti Shah heard about the revolt he rushed to the spot to pacify the citizens (Bhaktadarshan, 1976).

The contradiction between the people's basic needs and the State's revenue requirements remained unresolved and in due course they intensified. In 1930 the people of Garhwal began the non-cooperation movement mainly around the issue of forest resources. Satyagraha to resist the new oppressive forest laws was most intense in the Rawain region. The King of Tehri was in Europe at that time. His Dewan, Chakradhar Jayal, crushed the peaceful satyagraha with armed force. A large number of unarmed Satyagrahis were killed and wounded, while many others lost their lives in a desperate attempt to cross the rapids of the Yamuna River. While the right of access to forest resources remained a burning issue in the Garhwal Kingdom, the anti-imperialist freedom movement in India invigorated the Garhwali people's movement for democracy. The Saklana, Badiyargarh, Karakot, Kirtinagar, and other regions revolved against the King's rule in 1947 and declared themselves independent panchayats. Finally on 1 August 1949 the Kingdom of Tehri was liberated from feudal rule and became an integral part of the Union of India and the State of Uttar Pradesh.

The heritage of political struggle for social justice and ecological stability in Garhwal was strengthened in post-Independence India with the influence of eminent Gandhians, such as Mira Behn and Sarala Behn.

The Chipko Movement is, historically, philosophically and organisationally, an extension of traditional Gandhian Satyagraha. Its special significance is that it is taking place in post-Independence India. The continuity between the pre-Independence and post-Independence forms of this satyagraha has been provided by Gandhians, such as Sri Dev Suman, Mira Behn, and Sarala Behn. Sri Dev Suman was initiated into Gandhian Satyagraha at the time of the Salt Satyagraha. He died as a martyr for the cause of the

Garhwali people's right to survive with dignity and freedom. Both Mira Behn and Sarala Behn were close associates of Gandhiji. After his death, they both moved to the interior of the Himalaya and established ashrams. Sarala Behn settled in Kumaun and Mira Behn lived in Garhwal until her departure for Vienna due to ill health. Equipped with the Gandhian world-view of development based upon justice and ecological stability, they contributed silently to the growth of woman-power and ecological consciousness in the hill areas of Uttar Pradesh. Sunderlal Bahuguna is prominent among the new generation of workers deeply inspired by these Gandhians. Influenced by Sri Dev Suman, he joined the Independence Movement at the age of 13. Now, at nearly 60, he is busy strengthening the philosophical base of the Chipko Movement from the Gandhian view of nature. The rapid spread of resistance, based on the Movement, in the hills of Uttar Pradesh and its success in enforcing changes in forest management was largely due to the awareness created by folk poets, such as Chanshyam Raturi, and grass-roots organisational efforts of a number of activists, such as Chandi Prasad Bhatt in Chamoli and Dhoom Singh Negi in Tehri Garhwal.

The Gandhian movement in Garhwal in the post-Independence period had organised itself around three central issues: (1) organisation of women power; (2) struggle against the liquor menace; and (3) the forest problem. The organisational platform for the Chipko Movement was ready, therefore, when in the 1960s destruction of Himalayan forests through commercial exploitation became the major cause of ecological instability in the Himalaya. Since forest exploitation was carried out by private contractors, the Movement, in its initial stages, attempted to stop the auctioning of forests for felling by contractors. Auctions were held up by protestors in Nainital, Dehradun, Narendranagar, Tehri and Uttarkashi. Songs by the folk poet Ghanashyam Raturi were central to the mobilisation of support for these protests. The songs reminded the hill people of their forest-based culture and created an environment within which the hill people became more aware of the need for forest protection. In particular, one popular folk-song by Raturi, written in 1973, identifies embracing the trees as a method of saving them from the axe men. It is this cultural and political climate and heritage which marks the birth of the now famous Chipko Movement.

There has been a lot of confusion in the search for the originator of the Chipko Movement. However, the Movement is not the conceptual creation of any one individual. It is the expression of an old social consciousness in a new context. Chipko, like the earlier forest satyagrahas and movements in Garhwal, is aimed jointly at protecting forests, preserving a culture, and maintaining livelihoods. It is the response of a whole culture to the central problems related to the survival of the hill people. Today, the women of Garhwal are the main bearers of this culture.

This is the primary reason why the contemporary struggle to save the survival base in the Himalaya is led by the women. The first Chipko action took place spontaneously in April 1973, when the villagers demonstrated against felling of ash trees in Mandal forest. Again, in March 1974, 27 women under the leadership of Goura Devi saved a large number of trees from a contractor's axe. After this, the government stopped the contract system of felling and formed the Uttar Pradesh Forest Corporation. During the next five years Chipko resistance to felling took place in various parts of Garhwal Himalaya. In May 1977 Chipko activists in Henwal Valley organised themselves for future action. In June 1977 Sarala Behn planned a meeting of all activists in the hill areas of Uttar Pradesh State which further strengthened the movement and consolidated the resistance to commercial fellings as well as excessive tapping of resin from the Chir pine trees. In Gotars forest in the Tehri range the forest ranger was transferred because of his inability to control illegal over-tapping of resin. Consciousness was so high that, in the Joidanda area of Saklana range, the public sector agency, Garhwal Mandal Vikas Nigam, was asked to regulate its resin-tapping activity.

Among the numerous instances of Chipko successes through the Garhwal Himalaya in the years to follow, the instances in Adwani, Amarsar, and Badiargarh merit special mention. The auction of Adwani forests took place in October 1977 in Narendernagar, the district headquarters. Bahuguna undertook a fast against the auction and appealed to the forest contractors and the district authorities to refrain from auctioning the forests. The auction was undertaken despite the expression of popular discontent. In the first week of December 1977, the Adwani forests were scheduled to be felled. Large groups of women led by Bachhni Devi came forward to save the forests.

Interestingly, Bachhni Devi was the wife of the local village head, who was himself a contractor. Dhoom Singh Negi supported the women's struggle by undertaking a fast in the forest itself. The women tied sacred threads to the trees as a token of a vow of protection. Between 13 and 20 December large numbers of women from 15 villages guarded the forests while discourses on the role of forests in Indian life from ancient texts went on non-stop. It was here in Advani that the ecological slogan 'What do the forests bear? soil, water and pure air' was born.

The axe-man withdrew only to return on 1 February 1978 with two truckloads of the armed police. The plan was to encircle the forests with the help of the police in order to keep the people away during the felling operation. Even before the police reached the area the volunteers of the Movement entered the forest and explained their case to the forest labourers who had been brought in from far distant places. By the time the contractors arrived with the policemen each tree was being guarded by three embracing volunteers. The police, having been defeated in their own plan and seeing the awareness among the people, hastily withdrew before nightfall.

In March 1978 a new auction was planned in Narendranagar. A large popular demonstration took place against it and the police arrested 23 Chipko volunteers, including women. In December 1978 a large felling was planned by the public sector U.P. Forest Development Corporation in the Badiyargarh area. The local people instantly informed Bahuguna who started a fast unto death at the felling site. On the eleventh day of his fast Bahuguna was arrested in the middle of the night and taken to jail. This act only served to futher steel the commitment of the people. Folk poet Ghanashyam Raturi and priest Khima Shastri led the movement as thousands of men and women from all villages around joined them in the Badiyargarh forests. The people remained in the forests and guarded the trees for eleven days, when the contractors withdrew.

The cumulative impact of the sustained grass-roots struggles to protect the forests was a re-thinking of the forest management strategy in the hill areas. The Chipko demand for declaration of Himalayan forests as protection forests instead of production forests for commercial exploitation was recognised at the highest policy-making level. The late Prime Minister, Indira Gandhi, after meeting with Bahuguna, issued a directive for a 15-year ban on commercial green felling in the Himalayan forests of Uttar Pradesh.

ECOLOGICAL FOUNDATION OF THE CHIPKO MOVEMENT

Both the earlier forest satyagrahas and their contemporary form, the Chipko Movement, have arisen from conflicts over forest resources and are similar cultural responses to forest destruction. What differentiates Chipko from the earlier struggle is its ecological basis. The new concern to save and protect forests through Chipko Satyagraha did not arise from a resentment against further encroachment on the people's access to forest resources. It arose from the alarming signals of rapid ecological destabilisation in the hills. Villages that were self-sufficient in food had to resort to food imports as a result of declining food productivity. This, in turn, was related to the reduction of soil fertility in the forests. Water sources began to dry up as the forests disappeared. The so-called 'natural disasters', such as floods and landslides, began to occur in river systems which had hitherto been stable. The Alaknanda disaster of July 1970 inundated 1,000 km^2 of land in the hills and washed away many bridges and roads. In 1977 the Tawaghat tragedy took an even heavier toll. In 1978 the Bagirathi blockade above Uttarkashi resulted in massive floods across the entire Gangetic plains.

The over-exploitation of forest resources and the resulting threat to communities living in the forests have thus evolved from concerns for distribution of material benefits to concerns for distribution of ecologically-generated material costs. At the first stage, the growth of commercial interests resulted in efforts to exclude competing demands. The commercial exploitation of India's forest resources thus created the need for a forest legislation which denied village communities' access to forest resources. The forest satyagrahas of the 1930s were a result of the Forest Act of 1927 which denied the people access to biomass for survival while increasing biomass production for industrial and commercial growth. The growth imperative, however, drove production for commercial purposes into the second stage of conflict which is at the ecological level. Scientific and technical knowledge of forestry generated in the existing model of forest management is limited to viewing forests only as sources of commercial timber. This gives rise to prescriptions for forest management which are manipulations to maximise immediate growth of commercial wood. This is achieved initially by the destruction of other biomass forms that have lower commercial value but may be very important to the people, or have great ecological significance. The silvicultural system of modern forestry embraces prescriptions for destruction of non-commercial biomass forms to ensure the increased production of commercial forms. The encouragement given to the replacement of ecologically valuable oak forests by commercially valuable conifers is an indicator of this shift. Ultimately, this increase in production may be described as mining of the ecological capital of the forest ecosystems which have evolved through thousands of years.

The contemporary Chipko Movement, which has become a national campaign, is the result of these multi-dimensional conflicts over forest resources at the scientific, technical, economic and especially the ecological levels. It is not a narrow conflict over the local or non-local distribution of forest resources, such as timber and resin. The Chipko demand is not for a bigger share for the local people in the immediate commercial benefits of an ecologically destructive pattern of forest resource exploitation. Since the Chipko Movement is based upon the perception of forests in their ecological context, it exposes the social and ecological costs of growth-oriented forest management. This is clearly seen in the slogan of the Chipko Movement which claims that the main products of the forests are not timber or resin, but soil and water. Basic biomass needs of food, fuel, fodder, small timber and fertiliser can, in the Chipko vision and the Garhwal practice, be satisfied as positive externalities of biomass production primarily aimed at soil and water conservation to stabilise the local agro-pastoral economy.

The Chipko Movement has been successful in forcing a fifteen-year ban on commercial green-felling in the hills of Uttar Pradesh, in stopping clear-felling in the Western Ghats and the Vindhyas, and in generating pressure for a national forest policy which is more sensitive to the people's needs and to the ecological requirements of the country. Unfortunately, the Chipko Movement has often been naively presented by vested interests as a reflection of a conflict between 'development' and 'ecological concern', implying that 'development' relates to material and objective bases of life while 'ecology' is concerned with non-material and subjective factors, such as scenic beauty. The deliberate introduction of this false and dangerous dichotomy between 'development' and 'ecology' disguises the real dichotomy between ecologically sound development and unsustainable and ecologically destructive economic growth. The latter is always achieved through destruction of life-support systems and material deprivation of marginal communities. Genuine development can only be based on ecological stability which ensures sustainable supplies of vital resources. Gandhi and his later disciples, Mira Behn and Sarala Behn, clearly described how and why development is not necessarily contradictory to ecological stability. Conflict between exploitive economic growth and ecological development implies that, by questioning the destructive process of growth, ecological movements like Chipko are never an obstacle to the process of development. On the contrary, by constantly keeping ecological stability in focus, they provide the best guarantee for ensuring a stable material basis for life.

ECOLOGICAL DEVELOPMENT OR ECO-DEVELOPMENT?

The philosophical confusion created by taking sectoral growth as synonymous with development, however, has permeated movements such as Chipko. There is a growing tension between two streams of the Chipko Movement; one, guided by the ecological world-view of Sunderlal Bahuguna, and the other, represented by the eco-development model of Chandi Prasad Bhatt (Agarwal, 1982; Gadgil, 1984).

The Bahuguna philosophy is based on the ecological thesis that protection of livelihood and economic productivity is directly dependent on the maintenance of the life-support systems. The contemporary economic crises can be solved only by directly addressing the ecological crises symptomised by the destabilisation of the hydrological system and the disruption of nutrient cycles. Ecological rehabilitation of the hill areas is the primary task, and this involves a temporary moratorium on green-felling for commercial objectives, both local and non-local, to facilitate regeneration. Economic development in this perspective can only be based on minimising the ecological costs of growth while maximising the sustainable productivity of nature for the satisfaction of primary human needs.

The eco-development model of Bhatt (1980) is based on the acceptance of present modes of resource utilisation with a new emphasis on the location of manufacturing activities in the hill areas and strengthening of their raw material base. This model explains poverty as the absence of processing industries and not in the impoverishment of the environment. Poverty is seen by Bhatt as having a technological solution, in contrast to Bahuguna who sees the solution to poverty in the ecological rebuilding of nature's productivity. For Bahuguna, material benefits arise from lowering ecological costs due to resource destruction and increasing productivity of natural and man-made systems. For Bhatt, material benefits are not seen in the perspective of essential ecological processes. The instruments of production do not include nature and its ecological processes, and productivity is defined through the technological productivity of labour alone. In this respect Bhatt's model is subsumed by the dominant development paradigm which equates economic growth with social and economic development. The development prescription is that, 'with the help of modern scientific knowledge the instruments of production are improved and the standard of living is raised' (Bhatt, 1980). Co-operative felling and the use of trees by the local people can provide employment and thus regenerate the hill economy (Kowal, 1984). There is no consideration of ecological limits to commercial exploitation of natural resources in order to sustain the productivity of nature; water, for instance, whose economic significance is immense, is ignored in modern economic analysis.

The absence of an ecological perspective in the eco-development model results in the neglect of special strategies to regenerate and stabilise vital soil and water resources. It also leads to failure to assess the impact of other economic activities, including afforestation programmes, on the essential processes of soil and water conservation. The political economy of eco-development is based upon a new distribution of the goods produced by the existing resource-intensive and resource-wasteful technologies. In contrast, the political economy of ecological development is based on the distribution of both the benefits and the costs created through ecological disruption. It involves a development shift to resource-prudent and resource-conserving technologies which are more productive at the systems level.

In the ecological view, the old restricted notion of productivity as an increase of labour productivity is counterproductive at two levels. At the resource level, it consumes more resources to produce less useful goods. At the human level, it displaces labour in a labour-surplus context and thus destroys livelihoods instead of creating them. Gandhi critically articulated the fallacy of increasing labour productivity independent of the social and material context. Gandhi's followers in the Chipko Movement continue to critically evaluate restricted notions of productivity. It is this concern with resources and human needs that is captured in Bahuguna's well-known slogan that 'ecology is permanent economy'.

Growth for its own sake has been the overriding concern in resource use in India in the past. The threat to survival from ecological disruption is becoming the major concern in resource use for the future. And human survival in sensitive ecosystems, such as the Himalaya, is more severely threatened than elsewhere. The urgency to establish a new economy of permanence based on ecological principles is created with each environmental disaster in the Himalayan region which spells destruction throughout the Ganges basin. Chipko's search for a strategy for survival has global implications. What Chipko is trying to conserve is not merely local forest resources but the entire life-support system, and with it the option for human survival. Gandhi's mobilisation for a new society, where neither man nor nature is exploited and destroyed, was the beginning of this civilisational response to a threat to human survival. Chipko's agenda is the carrying forward of that vision against the heavier odds of contemporary crises. Its contemporary relevance, and its significance for the future world, is clearly indicated in the rapid spread of the ecological world view throughout the whole Himalaya, following the historical 5,000-km trans-Himalaya Chipko footmarch led by Bahuguna, and subsequently through other vulnerable mountain systems such as the Western Ghats, Central India and Aravalli.

Since the ecological crises threaten survival irrespective of the industrial status of societies, the philosophical significance of re-directing development onto an ecologically sustainable path relates to the industralised North as much as to countries of the South. This is why the ecological strategy of Chipko finds new application in the people's movement in European countries such as Switzerland, Germany, and Holland. The spread of the message of an alternate world-view is crucial to the creation of a sustainable world, particularly in the context of a highly integrated global economic system. The ecological world-view of Chipko provides a strategy for survival not only for tiny villages in the Garhwal Himalaya, but for all human societies threatened by environmental disasters.

ACKNOWLEDGEMENTS

The analysis and information presented here has evolved from a decade of interaction with the Chipko Movement. Participation in Chipko footmarches in the Garhwal Himalaya and in the Western Ghats has provided the experience for understanding the ecological crises more clearly. The firsthand opportunity to live with, and learn from, the rural people in the Chipko areas has led to major shifts in perception and has corrected many mistaken assumptions about resources and development. Opportunities of close interaction with Sarala Behn, Sunderlal Bahuguna, Vimala Bahuguna, Visveswar Dutt Saklani, Ghanashyam Raturi, and Dhum Sing Negi, have helped us appreciate the strength of non-violent satyagraha, not merely as a political weapon, but as a life-style.

REFERENCES

Agarwil Anil (1982), The State of India's Environment, Centre for Science and Environment, New Delhi, 42pp.

Bahuguna, S. (1976), Bagi Tehri Ki Ek Jhanki, in Bhaktdarshan (ed.), Suman Smriti Granth, Parvatiya Navjeeven Mandal, Silyara, Tehri-Garhwal

Bandyopadhyay, J. et al. (1984), The Doon Valley Ecosystem: A Report on the Natural Resource Utilisation in Doon Valley. Department of Environment of the Government of India, New Delhi, pp.17-18

Bhaktadarshan (1976), Suman Smriti Granth, Sunderlal Bahuguna, Silyara, 228pp.

Bhatt, Chandi Prasad (1980), Ecosystem of the Central Himalaya, Dasholi Gram Swarajya Mandal, Gopeshwar, 32pp.

Gadgil Madhav (1984), Whither Environmental Activism, Deccan Herald, Bangalore, February 19, 1984

Kowal, Torsten M. (1984), Environmentalism and Forest Management in the Garhwal Himalaya, Report of the School of Environmental Sciences, University of East Anglia, United Kingdom, 15pp.

Moench, N. and Bandyopadhyay, J. (1985), Local needs and forest resource management in the Himalaya, in Bandyopadhyay, J. et al. (eds.), India's Environment: Crisis and Responses, Natraj Publishers, Dehradun, pp.52-77

Nair, C.T.S. (1985), Crisis in forest resource management, in Bandyopadhyay, J. et al. (eds.), India's Environment: Crises and Responses, Natraj Publishers, Dehradun, pp.7-25

Raturi, Padma Dutt (1932), Working Plan of the Jamuna Forest Division, Tehri Garhwal State, Tehri, pp.48-51

Shiva, Vandana and Bandyopadhyay, J. (1985), Ecological Audit of Eucalyptus Cultivation in Rainfed Regions, English Book Depot, Dehradun, in press

9

CONCLUSION

M.E.D. Poore

It is time for a positive approach to deforestation. There has been much public concern and alarm about some aspects of the problem. The possibility exists that the end of the century will see serious shortages in the supply of industrial wood; the catastrophic erosion and floods accompanying the stripping of forests from mountainous land - especially in the Andes and the Himalayas; the acute shortages of fuelwood in much of the developing world; the spread of desert conditions at an alarming rate in the arid and semi-arid regions of the world; and the many environmental effects of the destruction of tropical rain forests.

These issues, all connected with the destruction or mismanagement of forest lands and forest resources, have tended to breed an attitude of despair and fatalism about the inevitability of it all. This is the way it has always gone; nothing seems to stop the rot. This is why we are deliberately focussing on replenishment rather than deforestation. We hope to instil a sense of urgency and purpose in place of the prevailing pessimism. For there are some bright patches in the clouds, there is action; some constructive measures are being taken. If these actions could be expanded and multiplied, there need be no problem. Can it be done?

Most of the history of mankind seems to have consisted in driving back the boundaries of the forest - first for grazing land and shifting cultivation, then for permanent agriculture. Most of our present cultivated and inhabited lands have been derived from forest; we owe most of our prosperity and civilisation to the stored fertility of forest soils. In favourable sites - such as the deltas of the Mekong

242

and Nile, or on the fertile volcanic soils of Java, the agricultural experiment has been successful. In unsuitable sites, on the other hand, it has led to land degradation; and in some, over-exploitation has been shown to cause catastrophic erosion and the collapse of civilisations, as that of the Mayans in Guatemala. Forests, too, have been, for centuries, creamed of their desirable species; and this has sometimes led to the near-extermination of some varieties. The cedars of Lebanon and of Cyprus were an early and notorious example.

In fact forests have too often been looked upon as a source of free goods - of unlimited wealth that could be tapped at will. Forest soils were there to be cleared and tilled; timber, fuelwood, animals for meat and skins, and other forest produce were there to be harvested. The numerous environmental benefits - the moderation of local climates, clear and regular water, freedom from soil erosion, protection from avalanches and abundant wild nature - were just part of the natural order of things and taken for granted.

The values of forests only began to be appreciated when they had nearly disappeared - this seems a sad but recurrent characteristic of human nature. Occasionally a warning was sounded in advance by some far-sighted observer (you may remember that remarkable passage about the ravaged forests of Attica in Plato's Kritias); but people seldom took notice until too late. Greek foresters are only now working to undo the damage done in the 3rd century BC. Sustained management only began in English woodlands in the Middle Ages when just enough woodlands were left to meet the needs of local markets. The Swiss forest law was passed in the late 19th century in response to the alarming effects of over-exploitation of the forests in the alpine valleys. Forest restoration began in Cyprus at much the same time as a reaction to the devastated state of the forest there, found by the incoming British administration. Each of these was a local reaction and confined to the forest values considered important at that place and time - timber supply, soil erosion, water, danger of avalanches.

Little has changed in the world of today. It is to the forest that people look for new, fertile soils to open up for agriculture. A substantial part of the published 'production' figures for timber are not, as in agriculture, the regularly expected annual yield (or production in the true sense), but the first cut from previously unexploited virgin forest. And

243

this deception applies not only to the tropical rain forest but also to the coniferous boreal forests. Forests have been, and often still are, mined with little thought for the future, used as 'an instant withdrawal account producing vital foreign exchange via timber'.

When capital has for centuries been used as income, there comes a day of reckoning - and a need to invest once again.

Forestry has very much to offer in a world where population is pressing against resources. Trees are, at one and the same time, a source of renewable material and of renewable energy. They are equally important to simple, rural communities (for fuel, construction, tools, fodder, shade and many other uses) as to industrial man. As a construction material, wood uses one-ninth of the energy of concrete, one-sixteenth that of cast iron and one-thirty-ninth that of aluminium. Moreover, if forest land is managed well and with restraint, it can yield valuable produce while continuing to provide its many environmental benefits.

The author is convinced that we need a fundamental change of attitude from those with the power and the money - towards looking upon forests as a capital reserve of natural wealth, and reforestation as a long-term investment in the future; a change from exploitation to resource building. Sustainable use should become the rule in forest management rather than alternating phases of plunder and emergency remedial treatment.

The time has come to build up this wealth again. This will require massive investment, some of it with an apparently low rate of return. If treated with patience, restraint and careful management, the trees themselves do most of the work. One has only to look at Switzerland or Cyprus today to see the advantages of a century of forest renewal. Surely no one would accuse the Almighty of a bad investment when He created the dipterocarp forests of Asia.

There are many open questions. Can we conquer inertia and vested interests? Can we marshal the investment, the organisation, the consistency of policy, the trained manpower? Have we the vision and environmental statesmanship? The questions are left with you.

INDEX

afforestation 106, 124
age groups 183
agriculture 77, 92, 99, 103
  agricultural land 59
  cropping 76, 77, 78, 146
  production rates 193
associations 182
Australia 81, 84, 85, 87, 88, 90
Azad Kashmir Hill Farming Technical Development Project 163

Bahuguna 5, 237
  see also Chipko
basic needs 203
  see also food, health, water, nutrition, etc.
Bengal, bay of 56, 65, 67
  Bengal West 181
Bhutan 191, 219

calories 199
  see also nutrition
canopy, forest 106
catchment areas 116
Central Water Commission 64
child labour 210
Chipko movement 65, 103, 122, 218, 224 ff.
cloud forests 82, 85, 99, 104
commons 175
community use of forests 174
consumption
  household 150
cooperatives 215 ff.
  see also community
coping
  farmers 142
crisis 55, 69
  crisis definition 139
cutting 76, 77, 80, 81, 82, 83, 84, 85, 86, 91, 104

dams 63
decision making 152
  see also political ecology
degradation
  land 132

education 211 ff.
  see also literacy
energy 143, 150
erosion
  see soil erosion

family forestry 176
farmers 142

245